2018

CANADIAN INSURANCE CLAIMS DIRECTORY

86th Annual Edition

Edited by

GWEN PERONI

Advertising Sales Co-ordinator: Gwen Peroni
Advertising Production Co-ordinator: Ruth Welch

ALL ADJUSTERS AND INSURANCE COUNSEL LISTED HEREIN ARE EXPERIENCED AND COMPETENT AS THEY ACT FOR INSURANCE COMPANIES SELECTION CAN BE MADE WITH EVERY CONFIDENCE

The Canadian Insurance Claims Directory has been completely revised and edited to 8 March 2018. Please send all corrections and additions to Canadian Insurance Claims Directory, University of Toronto Press, 800 Bay Street, Mezzanine, Toronto, Ontario M5S 3A9, or telephone (416) 978-2239 ext. 2245. Although every care is exercised in compiling these listings, some errors may occur. Under no circumstances will the publishers bear the responsibility of informing subscribers of errors or omissions, nor assume liability for damages arising out of any such errors.

utorontopress.com

ISSN 0318-0352 • ISBN 978-1-4875-2300-8
University of Toronto Press
800 Bay Street, Mezzanine, Toronto, Ontario M5S 3A9
Phone: (416) 978-2239 ext. 2245 Fax: (416) 921-6353
Orders: 1-800-565-9523 Fax: (416) 667-7832
$55.00 (plus applicable taxes)

Contents

Index of Advertisers

Index of Insurance-Related Services

Index of Insurance Associations and Governing Bodies

ADJUSTERS AND INSURANCE COUNSEL IN CANADA

MACKENZIE
BRITISH COLUMBIA
SASKATCHEWAN
MONT.
ALBERTA
Scale of Miles
0 20 40 60 80 100
DIV. NO. 15
DIV. NO. 12
DIV. NO. 13
DIV. NO. 14
DIV. NO. 10
DIV. NO. 11
DIV. NO. 9
DIV. NO. 8
DIV. NO. 7
DIV. NO. 6
DIV. NO. 5
DIV. NO. 4
DIV. NO. 3
DIV. NO. 2
DIV. NO. 1
Indian Cabins Post
Fort Smith
Fort Fitzgerald
Upper Hay River Post
Fort Chipewyan
Ft. Vermilion
Carcajou
Manning
Mackay
McMurray
Waterways
Hines Creek
Peace River
Berwyn
Grimshaw
Fairview
Spirit River
Rycroft
Falher
McLennan
High Prairie
Kinuso
Hythe
Sexsmith
Beaverlodge
Grande Prairie
Valley View
Smith
Mirror Landing
Athabaska
Lac la Biche
Cold Lake
Bonnyville
Whitecourt
Barrhead
Westlock
St. Paul
Heinsburg
Legal
Morinville
Redwater
Andrew
Lamont
Two Hills
Myrnam
Edson
Onoway
St. Albert
Fort Saskatchewan
Mundare
Stony Plain
Beverly
Vegreville
Vermilion
Edmonton
Jasper Pl.
Tofield
Mannville
Lloydminster
Devon
Leduc
Calmar
Holden
Viking
Coalspur
Drayton Valley
Millet
Camrose
Cadomin
Jasper
Mountain Park
Wetaskiwin
Daysland
Killam
Wainwright
Hardisty
Chauvin
Rimbey
Ponoka
Galahad
Hughenden
Bentley
Lacombe
Provost
Nordegg
Alix
Stettler
Rocky Mountain House
Sylvan Lake
Red Deer
Castor
Coronation
Consort
Big Valley
Innisfail
Bowden
Olds
Trochu
Compeer
Three Hills
Morrin
Delia
Hanna
Didsbury
Nacmine
Drumheller
Beiseker
Newcastle
Rosedale
Oyen
Lake Louise
East Coulee
Banff
Cochrane
Empress
Canmore
Bowness
Forest Lawn
Strathmore
Calgary
Gleichen
Bassano
Black Diamond
Okotoks
Brooks
Turner Valley
High River
Tilley
Vulcan
Suffield
Nanton
Champion
Redcliff
Stavely
Carmangay
Medicine Hat
Claresholm
Irvine
Picture Butte
Bow Island
Granum
Taber
Burdett
Fort Macleod
Coleman
Blairmore
Lethbridge
Coaldale
Bellevue
Stirling
Foremost
Hillcrest
Pincher Creek
Raymond
Magrath
Warner
Cardston
Milk River
Waterton Park
Carway
Coutts

Alberta

CALGARY–Adjusters

CRAWFORD & COMPANY

General Insurance Adjusters
3165 – 114 Avenue S.E., Suite 200
Calgary, AB T2Z 3X2
Phone: (403) 266-3933, ext. 3681
E-mail: calgary.claims@crawco.ca
Graham Carstairs, Manager

D.S. COOK & ASSOCIATES LTD.

General Insurance Adjusters
110, 7710 – 5th Street S.E.
Calgary, AB T2H 2L9
Phone: (403) 319-0434
Fax: (403) 276-9594
Website: www.dscook.com
Doug Cook, B.Comm.
doug@dscook.com
Jim Moriarty, B.A.
jim@dscook.com
Duncan Cook, F.C.I.P., C.R.M.
duncan@dscook.com
Covering all of Southern Alberta.

CUNNINGHAM LINDSEY

807 Manning Road N.E.
Calgary, AB T2E 7M8
Phone: (403) 571-2050
Fax: (403) 266-2078
Website: www.cunninghamlindsey.com
After Hours/Emergencies – 1-800-235-8784
E-mail: charder@cl-na.com

CALGARY–Continued

HBA ADJUSTERS LTD.

General Insurance Adjusters
1209 – 59 Avenue S.E., Suite 185
Calgary, AB T2H 2P6
Phone: (403) 245-4599
Fax: (403) 287-1775
Mike Ander, BA, CIP
Office Manager
Direct line: (403) 802-4235
Cell: (403) 620-9927
E-mail: mander@hbaadj.com
Mark R. Van der Wee, CIP
Direct line: (403) 802-4244
Cell: (403) 861-2421
E-mail: mvanderwee@hbdaadj.com
Scott Thielen, CIP
Direct line: (403) 802-4240
Cell: (403) 991-9801
E-mail: sthielen@hbaadj.com
Glen Jakubowski, FCIP
Direct line: (403) 802-4243
Cell: (403) 836-6670
E-mail: gjakubowski@hbaadj.com
Website: www.hbaadj.com
Member: A.A.I.A.

KERNAGHAN ADJUSTERS

General Insurance Adjusters
106 –1935 27th Avenue N.E.
Calgary, AB T2E 7E4
Phone: (403) 250-3700
Toll-free: 1-866-406-5677
Fax: (403) 250-5764
E-mail: calgary@kernaghan.com
Michelle Short, CIP, Branch Manager
Servicing: Medicine Hat, Red Deer, Lethbridge, Canmore, Banff, and Lake Louise.

CALGARY–Forensic Accountants

MDD FORENSIC ACCOUNTANTS

Tracing its roots to 1933, MDD is an internationally recognized forensic accounting firm that focuses on economic damage quantification assessments. Our highly trained experienced professionals provide expert, consultant, and fact witness testimony. We have qualified as experts in courts around the world. Regardless of the nature of the assignment, MDD's exceptional dedication and demonstrated results have long been the hallmark of the firm.

Our practice areas include: Agriculture, Builders Risk, Business Disputes, Business Interruption, Business Valuation, Catastrophe Services, Class Actions, Construction, Contingency Entertainment, Disability, Matrimonial Disputes, Environmental Damages, Expropriation, Extra Expenses, Franchise, Fraud Investigations, Government Services, Intellectual Property, Liability Losses, Litigation, Lost Profits, Maritime, Mining & Refining, Oil & Gas, Personal Injury, Physical Damages, Power Generation, Product Liability, Reported Insurance, Stocks & Contents, Subrogation, Surety Funds, Toxic Tort, Transportation, and Valuable Papers.

407 – 2nd Street S.W.
Suite 1030
Calgary, AB T2P 2Y3
Phone: (403) 218-4050
Fax: (403) 218-4051
Website: www.mdd.com
Scott Schellenberg,
CPA, CA•IFA, CBV, CFA, CFF
Partner, Senior Vice President
E-mail: scotts@mdd.com
Dean Das, CPA, CA, CBV
Partner, Senior Vice President
E-mail: ddas@mdd.com

CALGARY–Insurance Counsel

McLENNAN ROSS LLP

Insurance and Risk Management Lawyers: experience includes property losses; casualty; auto liability; comprehensive liability; fiduciary matters; business interruption; professional liability and malpractice; fidelity and surety; errors & omissions; directors' and officers' liability; home owners', life, accident and sickness insurance; aviation; employment liability; bad faith litigation; specialty lines; reinsurance; and licensing.

1000 First Canadian Centre
350 7th Avenue S.W.
Calgary, AB T2P 3N9
Phone: (403) 543-9120
Fax: (403) 543-9150
Toll-free: 1-888-543-9120
Alexis N. Moulton
amoulton@mross.com
Don W. Dear, Q.C.
ddear@mross.com
Website: www.mross.com

McLennan Ross has enjoyed a long and valued association with Canada's insurance industry, serving as counsel for numerous national and international insurance companies. Over the years, our firm has developed a top-notch team of legal professionals who truly understand the legal and business needs of the insurance industry.

Member: ARC Group Canada Inc. (a network of independent law firms across Canada committed to delivering new standards for client satisfaction through heightened responsiveness, added value, and seamless expertise across the country).

CALGARY–Continued

WHITELAW TWINING
Legal Counsel
675 – 333 7th Avenue S.W.
Calgary, AB T2P 2Z1
Phone: (403) 775-2200
Fax: (403) 536-3540
E-mail: kwigmore@wt.ca
Website: www.wt.ca

CALGARY–Insurance Loss Accountants

PRICEWATERHOUSECOOPERS LLP
Throughout Canada and around the world, PwC provides strategic assistance to insurance companies and legal counsel in investigating and resolving claims.
- *Business interruption losses*
- *Inventory assessment and valuation*
- *Economic loss quantification in liability claims, including product liability*
- *Product recall*
- *Assessment of financial motivation*
- *Personal injury tort claims for economic loss*
- *Valuation of fidelity and employee dishonesty claims*

Suncor Energy Centre
111 – 5th Avenue S.W., Suite 3100
Calgary, AB T2P 5L3
Phone: (403) 509-7500
Fax: (403) 781-1825
Website: www.pwc.com/ca/dai
PwC has over twenty offices across Canada.

EDMONTON–Adjusters

CRAWFORD & COMPANY
General Insurance Adjusters
3114 Calgary Trail N.W., Unit 203
Edmonton, AB T6J 6V4
Phone: (780) 486-8000
E-mail: edmonton.claims@crawco.ca
Bruce Toma, Manager

EDMONTON–Continued

CUNNINGHAM LINDSEY
400 West Tower, Suite 400W
14310 – 111th Avenue
Edmonton, AB T5M 2P4
Phone: (780) 451-0370
Fax: (780) 454-3083
Website: www.cunninghamlindsey.com
After Hours/Emergencies – 1-800-235-8784
E-mail: charder@cl-na.com

KERNAGHAN ADJUSTERS
General Insurance Adjusters
103 – 4246 97 Street N.W.
Edmonton, AB T6E 5Z9
Phone: (780) 488-2371
Toll-free: 1-866-988-2371
Fax: (780) 488-0243
E-mail: edmonton@kernaghan.com
Russell G. Fitzgerald CIP, Vice President, Alberta Operations
Servicing: Fort McMurray, Lloydminster, Edson, Red Deer, Jasper, Hinton, Whitecourt, and Grande Prairie.

EDMONTON–Forensic Accountants

MDD FORENSIC ACCOUNTANTS
Tracing its roots to 1933, MDD is an internationally recognized forensic accounting firm that focuses on economic damage quantification assessments. Our highly trained experienced professionals provide expert, consultant, and fact witness testimony. We have qualified as experts in courts around the world. Regardless of the nature of the assignment, MDD's exceptional dedication and demonstrated results have long been the hallmark of the firm.

... continued on next page

EDMONTON–Continued

MDD FORENSIC ACCOUNTANTS–Continued

Our practice areas include: Agriculture, Builders Risk, Business Disputes, Business Interruption, Business Valuation, Catastrophe Services, Class Actions, Construction, Contingency Entertainment, Disability, Matrimonial Disputes, Environmental Damages, Expropriation, Extra Expenses, Franchise, Fraud Investigations, Government Services, Intellectual Property, Liability Losses, Litigation, Lost Profits, Maritime, Mining & Refining, Oil & Gas, Personal Injury, Physical Damages, Power Generation, Product Liability, Reported Insurance, Stocks & Contents, Subrogation, Surety Funds, Toxic Tort, Transportation, and Valuable Papers.

900, First Edmonton Place
10665 Jasper Avenue
Edmonton, AB T5J 3S9
Phone: (780) 497-0190
Fax: (780) 497-0109
Website: www.mdd.com
Scott Schellenberg,
CPA, CA•IFA, CBV, CFA, CFF
Partner, Senior Vice President
E-mail: scotts@mdd.com

EDMONTON–Insurance Counsel

McLENNAN ROSS LLP

Insurance and Risk Management Lawyers: experience includes property losses; casualty; auto liability; comprehensive liability; fiduciary matters; business interruption; professional liability and malpractice; fidelity and surety; errors & omissions; directors' and officers' liability; home owners', life, accident and sickness insurance; aviation; employment liability; bad faith litigation; specialty lines; reinsurance; and licensing.

600 McLennan Ross Building
12220 Stony Plain Road
Edmonton, AB T5N 3Y4
Phone: (780) 482-9200
Fax: (780) 482-9100
Toll-free: 1-800-567-9200
Douglas J. Boyer
dboyer@mross.com
Sandra J. Weber
sweber@mross.com
Website: www.mross.com

McLennan Ross has enjoyed a long and valued association with Canada's insurance industry, serving as counsel for numerous national and international insurance companies. Over the years, our firm has developed a top-notch team of legal professionals who truly understand the legal and business needs of the insurance industry.

Member: ARC Group Canada Inc. (a network of independent law firms across Canada committed to delivering new standards for client satisfaction through heightened responsiveness, added value, and seamless expertise across the country).

EDMONTON–Insurance Loss Accountants

PRICEWATERHOUSECOOPERS LLP
Throughout Canada and around the world, PwC provides strategic assistance to insurance companies and legal counsel in investigating and resolving claims.
- *Business interruption losses*
- *Inventory assessment and valuation*
- *Economic loss quantification in liability claims, including product liability*
- *Product recall*
- *Assessment of financial motivation*
- *Personal injury tort claims for economic loss*
- *Valuation of fidelity and employee dishonesty claims*

Toronto-Dominion Tower
Edmonton City Centre
10088 – 102 Avenue N.W., Suite 1501
Edmonton, AB T5J 3N5
Phone: (780) 441-6700
Fax: (780) 441-6776
Website: www.pwc.com/ca/dai

FORT MCMURRAY–Adjusters

CRAWFORD & COMPANY
General Insurance Adjusters
149 – 395 Loutit Road
Fort McMurray, AB T9K 0Z4
Phone: 1-877-323-7874
E-mail: fortmcmurray.claims@crawco.ca
Bruce Toma, Manager

GRANDE PRAIRIE–Adjusters

CUNNINGHAM LINDSEY
P.O. Box 21085
Grande Prairie Co-op
Grande Prairie, AB T8V 6W7
Phone: (780) 532-5570
Fax: (780) 532-5579
Website: www.cunninghamlindsey.com
E-mail: charder@cl-na.com

GRANDE PRAIRIE–Continued

KERNAGHAN ADJUSTERS
General Insurance Adjusters
No. 3, 9899 112 Avenue, Suite 2033
Grande Prairie AB T8V 7T2
Phone: (780) 978-2707
Fax: (780) 488-0243
E-mail: grandeprairie@kernaghan.com
Servicing: Peace Region and Northern BC: Dawson Creek and Fort St. John.

LAURIN ADJUSTERS LTD.
Property (Residential & Commercial), Auto, Equipment, Marine, Liability, E & O, Employee Dishonesty
No. 207, 10055 – 120 Avenue
Grande Prairie, AB T8V 8H8
After Hours & Office Phone:
(780) 539-5065
Fax: (780) 532-2522
24-hour emergency claims:
1-800-362-1367
Website: www.laurinadjusters.ca
Marlene Lefebvre, CIP
E-mail: marlene@laurinadjusters.ca
Jim DeVito, CIP
E-mail: jim@laurinadjusters.ca
Tina Vangroningen
E-mail: tina@laurinadjusters.ca
Karen Penner, CIP
E-mail: karen@laurinadjusters.ca
Melissa Kluyt
E-mail: melissa@laurinadjusters.ca
New Claims: info@laurinadjusters.ca
Licensed in British Columbia, Alberta, and Saskatchewan.
Member: A.A.I.A., C.I.A.A.

LETHBRIDGE–Adjusters

CRAWFORD & COMPANY
General Insurance Adjusters
1211 3rd Avenue South, Suite 200
Lethbridge, AB T1J 0J7
Phone: (403) 328-5545
E-mail: lethbridge.claims@crawco.ca
David Leavitt, Manager

LETHBRIDGE–Continued

CUNNINGHAM LINDSEY
1253 – 6A Avenue South
Lethbridge, AB T1J 1G9
Phone: (403) 381-1103
Website: www.cunninghamlindsey.com
After Hours/Emergencies –
1-800-235-8784
E-mail: charder@cl-na.com

LLOYDMINSTER–Adjusters

CUNNINGHAM LINDSEY
P.O. Box 11981
Lloydminster, AB T9V 3C3
Phone: 1-855-408-6846
Fax: (780) 871-1781
Website: www.cunninghamlindsey.com
After Hours/Emergencies –
1-800-235-8784
E-mail: jjory@cl-na.com

MEDICINE HAT–Adjusters

CRAWFORD & COMPANY
General Insurance Adjusters
1290 Trans Canada Way S.E., Suite 202
Medicine Hat, AB T1B 1J5
Phone: (403) 527-4205
E-mail: medicinehat.claims@crawco.ca
David Leavitt, Manager

PEACE RIVER–Adjusters

LAURIN ADJUSTERS LTD.
General Insurance Adjusters
P.O. Box 6777
Peace River, AB T8S 1S5
Phone: (780) 624-3322
Fax: (780) 624-8030
Website: laurinadjusters.ca
E-mail: info@laurinadjusters.ca
Member: C.I.A.A., A.A.I.A.

RED DEER–Adjusters

CRAWFORD & COMPANY
General Insurance Adjusters
5020 68 Street, Suite 4
Red Deer, AB T4N 7B4
Phone: (403) 347-7747
E-mail: reddeer@crawco.ca
Graham Carstairs, Manager

CUNNINGHAM LINDSEY
571 – 2050 807 Manning Road N.E.
Calgary, AB T2E 7M8
Phone: (403) 571-2050
Fax: (403) 266-2078
Website: www.cunninghamlindsey.com
After Hours/Emergencies –
1-800-235-8784
E-mail: charder@cl-na.com

British Columbia

COURTENAY-COMOX–Adjusters

KERNAGHAN ADJUSTERS
General Insurance Adjusters
201 – 2435 Mansfield Drive
Courtenay, BC V9N 2M2
Phone: (250) 338-1213
Fax: (250) 338-1215
E-mail:
courtenaycomox@kernaghan.com
Debbie Halstead, CIP,
Vancouver Island Manager
Servicing: Tofino, Ucluelet, Port Alberni, Powell River, Sechelt, and the Northern Gulf Islands.

CRANBROOK–Adjusters

CRAWFORD & COMPANY
General Insurance Adjusters
125 – 10th Avenue
Suite 104
Cranbrook, BC V1C 2N1
Phone: (403) 328-5545
E-mail: cranbrook.claims@crawco.ca
David Leavitt, Manager

CUNNINGHAM LINDSEY
P.O. Box 310
Cranbrook, BC V1C 4H8
Phone: (250) 426-6651
Fax: (250) 426-2009
Website: www.cunninghamlindsey.com
After Hours/Emergencies –
1-800-235-8784
E-mail: lmccabe@cl-na.com

CRANBROOK–Continued

KERNAGHAN ADJUSTERS
General Insurance Adjusters
250 – 100 Cranbrook Street North
Cranbrook, BC V1C 3P9
Phone (778) 517-3461
Fax: (778) 517-3462
E-mail: cranbrook@kernaghan.com
Mark Graw, CIP, Senior Adjuster
Servicing: Fernie, Sparwood, Elkford, Kimberley, Elko, Jaffray, and Creston.

FRASER VALLEY–Adjusters

CUNNINGHAM LINDSEY
6325 – 204th Street, Suite 316
Langley, BC V2Y 3B3
Phone: (604) 539-8206
Fax: (604) 539-1622
Website: www.cunninghamlindsey.com
After Hours/Emergencies –
1-800-235-8784
E-mail: lmccabe@cl-na.com

KAMLOOPS–Adjusters

CRAWFORD & COMPANY
General Insurance Adjusters
230 – 1210 Summit Drive, Unit 421
Kamloops, BC V2C 6M1
Phone: (250) 819-7547
E-mail: kamloops.claims@crawco.ca
Dave Lemire, Manager

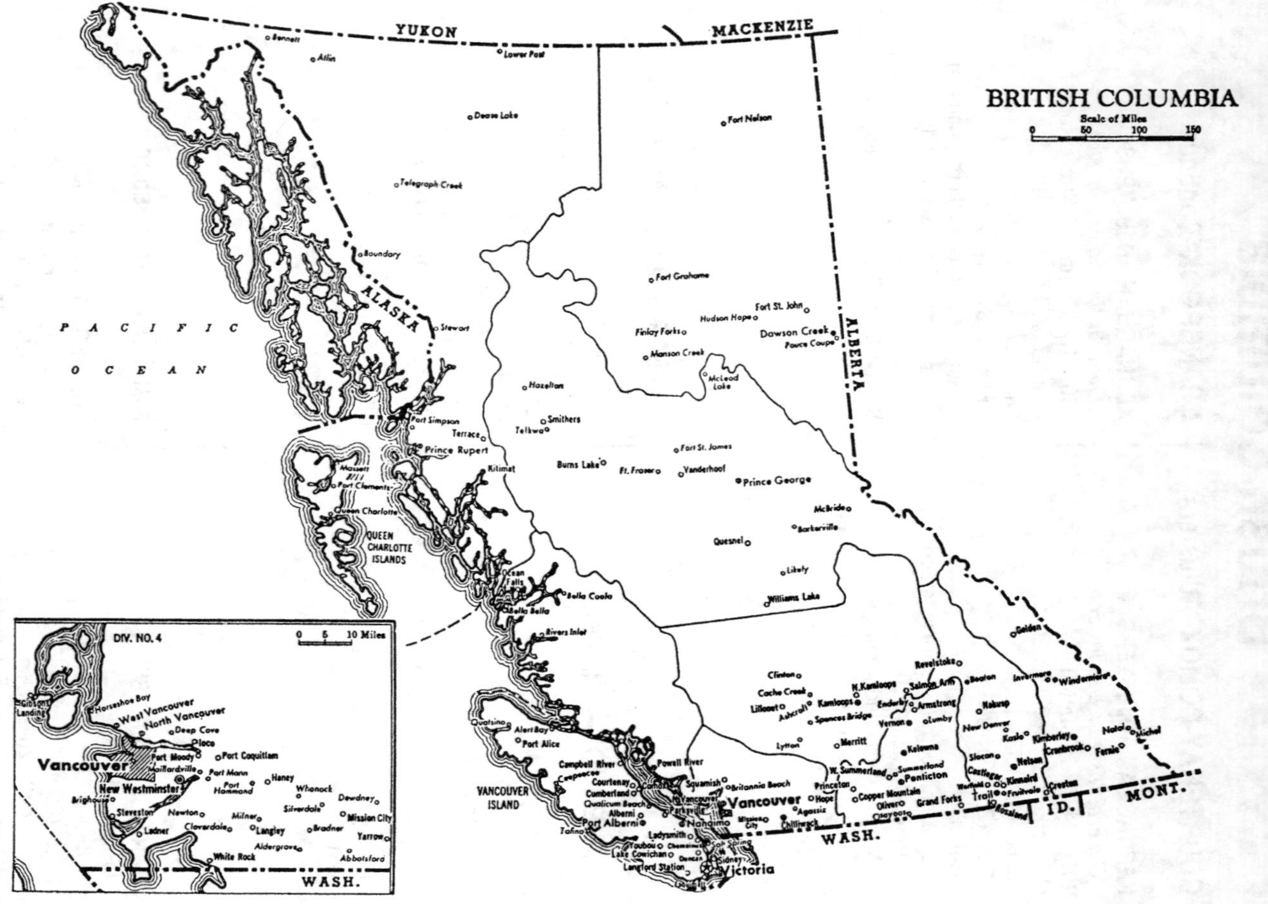

BRITISH COLUMBIA
Scale of Miles
0
50
100
150
YUKON
MACKENZIE
ALBERTA
ALASKA
MONT.
ID.
WASH.
PACIFIC
OCEAN
QUEEN CHARLOTTE ISLANDS
VANCOUVER ISLAND
Bennett
Atlin
Lower Post
Dease Lake
Telegraph Creek
Boundary
Stewart
Fort Nelson
Fort Grahame
Fort St. John
Hudson Hope
Finlay Forks
Dawson Creek
Pouce Coupe
Manson Creek
McLeod Lake
Hazelton
Smithers
Telkwa
Port Simpson
Terrace
Prince Rupert
Kitimat
Masset
Port Clements
Queen Charlotte
Fort St. James
Burns Lake
Ft. Fraser
Vanderhoof
Prince George
McBride
Barkerville
Quesnel
Likely
Williams Lake
Ocean Falls
Bella Coola
Bella Bella
Rivers Inlet
Golden
Revelstoke
Clinton
Cache Creek
N. Kamloops
Salmon Arm
Beaton
Invermere
Windermere
Lillooet
Ashcroft
Kamloops
Enderby
Armstrong
Nakusp
Spences Bridge
Vernon
Lumby
New Denver
Kaslo
Kimberley
Natal
Michel
Cranbrook
Fernie
Lytton
Merritt
Kelowna
Slocan
Nelson
Castlegar
Kinnaird
Creston
W. Summerland
Summerland
Penticton
Princeton
Copper Mountain
Oliver
Osoyoos
Grand Forks
Trail
Fruitvale
Rossland
Quatsino
Alert Bay
Port Alice
Campbell River
Powell River
Courtenay
Comox
Cumberland
Qualicum Beach
Alberni
Port Alberni
Parksville
Squamish
Britannia Beach
Vancouver
Hope
Agassiz
Chilliwack
Mission City
Nanaimo
Ladysmith
Tofino
Youbou
Chemainus
Lake Cowichan
Duncan
Sidney
Langford Station
Victoria
DIV. NO. 4
0
5
10 Miles
Gibsons Landing
Horseshoe Bay
West Vancouver
North Vancouver
Deep Cove
Ioco
Port Moody
Port Coquitlam
Vancouver
Maillardville
Port Mann
New Westminster
Port Hammond
Haney
Whonock
Dewdney
Brighouse
Silverdale
Steveston
Newton
Milner
Mission City
Ladner
Cloverdale
Langley
Bradner
Yarrow
Aldergrove
White Rock
Abbotsford
WASH.

KAMLOOPS–Continued

KERNAGHAN ADJUSTERS
General Insurance Adjusters
230 – 1210 Summit Drive, Suite 301
Kamloops, BC V2C 6M1
Phone: (236) 425-4224
Fax: (250) 860-6609
E-mail: Kamloops@kernaghan.com
Cam Fortems, Adjuster
Servicing: Merritt, Lytton, Lillooet, Williams Lake, Clearwater, Valemont, 100 Mile House, Cache Creek, and Hope.

KELOWNA–Adjusters

CRAWFORD & COMPANY
General Insurance Adjusters
160 Dougall Road South, Suite 201
Kelowna, BC V1X 3J4
Phone: (250) 491-0317
E-mail: kelowna.claims@crawco.ca
Dave Lemire, Manager

CUNNINGHAM LINDSEY
347 Leon Avenue, Suite 210
Kelowna, BC V1W 3A5
Phone: (250) 762-4785
Fax: (778) 754-0293
Website: www.cunninghamlindsey.com
After Hours/Emergencies – 1-800-235-8784
E-mail: lmccabe@cl-na.com

KERNAGHAN ADJUSTERS
General Insurance Adjusters
210 – 307 Banks Road
Kelowna, BC V1X 6A1
Phone (250) 860-8066
Fax: (250) 860-6609
E-mail: kelowna@kernaghan.com
Tony Read, BC Interior Manager
Servicing: Penticton, Kamloops, Salmon Arm, Vernon, Enderby, Falkland, Armstrong, Westbank, Merritt, and Chase.

KELOWNA–Insurance Counsel

OLAND BAXTER
Maritime/Transportation & Personal Injury Law
803 Bernard Avenue
Kelowna, BC V1Y 6P6
Phone: (250) 762-8092
Fax: (250) 762-2857
E-mail: oland@olandbaxter.com
Website: www.olandbaxter.com
Contacts: Barry Oland or Leona Baxter

KELOWNA–Restoration Services

TOTAL RESTORATION SERVICES INC.
Restoration Services
707 Finns Road
Kelowna, BC V1X 5B7
Phone: (250) 491-3828
Toll-free phone: 1-888-491-3828 (24/7)
Fax: (250) 491-3132
E-mail: info@totalrestore.ca
Website: www.totalrestore.ca
Offices in Kelowna, Penticton and Vernon serving the Okanagan, Shuswap and Similkameen areas.

NANAIMO–Adjusters

CRAWFORD & COMPANY
General Insurance Adjusters
235 Bastion Street, Suite 203
Nanaimo, BC V9R 3A3
Phone: (250) 741-8134
E-mail: nanaimo.claims@crawco.ca
Jennifer, Tims, Manager

KERNAGHAN ADJUSTERS
General Insurance Adjusters
201 Selby Street
Nanaimo, BC V9R 2R2
Phone: (250) 740-3999
Fax: (250) 740-3998
E-mail: nanaimo@kernaghan.com
Debbie Halstead, CIP, Vancouver Island Manager
Servicing: Port Alberni, Tofino, Ucluelet, Qualicum Beach, Parksville, and Bowser.

PENTICTON–Adjusters

CUNNINGHAM LINDSEY
113 – 437 Martin Street, Suite 368
Penticton, BC V2A 5L1
Phone: (250) 490-9689
Fax: (844) 818-9951
Website: www.cunninghamlindsey.com
After Hours/Emergencies –
1-800-235-8784
E-mail: lmccabe@cl-na.com

PENTICTON–Restoration Services

TOTAL RESTORATION SERVICES INC.
Restoration Services
505 Dawson Avenue
Penticton, BC V2A 6S5
Phone: (250) 493-8028
Toll-free phone: 1-888-491-3828 (24/7)
Fax: (250) 493-8058
E-mail: info@totalrestore.ca
Website: www.totalrestore.ca
Offices in Kelowna, Penticton and Vernon.

PORT MOODY–Adjusters

CUNNINGHAM LINDSEY
3003 St. Johns Street, Suite 210
Port Moody, BC V3H 2C4
Phone: (604) 949-2170
Fax: (604) 949-1251
Website: www.cunninghamlindsey.com
After Hours/Emergencies –
1-800-235-8784
E-mail: lmccabe@cl-na.com

PRINCE GEORGE–Adjusters

KERNAGHAN ADJUSTERS
General Insurance Adjusters
9925 Shad Road
Prince George, BC V2N 6L7
Phone: (778) 281-2619
Fax: (604) 688-5676
E-mail: princegeorge@kernaghan.com
Nadine Furnell, Branch Manager
Servicing: Terrace, Valemount, Huston, and 100 Mile House.

SURREY–Adjusters

CRAWFORD & COMPANY
General Insurance Adjusters
5455 – 152nd Street, Suite 211
Surrey, BC V3S 5A5
Phone: (604) 574-6275
E-mail: surrey.claims@crawco.ca

KERNAGHAN ADJUSTERS
General Insurance Adjusters
15290 103A Avenue, Suite 102
Surrey, BC V3R 7A2
Phone: (604) 282-7932
Fax: (604) 688-5676
E-mail: surrey@kernaghan.com
Tony McVicker, BA, Vice President, British Columbia Operations
Servicing: Langley, Mission, Maple Ridge, Chilliwack, Aldergrove, Delta, Richmond, White Rock, and Hope.

VANCOUVER–Adjusters

BBCG CLAIM SERVICES
a division of ClaimsPro
Specializing in surety and fidelity bond claims, E&O, D&O and trade credit claims
8333 Eastlake Drive, Suite 101
Burnaby, BC V5A 4W2
Phone: (604) 742-9929
Toll-free: 1-866-714-0005
Fax: (604) 742-9928
Jamie O'Connor
E-mail: joconnor@bbcg.ca
Offices in Ontario and Quebec.
Servicing all of Canada.
Member: C.I.A.A.

CRAWFORD & COMPANY
General Insurance Adjusters
2985 Virtual Way, Suite 280
Vancouver, BC V5M 4X7
Phone: (604) 739-3816
E-mail: vancouver.claims@crawco.ca

VANCOUVER–Continued

CUNNINGHAM LINDSEY

1200 West 73rd Avenue, Suite 410
Vancouver, BC V6P 6G5
Phone: (604) 683-2521
Fax: (604) 669-4711
Website: www.cunninghamlindsey.com
After Hours/Emergencies – 1-800-235-8784
E-mail: lmccabe@cl-na.com

KERNAGHAN ADJUSTERS

General Insurance Adjusters
Corporate Office
300-1445 West Georgia Street
Vancouver, BC V6G 2T3
Phone: (604) 688-5651
Fax: (604) 688-5676
E-mail: vancouver@kernaghan.com
Tony McVicker, BA, Vice President, British Columbia Operations
Servicing: Greater Vancouver, Squamish, North Vancouver, West Vancouver, Richmond, Delta, Burnaby, New Westminster, Coquitlam, Maple Ridge, Mission, White Rock, Langley, Aldergrove, Chilliwack, Hope, and Whistler.

VANCOUVER–Forensic Accountants

MDD FORENSIC ACCOUNTANTS

Tracing its roots to 1933, MDD is an internationally recognized forensic accounting firm that focuses on economic damage quantification assessments. Our highly trained experienced professionals provide expert, consultant, and fact witness testimony. We have qualified as experts in courts around the world. Regardless of the nature of the assignment, MDD's exceptional dedication and demonstrated results have long been the hallmark of the firm.

VANCOUVER–Continued

MDD FORENSIC ACCOUNTANTS–Continued

Our practice areas include: Agriculture, Builders Risk, Business Disputes, Business Interruption, Business Valuation, Catastrophe Services, Class Actions, Construction, Contingency Entertainment, Disability, Matrimonial Disputes, Environmental Damages, Expropriation, Extra Expenses, Franchise, Fraud Investigations, Government Services, Intellectual Property, Liability Losses, Litigation, Lost Profits, Maritime, Mining & Refining, Oil & Gas, Personal Injury, Physical Damages, Power Generation, Product Liability, Reported Insurance, Stocks & Contents, Subrogation, Surety Funds, Toxic Tort, Transportation, and Valuable Papers.

555 Burrard Street, Suite 1725, Box 211
Two Bentall Centre
Vancouver, BC V7X 1M9
Phone: (604) 331-8787
Fax: (604) 331-8799
Website: www.mdd.com
Tony Volpe, CPA, CMA
Partner, Senior Vice President
E-mail: tvolpe@mdd.com

VANCOUVER–Insurance Counsel

WHITELAW TWINING

Legal Counsel
2400 – 200 Granville Street
Vancouver, BC V6C 1S4
Phone: (604) 682-5466
Fax: (604) 682-5217
E-mail: kwigmore@wt.ca
Website: www.wt.ca

VANCOUVER–Insurance Loss Accountants

PRICEWATERHOUSECOOPERS LLP

Throughout Canada and around the world, PwC provides strategic assistance to insurance companies and legal counsel in investigating and resolving claims.

- *Business interruption losses*
- *Inventory assessment and valuation*
- *Economic loss quantification in liability claims, including product liability*
- *Product recall*
- *Assessment of financial motivation*
- *Personal injury tort claims for economic loss*
- *Valuation of fidelity and employee dishonesty claims*

250 Howe Street
Suite 1400
Vancouver, BC V6C 3S7
Phone: (604) 806-7000
Fax: (604) 806-7806
Website: www.pwc.com/ca/dai
PwC has over twenty offices across Canada.

VERNON–Restoration Services

TOTAL RESTORATION SERVICES INC.

Restoration Services
8121 Highland Place
Vernon, BC V1B 3W6
Phone: (250) 558-1412
Toll-free phone: 1-888-491-3828 (24/7)
Fax: (250) 558-5341
Nights: 1-888-491-3828
E-mail: info@totalrestore.ca
Website: www.totalrestore.ca
Offices in Kelowna, Penticton and Vernon serving the Okanagan, Shuswap and Similkameen areas within southern British Columbia.

VICTORIA–Adjusters

CRAWFORD & COMPANY

General Insurance Adjusters
3318 Oak Street, Suite 22
Victoria, BC V8X 1R1
Phone: (250) 360-0304
E-mail: victoria.claims@crawco.ca
Jennifer Tims, Manager

CUNNINGHAM LINDSEY

19 DeGoutiere Place
Victoria, BC V9B 0H3
Phone: (250) 474-1213
Fax: (250) 474-1248
Website: www.cunninghamlindsey.com
After Hours/Emergencies – 1-800-235-8784
E-mail: lmccabe@cl-na.com

KERNAGHAN ADJUSTERS

General Insurance Adjusters
309 – 1834C Oak Bay Ave.
Victoria, BC V8R 0A4
Phone: (250) 338-1213
Fax: (250) 338-1215
E-mail: victoria@kernaghan.com
Colleen Stevens, CIP, General Adjuster
Servicing: Southern Vancouver Island.

WHISTLER–Adjusters

KERNAGHAN ADJUSTERS

General Insurance Adjusters
P.O. Box 850, Garibaldi Highlands
Squamish, BC V0N 1T0
Phone: (604) 892-9229
Fax: (604) 357-1461
E-mail: whistler@kernaghan.com
Andrea G. Symons, BFA, Executive Adjuster
Servicing: Lions Bay, Britannia Beach, Furry Creek, Squamish, Garibaldi Highlands, Brackendale, Black Tusk Village, Pine Crest, Whistler, Pemberton, Mount Currie, Birken, D'Arcy, Braelorn, Ivy Lake, Owl Ridge, Gold Bridge, Tyax, Seaton Portage, Shallath, and Lillooet.

Manitoba

BRANDON–Adjusters

JAMES DUBÉ SPRAGGS ADJUSTERS LTD.

All lines of general adjusting including auto and equipment appraisals
Unit No. 7A – 2010 Currie Boulevard
Brandon, MB R7B 4E7
Phone: (204) 728-6126
Fax: (204) 728-6044
Nights: (204) 728-6126
E-mail: jdsbdn@mts.net
Website: www.jdsadj.ca
Gary Pilloud, Manager
Serving city of Brandon and western Manitoba.
Member: M.I.A.A.

FLIN FLON–Adjusters

KERNAGHAN ADJUSTERS

General Insurance Adjusters
49 Main Street
Flin Flon, MB R8A 1J7
Phone: (204) 687-7260
Fax: (204) 687-4131
E-mail: flinflon@kernaghan.com
Stephanie Straile, General Adjuster
Servicing: The Pas, Snow Lake, Grand Rapids, and Creighton, Saskatchewan.

THOMPSON–Adjusters

KERNAGHAN ADJUSTERS

General Insurance Adjusters
304 – 83 Churchill Drive
Thompson, MB R8N 0L5
Phone: (204) 677-2351
Fax: (204) 677-9961
E-mail: thompson@kernaghan.com
Toni Burt, Adjuster
Servicing: Churchill, Leaf Rapids, Shamattawa, Rankin Inlet, and Arviat, Nunavut.

WINNIPEG–Adjusters

CRAWFORD & COMPANY

General Insurance Adjusters
1250 Waverley Street
Unit 1
Winnipeg, MB R3T 6C6
Phone: (204) 947-2340
E-mail: winnipeg.claims@crawco.ca
Jacqueline Desrochers, Manager

CUNNINGHAM LINDSEY

2703-A, 83 Garry Street
Winnipeg, MB R3C 4J9
Phone: (204) 942-2608
Fax: (204) 943-2239
Website: www.cunninghamlindsey.com
After Hours/Emergencies – 1-800-235-8784
E-mail: skarpenko@cl-na.com

JAMES DUBÉ SPRAGGS ADJUSTERS LTD.

All lines of general adjusting including auto and equipment appraisals
5 Scurfield Boulevard
Unit 5
Winnipeg, MB R3Y 1G3
Phone: (204) 985-1200
Fax: (204) 475-0221
Nights: (204) 985-1200
E-mail: jdsadj@mts.net
Website: www.jdsadj.ca
David Dubé, Manager
Serving city of Winnipeg and province of Manitoba.
Member: M.I.A.A., C.A.F.I.

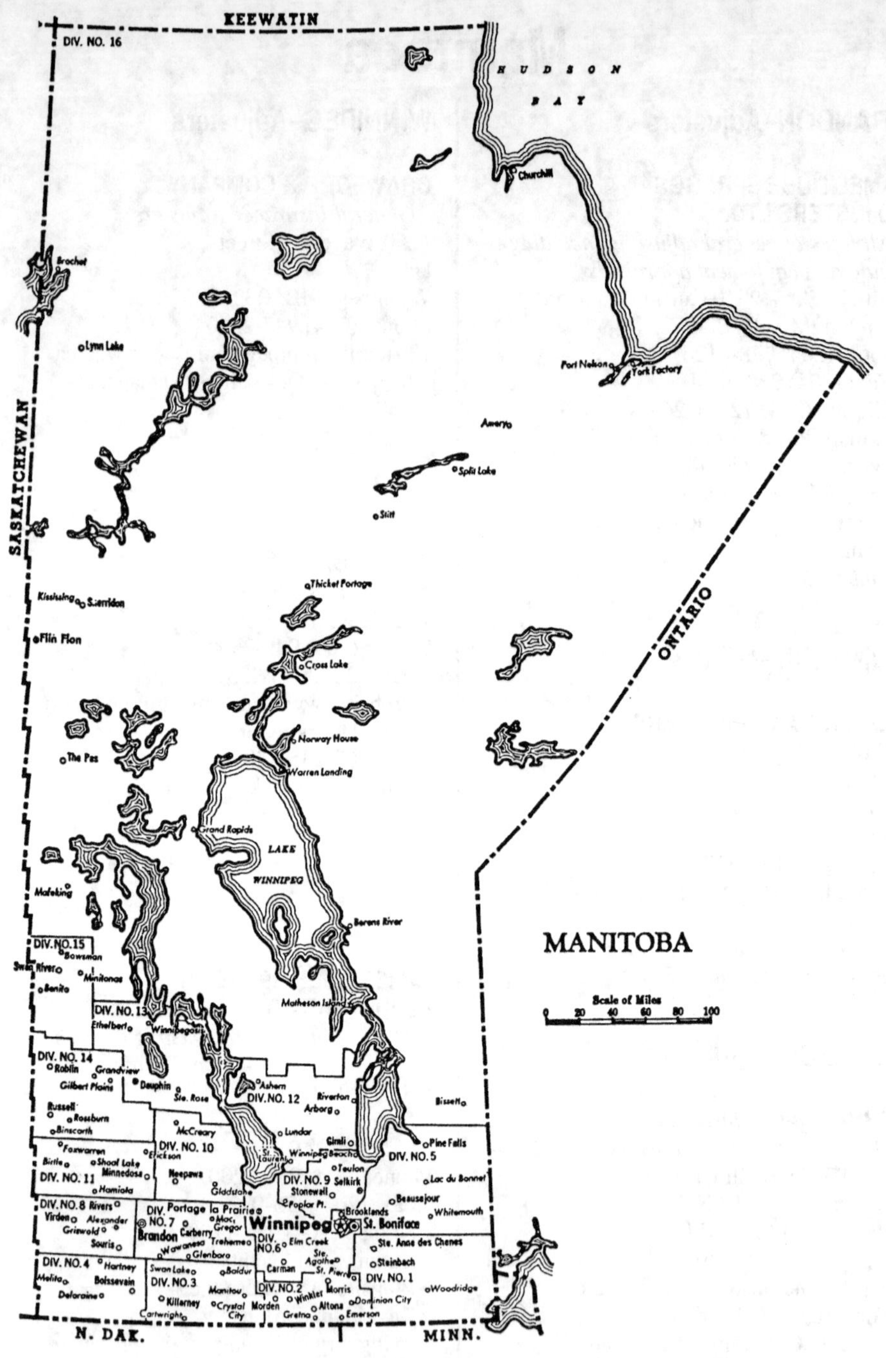
KEEWATIN
DIV. NO. 16
HUDSON
BAY
Churchill
Brochet
Lynn Lake
Port Nelson
York Factory
Amery
Split Lake
Stitt
SASKATCHEWAN
ONTARIO
Thicket Portage
Kississing
Sherridon
Flin Flon
Cross Lake
Norway House
The Pas
Warren Landing
Grand Rapids
LAKE
WINNIPEG
Mafeking
Berens River
MANITOBA
Scale of Miles
0 20 40 60 80 100
DIV. NO. 15
Bowsman
Swan River
Minitonas
Benito
Matheson Island
DIV. NO. 13
Ethelbert
Winnipegosis
DIV. NO. 14
Roblin
Grandview
Gilbert Plains
Dauphin
Ste. Rose
Ashern
DIV. NO. 12
Riverton
Arborg
Bissett
Russell
Rossburn
Binscarth
McCreary
Lundar
Gimli
Pine Falls
Foxwarren
DIV. NO. 10
Erickson
St. Laurent
Winnipeg Beach
DIV. NO. 5
Birtle
Shoal Lake
Minnedosa
Neepawa
Teulon
DIV. NO. 11
Hamiota
Gladstone
DIV. NO. 9
Selkirk
Lac du Bonnet
Stonewall
Beausejour
Poplar Pt.
DIV. NO. 8
Rivers
Virden
Alexander
Griswold
Souris
DIV. NO. 7
Portage la Prairie
Brandon
Carberry
Mac Gregor
Wawanesa
Treherne
Glenboro
Winnipeg
Brooklands
St. Boniface
Whitemouth
DIV. NO. 6
Elm Creek
Ste. Anne des Chenes
Ste. Agathe
Carman
Steinbach
DIV. NO. 4
Hartney
Melita
Boissevain
Deloraine
Swan Lake
Baldur
DIV. NO. 3
Manitou
Killarney
Crystal City
Cartwright
DIV. NO. 2
St. Pierre
Morris
Winkler
Morden
Altona
Gretna
Dominion City
Emerson
DIV. NO. 1
Woodridge
N. DAK.
MINN.

WINNIPEG–Continued

KERNAGHAN ADJUSTERS

General Insurance Adjusters
203 – 90 Garry Street
Winnipeg, MB R3C 4H1
Phone: (204) 956-2550 or
(204) 943-0003
Fax: (204) 943-5760
E-mail: winnipeg@kernaghan.com
Grant Rerie, CRM,
Manitoba Regional Manager
Servicing: Brandon, Altona, Ste Anne, Selkirk, Beausejour, and Pine Falls.

WINNIPEG–Forensic Accountants

MDD FORENSIC ACCOUNTANTS

Tracing its roots to 1933, MDD is an internationally recognized forensic accounting firm that focuses on economic damage quantification assessments. Our highly trained experienced professionals provide expert, consultant, and fact witness testimony. We have qualified as experts in courts around the world. Regardless of the nature of the assignment, MDD's exceptional dedication and demonstrated results have long been the hallmark of the firm.

Our practice areas include: Agriculture, Builders Risk, Business Disputes, Business Interruption, Business Valuation, Catastrophe Services, Class Actions, Construction, Contingency Entertainment, Disability, Matrimonial Disputes, Environmental Damages, Expropriation, Extra Expenses, Franchise, Fraud Investigations, Government Services, Intellectual Property, Liability Losses, Litigation, Lost Profits, Maritime, Mining & Refining, Oil & Gas, Personal Injury, Physical Damages, Power Generation, Product Liability, Reported Insurance, Stocks & Contents, Subrogation, Surety Funds, Toxic Tort, Transportation, and Valuable Papers.

201 Portage Avenue, 18th Floor
Winnipeg, MB R3B 3K6
Phone: (204) 421-2800
Fax: (204) 416-2839
Website: www.mdd.com
Martin Pavelic, CPA, CMA, CFF
Partner, Senior Vice President
E-mail: mpavelic@mdd.com

WINNIPEG–Insurance Counsel

THOMPSON DORFMAN SWEATMAN LLP

Barristers & Solicitors
Bruce S. Thompson
P. Michael Sinclair, Q.C.
Chrys Pappas, Q.C.
William G. Percy
Richard H.G. Adams
Robert J.M. Adkins
Donald G. Douglas
Bjorn Christianson
Paul J. Brett
Robert H. Johnston
Paul E. Roy
Gregory J. Tallon
A. Blair Graham, Q.C.
Gordon A. McKinnon
Robin M. Kersey
James A. Ripley
B. Douglas Tait
Arthur J. Stacey
Antoine F. Hacault
Vivian E. Rachlis
Jeffrey B. Hirsch
Barry N. MacTavish
John D. Stefaniuk
Glen W. Agar
Albina P. Moran
Jamie A. Kagan
Douglas J. Forbes
Maria L. Grande
Kelly L. Dickson
Jeffrey A. Kowall
Keith D. LaBossiere
Silvia V. de Sousa
Jeff Pniowsky
Anita R. Wortzman
Sheryl A. Rosenberg
Leilani J. Kagan
Lisa J. Stiver
Michael A. Choiselat
Adrian B. Frost
Elmer J. Gomes
Caroline G.S. Kiva
Ross A. McFadyen
Andrew L. Thompson
Sacha R. Paul
Jonathan M. Woolley
Gerald S. Ashcroft
Robert W. Olson
Lynda K. Troup

WINNIPEG–Continued

THOMPSON DORFMAN SWEATMAN LLP–Continued

Jennifer E. McRae
Drew M. Mitchell
Allan P. Fineblit
Richard M. Leipsic
Allan L.V. Stewart
Peter A. Sim
Lucy M.P. Kinnear
Scott J. Hoeppner
Melissa M. Malden
Melissa D.L. Beaumont
Bailey J. Harris
Andrea J. Hadley
Terra L. Welsh
Andrea R. Doyle
Stéphanie M. Tétreault
Danny C. Spencer
Lewis H. Allen
Meghan C. Ross
Andrew D.F. Sain
Matthew D. Dalloo
Catherine M. Hamilton
Stephen A. Porco
Nicholas E. Woelcke
Suzette Golden-Greenwood
Stephen P. Beernaert
John F. Murray
Megan A. Smith
Sarah S.R. Thomson
Stefan W. Drew
Danielle Grzybowski
Alexander H. Leaver
Kristin M. Kersey
Alyssa Mariani
Scott E.W. Birse
Mason Broadfoot
Sharyne Hamm
Colton M. Hnatiuk
Ali J. Hyde
Kelsey M. McIntyre
Courtney Weinstein
201 Portage Avenue, Suite 2200
Winnipeg, MB R3B 3L3
Telephone: (204) 957-1930
Toll-free: 1-855-483-7529
Fax: (204) 934-0570
E-mail: tds@tdslaw.com
Website: www.tdslaw.com

New Brunswick

CARAQUET–Adjusters

CUNNINGHAM LINDSEY
20 rue de Portage
Caraquet, NB E1W 1B7
Phone: (506) 727-6866
Fax: (506) 727-6093
Website: www.cunninghamlindsey.com
After Hours/Emergencies –
1-800-235-8784
E-mail: eporter@cl-na.com

C. LANDRY ADJUSTMENT LTD.
General Insurance Adjusters
42 Boulevard St-Pierre W.
P.O. Box 5696
Caraquet, NB E1W 1B7
Phone: (506) 726-1898
Fax: (506) 726-1911
E-mail: clandry_adj@nb.aibn.com
Nights: (506) 732-2875
Claude E. Landry, AIIC
Jocelyn Boudreau
Serving the areas of Caraquet, Shippagan, Lameque, Miscou, Neguac, Tracadie-Sheila, Grande-Anse, and Bathurst.

EDMUNDSTON–Adjusters

CUNNINGHAM LINDSEY
407 rue Principale
Saint-Léonard, NB E7E 2J1
Phone: (506) 735-5549
Fax: (506) 739-6725
Website: www.cunninghamlindsey.com
After Hours/Emergencies –
1-888-679-4455
E-mail: eporter@cl-na.com

FREDERICTON–Adjusters

CRAWFORD & COMPANY
General Insurance Adjusters
403 Regent Street, Suite 101
Fredericton, NB E3B 3X6
Phone: (506) 452-1909
E-mail: fredericton.claims@crawco.ca
Pierre Roy, Manager

NEW BRUNSWICK
QUEBEC
MAINE
GULF OF ST. LAWRENCE
BAY OF FUNDY
RESTIGOUCHE
MADAWASKA
VICTORIA
NORTHUMBERLAND
GLOUCESTER
CARLETON
YORK
SUNBURY
KENT
WESTMORLAND
QUEENS
KINGS
ALBERT
CHARLOTTE
ST. JOHN
Campbellton
Dalhousie
Charlo
Atholville
Balmoral
Petit Rocher
Grand Anse
Caraquet
Shippigan
Bathurst
E. Bathurst
S. Bathurst
Tracadie
Tabusintac
Kedgwick
St. Quentin
Edmundston
St. Leonard
Grand Falls
Plaster Rock
Aroostook
Arthurette
Andover
Perth
Loggieville
Newcastle
Chatham
Chatham Head
Red Bank
Blackville
Rogersville
St. Louis
Richibucto
Rexton
Buctouche
Doaktown
Boiestown
Bath
Centreville
Hartland
Woodstock
McGivney
Barker's Point
Chipman
Minto
Rothwell
Notre Dame
Cocagne
Shediac
Cape Tormentine
Dieppe
Moncton
Port Elgin
Sackville
Dorchester
Havelock
Petitcodiac
Hopewell Cape
Nashwaaksis
Marysville
Fredericton
Canterbury Sta.
Oromocto
Burton
Sheffield
Gagetown
Sussex
Alma
McAdam
Hampton
Rothesay
St. Martins
St. John
Lancaster
Moore's Mills
St. Stephen
Milltown
St. George
Pennfield
St. Andrews
Deer Island
Black's Harbour
Welchpool
Grand Harbour
Scale of Miles
0
20
40
60

MONCTON–Adjusters

CRAWFORD & COMPANY
General Insurance Adjusters
1133 St. George Boulevard, Suite 340
Moncton, NB E1E 4E1
Phone: (506) 863-0950
E-mail: moncton.claims@crawco.ca
Pierre Roy, Manager

CUNNINGHAM LINDSEY
1600 Main Street, Suite 240
Moncton, NB E1E 1G5
Phone: (506) 857-8660
Fax: (506) 859-7399
Website: www.cunninghamlindsey.com
After Hours/Emergencies – 1-800-235-8784
E-mail: eporter@cl-na.com

GREATER MONCTON ADJUSTMENT BUREAU INC.
General Insurance Adjusters
Specializing in detailed investigations – All Lines
428 Champlain Street
Dieppe, NB E1A 1P3
Phone: (506) 389-8377
Toll-free: 1-877-903-8377
Fax: (506) 389-8379
Evenings and weekends: (506) 389-8377 or (506) 866-6349
Paul R. Cyr, B.B.A., C.I.P., A.I.I.C.
President/General Manager
E-mail: pcyrgmab@nb.aibn.com
Covering the southeast regions of New Brunswick and the northeast regions of Nova Scotia, including all areas between Miramichi, Renous, Rogersville, Harcourt, Greater Moncton area, Sussex, Petitcodiac, Sackville, Shediac, Cap Pele, Port Elgin, Amherst, Springhill, Parrsboro, and Oxford, Nova Scotia.
Member: C.I.A.A.

MONCTON–Investigating Consultants and Forensics

KODSI ENGINEERING INC.
See Halifax, Nova Scotia, listing for full details

Phone: 1-800-263-6351

SAINT JOHN–Adjusters

CUNNINGHAM LINDSEY
14 King Street
Suite 101
Saint John, NB E2L 1G2
Phone: (506) 634-2100
Fax: (506) 632-0809
Website: www.cunninghamlindsey.com
E-mail: eporter@cl-na.com

SAINT JOHN–Investigating Consultants and Forensics

KODSI ENGINEERING INC.
See Halifax, Nova Scotia, listing for full details

Phone: 1-800-263-6351

SHIPPIGAN–Adjusters

C. LANDRY ADJUSTMENT LTD.
See Caraquet, New Brunswick, listing for full details
Phone: (506) 726-1898
Fax: (506) 726-1911

TRACADIE–Adjusters

C. LANDRY ADJUSTMENT LTD.
See Caraquet, New Brunswick, listing for full details
Phone: (506) 726-1898
Fax: (506) 726-1911

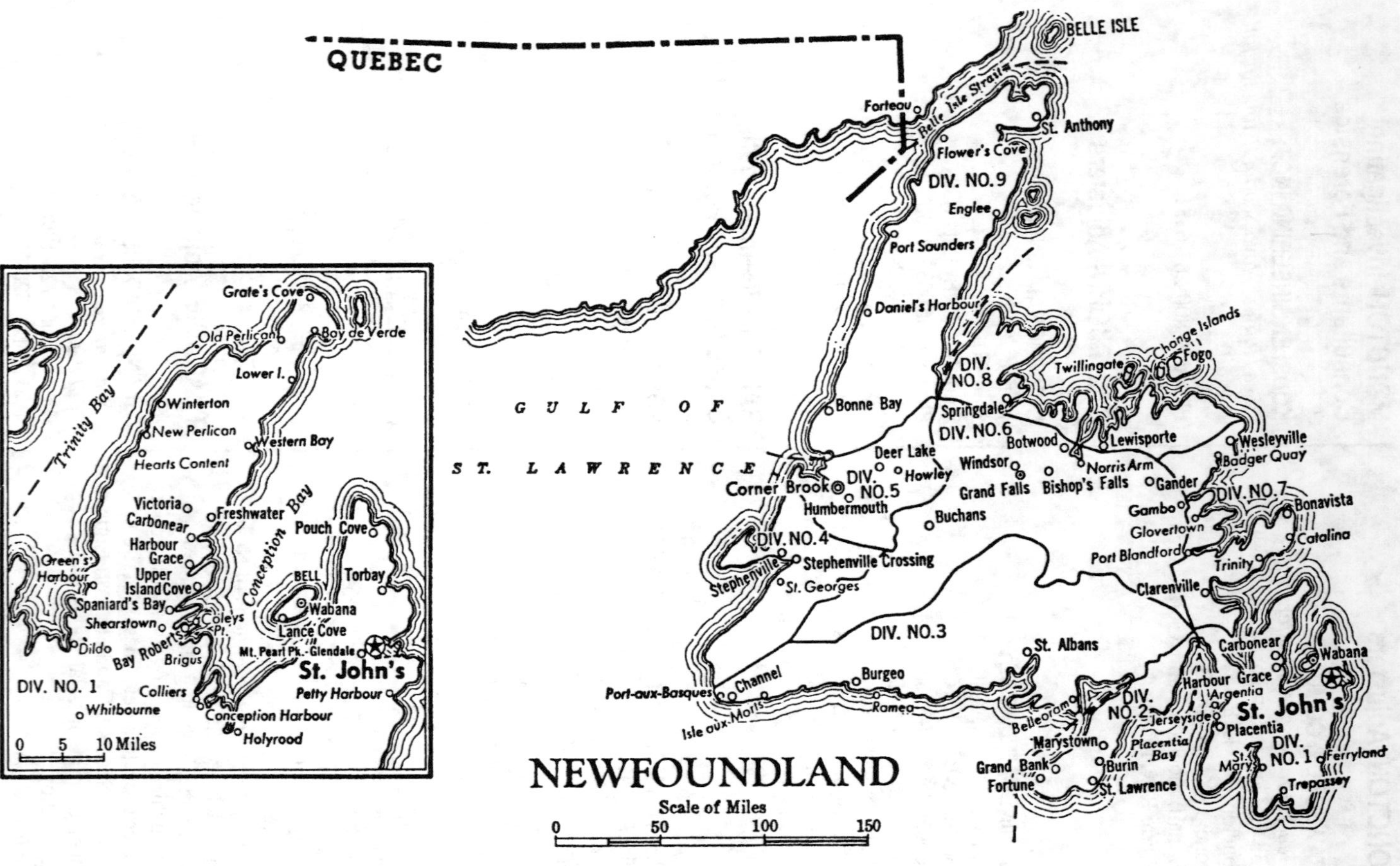
QUEBEC
BELLE ISLE
Belle Isle Strait
Forteau
St. Anthony
Flower's Cove
DIV. NO.9
Englee
Port Saunders
Daniel's Harbour
GULF OF
ST. LAWRENCE
DIV. NO.8
Bonne Bay
Springdale
DIV. NO.6
Twillingate
Change Islands
Fogo
Lewisporte
Botwood
Norris Arm
Wesleyville
Badger Quay
Deer Lake
Howley
Windsor
Grand Falls
Bishop's Falls
Gander
Corner Brook
DIV. NO.5
Humbermouth
Buchans
Gambo
DIV. NO.7
Bonavista
Catalina
Glovertown
Port Blandford
Trinity
DIV. NO.4
Stephenville
Stephenville Crossing
St. Georges
Clarenville
DIV. NO.3
St. Albans
Carbonear
Wabana
Harbour Grace
Argentia
St. John's
Burgeo
Port-aux-Basques
Channel
Isle aux Morts
Ramea
Belleoram
DIV. NO.2
Jerseyside
Placentia
Marystown
Placentia Bay
DIV. NO. 1
St. Mary's
Ferryland
Trepassey
Grand Bank
Fortune
Burin
St. Lawrence
NEWFOUNDLAND
Scale of Miles
0
50
100
150
Grate's Cove
Old Perlican
Bay de Verde
Lower I.
Trinity Bay
Winterton
New Perlican
Western Bay
Hearts Content
Victoria
Carbonear
Freshwater
Conception Bay
Pouch Cove
Harbour Grace
Green's Harbour
Upper Island Cove
BELL
Torbay
Wabana
Spaniard's Bay
Shearstown
Coleys Pt.
Lance Cove
Dildo
Bay Roberts
Brigus
Mt. Pearl Pk.-Glendale
St. John's
DIV. NO. 1
Colliers
Petty Harbour
Whitbourne
Conception Harbour
Holyrood
0 5 10 Miles

Newfoundland and Labrador

CORNER BROOK–Adjusters

CUNNINGHAM LINDSEY
4 Herald Avenue, Suite 502
Corner Brook, NL A2H 4B4
Phone: (709) 639-7545
Fax: (709) 639-8955
Website: www.cunninghamlindsey.com
After Hours/Emergencies – 1-800-235-8784
E-mail: eporter@cl-na.com

GRAND FALLS–WINDSOR–Adjusters

CUNNINGHAM LINDSEY
2A Mill Road
Grand Falls, NL A2A 2J7
Phone: (709) 489-7966
Fax: (709) 489-5169
Website: www.cunninghamlindsey.com
After Hours/Emergencies – 1-800-235-8784
E-mail: eporter@cl-na.com

ST. JOHN'S–Adjusters

CRAWFORD & COMPANY
General Insurance Adjusters
96 Clyde Avenue
Suite 310
Mount Pearl, NL A1N 4S2
Phone: (709) 753-6351
E-mail: st.johns.claims@crawco.ca
Shelley Landry

CUNNINGHAM LINDSEY
15 Hallett Crescent
Suite 204
St. John's, NL A1B 4C4
Phone: (709) 753-7700
Fax: (709) 753-2956
Website: www.cunninghamlindsey.com
After Hours/Emergencies – 1-800-235-8784
E-mail: eporter@cl-na.com

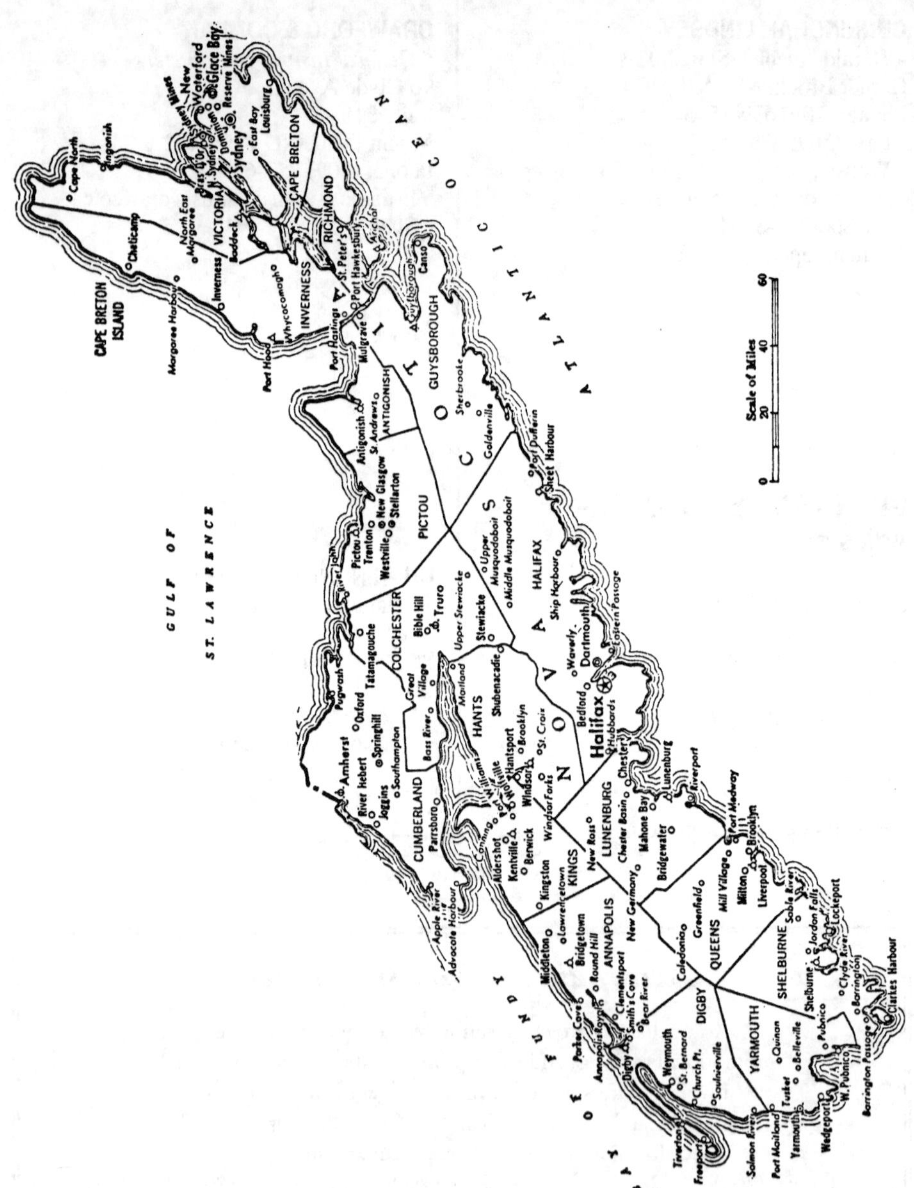
GULF OF ST. LAWRENCE
ATLANTIC OCEAN
NOVA SCOTIA
BAY OF FUNDY
CAPE BRETON ISLAND
Scale of Miles
0 20 40 60
CAPE BRETON
VICTORIA
INVERNESS
RICHMOND
GUYSBOROUGH
ANTIGONISH
PICTOU
COLCHESTER
CUMBERLAND
HANTS
HALIFAX
LUNENBURG
KINGS
ANNAPOLIS
QUEENS
DIGBY
SHELBURNE
YARMOUTH
Sydney
Glace Bay
New Waterford
Louisburg
Cheticamp
Inverness
Port Hawkesbury
Canso
Mulgrave
Port Hood
Antigonish
New Glasgow
Stellarton
Westville
Trenton
Pictou
Truro
Amherst
Springhill
Oxford
Pugwash
Parrsboro
Windsor
Hantsport
Wolfville
Kentville
Berwick
Middleton
Bridgetown
Annapolis Royal
Digby
Weymouth
Yarmouth
Halifax
Dartmouth
Bedford
Chester
Lunenburg
Mahone Bay
Bridgewater
Liverpool
Milton
Shelburne
Lockeport
Barrington Passage
Clarkes Harbour
Sheet Harbour
Sherbrooke
Stewiacke
Shubenacadie

Nova Scotia

DARTMOUTH–Adjusters

CUNNINGHAM LINDSEY

11 Morris Drive, Suite 200
Dartmouth, NS B3B 1M2
Phone: (902) 421-1519
Fax: (902) 429-7296
Website: www.cunninghamlindsey.com
After Hours/Emergencies –
1-800-235-8784
E-mail: eporter@cl-na.com

HALIFAX–Adjusters

CRAWFORD & COMPANY

General Insurance Adjusters
237 Brownlow Avenue, Suite 120
Dartmouth, NS B3B 2C7
Phone: (902) 468-7787
E-mail:
halifaxdartmouth.claims@crawco.ca
Walter Tingley, Manager

CUNNINGHAM LINDSEY

11 Morris Drive, Suite 200
Dartmouth, NS B3B 1M2
Phone: (902) 421-1519
Fax: (902) 429-7296
Website: www.cunninghamlindsey.com
After Hours/Emergencies –
1-800-235-8784
E-mail: eporter@cl-na.com

KERNAGHAN ADJUSTERS

General Insurance Adjusters
710 – 6009 Quinpool Road
Halifax, NS B3K 5J7
Phone: (902) 429-3440
Toll-free: 1-877-603-5677
Fax: (902) 425-0787
E-mail: halifax@kernaghan.com
Scott Lynds, CIP,
Senior Adjuster
Servicing: Mainland Nova Scotia and Southern Cape Breton.

HALIFAX–Forensic Accountants

MDD FORENSIC ACCOUNTANTS

Tracing its roots to 1933, MDD is an internationally recognized forensic accounting firm that focuses on economic damage quantification assessments. Our highly trained experienced professionals provide expert, consultant, and fact witness testimony. We have qualified as experts in courts around the world. Regardless of the nature of the assignment, MDD's exceptional dedication and demonstrated results have long been the hallmark of the firm.

Our practice areas include: Agriculture, Builders Risk, Business Disputes, Business Interruption, Business Valuation, Catastrophe Services, Class Actions, Construction, Contingency Entertainment, Disability, Matrimonial Disputes, Environmental Damages, Expropriation, Extra Expenses, Franchise, Fraud Investigations, Government Services, Intellectual Property, Liability Losses, Litigation, Lost Profits, Maritime, Mining & Refining, Oil & Gas, Personal Injury, Physical Damages, Power Generation, Product Liability, Reported Insurance, Stocks & Contents, Subrogation, Surety Funds, Toxic Tort, Transportation, and Valuable Papers.

1959 Upper Water Street, Suite 1301
Halifax, NS B3J 3N2
Phone: (902) 406-8886
Fax: (902) 422-2388
Website: www.mdd.com
Jarrett Reaume,
CPA, CA•IFA, CBV, CFE, CFF
Partner, Senior Vice President
E-mail: jreaume@mdd.com

HALIFAX–Insurance Loss Accountants

PRICEWATERHOUSECOOPERS LLP

Throughout Canada and around the world, PwC provides strategic assistance to insurance companies and legal counsel in investigating and resolving claims.

- *Business interruption losses*
- *Inventory assessment and valuation*
- *Economic loss quantification in liability claims, including product liability*
- *Product recall*
- *Assessment of financial motivation*
- *Personal injury tort claims for economic loss*

1601 Lower Water Street, Suite 400
Halifax, NS B3J 3P6
Phone: (902) 491-7400
Fax: (902) 422-1166
Website: www.pwc.com/ca/dai
PwC has over twenty offices across Canada.

HALIFAX–Investigating Consultants and Forensics

KODSI ENGINEERING INC.

Providing nation-wide engineering expertise from claim to settlement

We specialize in:

- *Accident Reconstruction*
- *Biomechanical Injury Assessments*
- *Mechanical Assessments*
- *Personal Injury – Slip/Trip and Fall Assessments*
- *Evidence Preservation*
- *Critiques of Opposing Expert Reports*
- *Expert Witness Testimony*

Phone: 1-800-263-6351
E-mail: info@kodsiengineering.com
Website: www.kodsiengineering.com
Sam Kodsi, P.Eng.
Shady Attalla, P.Eng.
Sami Shaker, B.Sc.
Kenneth Cowie, B.Sc.E.
Laurie Rogers, MBA

KENTVILLE–Adjusters

CRAWFORD & COMPANY

General Insurance Adjusters
237 Brownlow Avenue, Suite 120
Kentville Town Square
Dartmouth, NS B3B 2C7
Phone: (902) 678-7850
E-mail: kentville.claims@crawco.ca
Rannoch Harley, Manager

CUNNINGHAM LINDSEY

57 Webster Street, Suite 204
Kentville, NS B4N 1H6
Phone: (902) 678-1400
Fax: (902) 678-1490
Website: www.cunninghamlindsey.com
After Hours/Emergencies – 1-800-235-8784
E-mail: eporter@cl-na.com

NEW GLASGOW–Adjusters

CUNNINGHAM LINDSEY

342 Stewart Street
Suite 200
New Glasgow, NS B2H 2R7
Phone: (902) 755-4190
Fax: (902) 752-4429
Website: www.cunninghamlindsey.com
After Hours/Emergencies – 1-800-235-8784
E-mail: eporter@cl-na.com

STELLARTON–Adjusters

CRAWFORD & COMPANY

General Insurance Adjusters
195 North Foord Street
Suite 2
Stellarton, NS B0K 1S0
Phone: (902) 752-9388
E-mail: stellarton.claims@crawco.ca
Rannoch Harley, Manager

SYDNEY–Adjusters

CRAWFORD & COMPANY
General Insurance Adjusters
500 Kings Road, Suite 210
Sydney, NS B1S 1B1
Phone: (902) 564-4519
E-mail: sydney.claims@crawco.ca
Michael Tobin, Manager

CUNNINGHAM LINDSEY
200 James Street
Sydney, NS B1N 2S7
Phone: (902) 396-7022
Fax: (902) 270-2713
Website: www.cunninghamlindsey.com
After Hours/Emergencies – 1-800-235-8784
E-mail: eporter@cl-na.com

SYDNEY–Continued

KERNAGHAN ADJUSTERS
General Insurance Adjusters
30 Green Meadows Drive
Sydney, NS B1L 1C7
Phone: (902) 429-3900
Fax: (902) 425-0787
E-mail: sydney@kernaghan.com
Phil Harris BA, FCIP,
Nova Scotia Regional Manager
Servicing: Cape Breton Island and Antigonish areas.

YARMOUTH–Adjusters

CRAWFORD & COMPANY
General Insurance Adjusters
99 Water Street
Yarmouth, NS B5A 4P5
Phone: (902) 742-2021
E-mail: yarmouth.claims@crawco.ca
Rannoch Harley, Manager

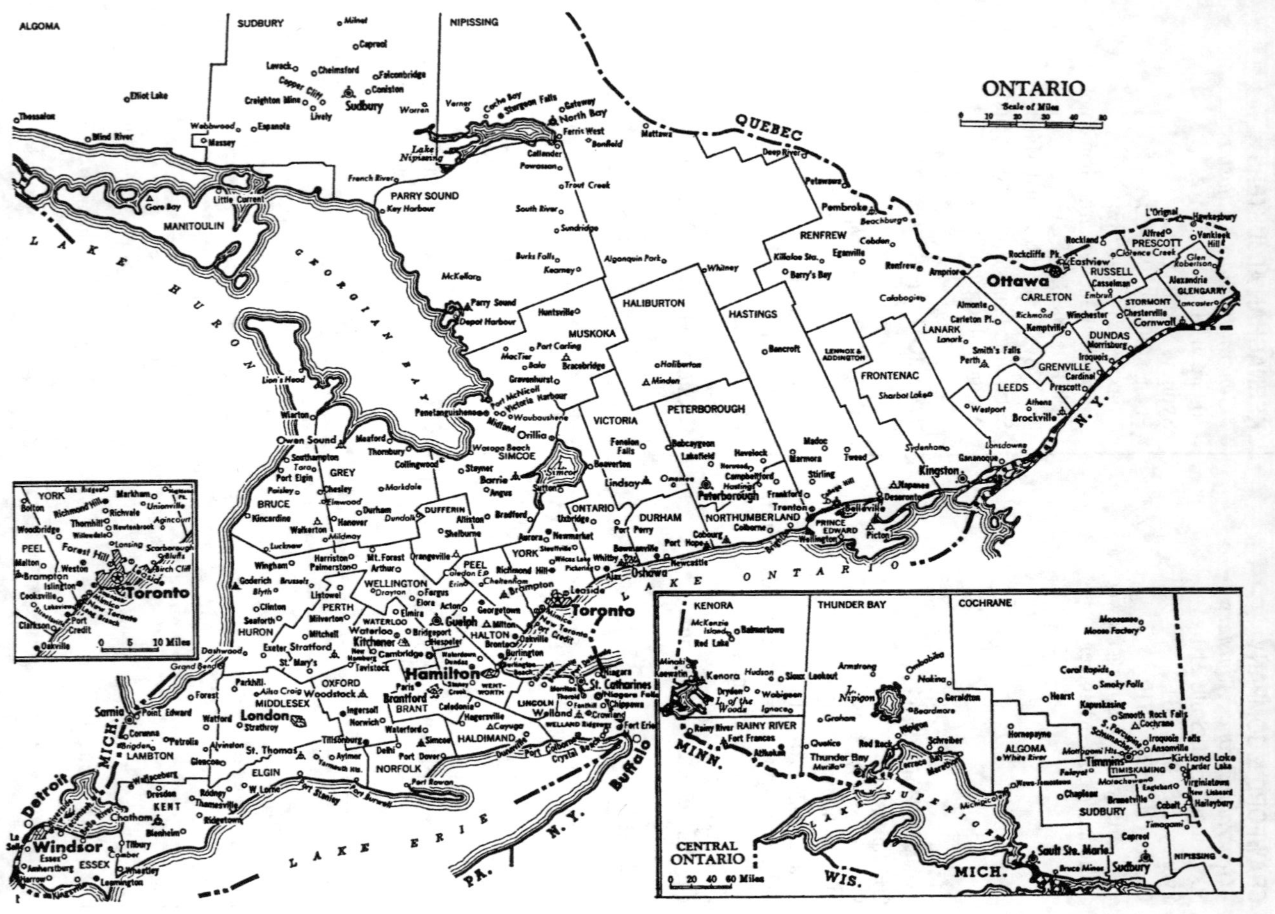
ONTARIO
Scale of Miles
QUEBEC
N.Y.
MICH.
PA.
LAKE ONTARIO
LAKE ERIE
LAKE HURON
GEORGIAN BAY
ALGOMA
SUDBURY
NIPISSING
PARRY SOUND
MANITOULIN
MUSKOKA
HALIBURTON
HASTINGS
RENFREW
FRONTENAC
LANARK
CARLETON
RUSSELL
PRESCOTT
GLENGARRY
STORMONT
DUNDAS
GRENVILLE
LEEDS
PETERBOROUGH
VICTORIA
DURHAM
NORTHUMBERLAND
SIMCOE
GREY
BRUCE
DUFFERIN
WELLINGTON
HURON
PERTH
WATERLOO
OXFORD
MIDDLESEX
LAMBTON
KENT
ESSEX
ELGIN
NORFOLK
HALDIMAND
BRANT
LINCOLN
HALTON
PEEL
YORK
ONTARIO
Ottawa
Toronto
Hamilton
London
Windsor
Kingston
Sudbury
Detroit
Buffalo
10 Miles
CENTRAL ONTARIO
0 20 40 60 Miles
KENORA
THUNDER BAY
COCHRANE
RAINY RIVER
TIMISKAMING
MINN.
WIS.

Ontario

BANCROFT–Adjusters

PCA ADJUSTERS LIMITED
122 Parks Drive, Suite 4
Belleville, ON K8N 4Z5
Phone: (613) 962-9566 (24 hours)
Toll-free: 1-888-962-9556
Fax: (613) 962-9596
Toll-free Fax: 1-800-722-7896
Phone and fax 24 hours
E-mail: claims@pca-adj.com
Website: www.pca-adj.com
Servicing all of the Eastern Ontario corridor.
Member: C.I.A.A., O.I.A.A., O.V.A.A., C.A.F.I.–A.M. Best Recommended 2018

D.R. SIEGEL INSURANCE ADJUSTERS LIMITED
Member of ClaimsPlus
129 Beckett View Drive
Pembroke, ON K8A 6W2
Phone: (613) 638-2400 (24 hours)
Fax: (613) 638-2402
E-mail: siegadj@nrtco.net
Don/Diane Siegel residence
(613) 638-1236
Servicing the Upper Ottawa Valley including Pembroke, west to Rolphton, south to Bancroft, east to Arnprior and all points between.
Member: CIAA, OIAA, OVAA, CAFI

BARRIE–Adjusters

CRAWFORD & COMPANY
General Insurance Adjusters
431 Bayview Drive, Unit 11
Barrie, ON L4N 8Y2
Phone: (705) 728-5597
E-mail: barrie.claims@crawco.ca
Mary Charman, Manager

BARRIE–Continued

CUNNINGHAM LINDSEY
74 Cedar Pointe Drive, Unit 1001
Barrie, ON L4N 5R7
Phone: (705) 728-8398
Fax: (705) 734-0559
Website: www.cunninghamlindsey.com
After Hours/Emergencies –
1-800-235-8784
E-mail: hpalma@cl-na.com

DSB CLAIMS SOLUTIONS
General Insurance Adjusters
92 Caplan Avenue, Suite 118
Barrie, ON L4N 9J2
Phone: (705) 315-0222
Fax: 1-866-641-3151
E-mail: claims@dsbclaims.com
Website: www.dsbclaims.com
Amanda Massie, Manager

KERNAGHAN ADJUSTERS
General Insurance Adjusters
P.O. Box 31042, Molson Park Road
Barrie, ON L4N 0B3
Phone: (705) 241-5474
Fax: (416) 251-3819
E-mail: barrie@kernaghan.com
Eric Gunnel, Senior Adjuster
Servicing: Barrie, Newmarket, Richmond Hill, Markham, Aurora, Orangeville, Tottenham, Keswick, Owen Sound, Collingwood, Orillia, Midland, and Gravenhurst.

BELLEVILLE–Adjusters

CRAWFORD & COMPANY
General Insurance Adjusters
365 North Front Street, Suite 210
Belleville, ON K8P 5A5
Manager: Brian Hambly
Phone: (613) 966-2872
E-mail: belleville.claims@crawco.ca
Brian Hambly, Manager

BELLEVILLE–Continued

CUNNINGHAM LINDSEY
334-A Pinnacle Street
Belleville, ON K8N 3B4
Phone: (613) 966-4755
Fax: (613) 966-2655
Website: www.cunninghamlindsey.com
E-mail: agallagher@cl-na.com

DSB CLAIMS SOLUTIONS
General Insurance Adjusters
110 North Front Street, A-3, Suite 358
Belleville, ON K8P 0A6
Phone: (613) 707-6778
Fax: 1-866-641-3151
E-mail: claims@dsbclaims.com
Website: www.dsbclaims.com
Nesar Sadeque, Manager

PCA ADJUSTERS LIMITED
122 Parks Drive, Suite 4
Belleville, ON K8N 4Z5
Phone: (613) 962-9566 (24 hours)
Toll-free: 1-888-962-9556
Fax: (613) 962-9596
Toll-free Fax: 1-800-722-7896
Phone and fax 24 hours
E-mail: claims@pca-adj.com
Website: www.pca-adj.com
Servicing all of the Eastern Ontario corridor.
Member: C.I.A.A., O.I.A.A., O.V.A.A., C.A.F.I.–A.M. Best Recommended 2018

BRACEBRIDGE–Adjusters

DSB CLAIMS SOLUTIONS
General Insurance Adjusters
505 Hwy 118 West, Suite 317
Bracebridge, ON P1L 2G7
Phone: (705) 646-3427
Fax: 1-866-641-3151
E-mail: claims@dsbclaims.com
Website: www.dsbclaims.com
David J. Rienzo, Manager

BRAMPTON–Adjusters

CUNNINGHAM LINDSEY
50 Burnhamthorpe Road West, Suite 1102
Mississauga, ON L5B 3C2
Phone: (905) 896-8181
Fax: (905) 896-3485
Website: www.cunninghamlindsey.com
After Hours/Emergencies – 1-800-235-8784
E-mail: rgreyling@cl-na.com

DSB CLAIMS SOLUTIONS
General Insurance Adjusters
204 Main Street North
Brampton, ON L6V 1P1
Phone: (905) 915-4683
Fax: (905) 915-4685
E-mail: claims@dsbclaims.com
Website: www.dsbclaims.com
Balvinder Cheema, Manager

BRANTFORD–Adjusters

CRAWFORD & COMPANY
General Insurance Adjusters
166 Charing Cross Street
Brantford, ON N3R 2J4
Phone: 519 759 5760
E-mail: brantford.claims@crawco.ca
Michael McLeod, Manager

CUNNINGHAM LINDSEY
P.O. Box 23004
Stn. Main
Brantford, ON N3T 6K4
Phone: 1-800-668-9922
Fax: (905) 684-5033
Website: www.cunninghamlindsey.com
After Hours/Emergencies – 1-800-235-8784
E-mail: tblack@cl-na.com

BROCKVILLE–Adjusters

CRAWFORD & COMPANY
General Insurance Adjusters
163 Ormond Street
Suite 306
Brockville, ON K6V 7E6
Phone: 1-877-579-890 ext. 2593
E-mail: brockville.claims@crawco.ca
Nancy Brooks, Manager

CUNNINGHAM LINDSEY
163P Ormond Street
Suite 202
Brockville, ON K6V 7E6
Phone: 1-866-874-4402
Website: www.cunninghamlindsey.com
After Hours/Emergencies – 1-800-235-8784
E-mail: agallagher@cl-na.com

BROCKVILLE–Continued

PCA ADJUSTERS LIMITED
234 Concession Street, Suite 201
Kingston, ON K7K 6W6
Phone: (613) 544-9771
Toll-free: 1-866-544-9771
Fax: (613) 544-3487
Phone and fax 24 hours
E-mail: claims@pca-adj.com
Website: www.pca-adj.com
Servicing all of the Eastern Ontario corridor.
Member: C.I.A.A., O.I.A.A., O.V.A.A., C.A.F.I.–A.M. Best Recommended 2018

CHATHAM–Adjusters

CUNNINGHAM LINDSEY
55 Dover Street, Suite 2
Chatham, ON N7L 1S7
Phone: (519) 352-4160
Fax: (519) 352-4169
Website: www.cunninghamlindsey.com

COBALT–Adjusters

ADJUSTERS SSA LIMITED
See North Bay, Ontario, listing for full details
Phone: (705) 476-1474
E-mail: ssanbay@vianet.on.ca

COBOURG–Adjusters

PCA ADJUSTERS LIMITED
122 Parks Drive, Suite 4
Belleville, ON K8N 4Z5
Phone: (613) 962-9566 (24 hours)
Toll-free: 1-888-962-9556
Fax: (613) 962-9596
Toll-free Fax: 1-800-722-7896
Phone and fax 24 hours
E-mail: claims@pca-adj.com
Website: www.pca-adj.com
Servicing all of the Eastern Ontario corridor.
Member: C.I.A.A., O.I.A.A., O.V.A.A., C.A.F.I.–A.M. Best Recommended 2018

COCHRANE–Insurance Counsel

WEAVER, SIMMONS LLP
Barristers & Solicitors

See Sudbury, Ontario, listing for full details
Phone: (705) 674-6421

CORNWALL–Adjusters

CUNNINGHAM LINDSEY
P.O. Box 158
Cornwall, ON K6J 1C5
Phone: (613) 774-1277
Fax: 1-855-580-5852
Website: www.cunninghamlindsey.com
After Hours/Emergencies – 1-800-235-8784
E-mail: agallagher@cl-na.com

PCA ADJUSTERS LIMITED
The Chambers of Queensview
2725 Queensview Drive, Suite 100
Ottawa, ON K2B 0A1
Phone: (613) 726-9556
Toll-free: 1-800-722-9556
Fax: (613) 726-0000
Toll-free Fax: 1-800-722-7896
Phone and fax 24 hours
E-mail: claims@pca-adj.com
Website: www.pca-adj.com
Servicing all of the Eastern Ontario corridor.
Member: C.I.A.A., O.I.A.A., O.V.A.A., C.A.F.I.–A.M. Best Recommended 2018

GUELPH–Adjusters

CUNNINGHAM LINDSEY
291 Woodlawn Road West
Unit 1, Block A
Guelph, ON N1H 7L6
Phone: (519) 822-7110
Fax: (519) 822-7063
Website: www.cunninghamlindsey.com
After Hours/Emergencies – 1-800-235-8784
E-mail: hpalma@cl-na.com

HAILEYBURY–Adjusters

ADJUSTERS SSA LIMITED
See North Bay, Ontario, listing for full details
Phone: (705) 476-1474
E-mail: ssanbay@vianet.on.ca

HAILEYBURY–Insurance Counsel

WEAVER, SIMMONS LLP
Barristers & Solicitors

See Sudbury, Ontario, listing for full details
Phone: (705) 674-6421

HAMILTON–Adjusters

BANNATYNE & COMPANY GENERAL INSURANCE ADJUSTERS LTD.
All Lines
481 Main Street East
Hamilton, ON L8N 1K1
Phone: (905) 528-0661 or 1-800-667-3102 24 hr. paging
Fax: (905) 528-9200
E-mail: claims@bannatyneadjusters.com
Nights:
Bob Phipps (905) 741-8136
Peter MacKinnon (416) 417-0577
Member: C.I.A.A., O.I.A.A., I.A.A.I., A.C.F.E.

HAMILTON–Continued

CRAWFORD & COMPANY

General Insurance Adjusters
4 Hughson Street South, 6th Floor
Hamilton, ON L8N 3Z1
Phone: (905) 529-9600
E-mail: hamilton.claims@crawco.ca
Kelly Stevens, Manager

CUNNINGHAM LINDSEY

4 Jackson Street East
Hamilton, ON L8N 1J1
Phone: (905) 521-0340
Fax: 1-800-767-9907
Website: www.cunninghamlindsey.com
After Hours/Emergencies – 1-800-235-8784
E-mail: rgreyling@cl-na.com or tblack@cl-na.com

DSB CLAIMS SOLUTIONS

General Insurance Adjusters
1 Hunter Street East, Ground Floor
Hamilton, ON L8N 3W1
Phone: (905) 218-6205
Fax: 1-866-641-3151
E-mail: claims@dsbclaims.com
Website: www.dsbclaims.com

KERNAGHAN ADJUSTERS

General Insurance Adjusters
22 Windsor Drive, P.O. Box 1001
St. George, ON N0E 1N0
Phone: (905) 522-6116
Fax: (416) 251-3819
E-mail: Hamilton@kernaghan.com
Peter Doublard, Senior Adjuster
Servicing: Brantford, Cambridge, Woodstock, Burlington, Oakville, Stoney Creek, Grimsby, Beamsville, Simcoe, Port Dover, Cayuga, and Niagara.

HAMILTON–Forensic Accountants

MDD FORENSIC ACCOUNTANTS

Tracing its roots to 1933, MDD is an internationally recognized forensic accounting firm that focuses on economic damage quantification assessments. Our highly trained experienced professionals provide expert, consultant, and fact witness testimony. We have qualified as experts in courts around the world. Regardless of the nature of the assignment, MDD's exceptional dedication and demonstrated results have long been the hallmark of the firm.

Our practice areas include: Accident Benefits, Agriculture, Builders Risk, Business Disputes, Business Interruption, Business Valuation, Catastrophe Services, Class Actions, Construction, Contingency Entertainment, Disability, Matrimonial Disputes, Environmental Damages, Expropriation, Extra Expenses, Franchise, Fraud Investigations, Government Services, Intellectual Property, Liability Losses, Litigation, Lost Profits, Maritime, Mining & Refining, Oil & Gas, Personal Injury, Physical Damages, Power Generation, Product Liability, Reported Insurance, Stocks & Contents, Subrogation, Surety Funds, Toxic Tort, Transportation, and Valuable Papers.

25 Main Street West, Suite 1105
Hamilton, ON L8P 1H1
Phone: (905) 523-6363
Fax: (905) 523-6362
Website: www.mdd.com
Martin Pavelic, CPA, CMA, CFF
Partner, Senior Vice-President
E-mail: mpavelic@mdd.com
HJ Ustler
Senior Consultant
E-mail: hjustler@mdd.com

HAMILTON–Insurance Counsel

EVANS, PHILP LLP

Barristers & Solicitors

Robert H. Rogers, LL.B.
rrogers@evansphilp.com
Linda M. O'Brien, LL.B.
lobrien@evansphilp.com
M. Kathleen Robb, LL.B.
krobb@evansphilp.com
Kieran C. Dickson, LL.B.
kdickson@evansphilp.com
Kevin H. Griffiths, LL.B.
kgriffiths@evansphilp.com
Carolynne J. Wahlman, LL.B.
cwahlman@evansphilp.com
Pamela J. Quesnel, LL.B.
pquesnel@evansphilp.com
Cara L. Boddy, LL.B.
cboddy@evansphilp.com
Leanne W. Zabudsky, LL.B
lzabudsky@evansphilp.com
Jessica L. Rogers, LL.B.
jrogers@evansphilp.com
Brendan M. Lanigan, J.D.
blanigan@evansphilp.com
Andrew M. Baerg, J.D.
abaerg@evansphilp.com
Kenneth J. Raddatz, J.D.
kraddatz@evansphilp.com
Amanda R.M. Faulkner, J.D.
afaulkner@evansphilp.com
Cameron R. Malcolm, J.D.
cmalcolm@evansphilp.com
David E.W. Koots, J.D.
dkoots@evansphilp.com
Samantha E. Slater, J.D.
sslater@evansphilp.com
Marcin J. Panasewicz, J.D.
mpanasewicz@evansphilp.com
Frank Kolenko, LL.B.
fkolenko@evansphilp.com
Orville M. Walsh, K.C.
(1919–1949)
F. John L. Evans, Q.C., LL.B.
(1931–1980)
Joseph M. Pigott, Q.C., LL.B.
(1971–2001)

HAMILTON–Continued

EVANS, PHILP LLP–Continued

One King Street West, Suite 1600
Hamilton, ON L8P 1A4
Telephone: (905) 525-1200
Fax: (905) 525-7897
Website: www.evansphilp.com

HUNTSVILLE–Adjusters

CRAWFORD & COMPANY

General Insurance Adjusters

12 High Street, Suite 4
Huntsville, ON P1H 1N9
Phone: (705) 789-2366
E-mail: huntsville.claims@crawco.ca
Mary Charman, Manager

KAPUSKASING–Adjusters

CRAWFORD & COMPANY

General Insurance Adjusters

9A Queen Street
Kapuskasing, ON P5N 1G5
Phone: (705) 337-6565
E-mail: kapuskasing.claims@crawco.ca
Michael Bottan, Manager

KINGSTON–Adjusters

CUNNINGHAM LINDSEY

1875 Bath Road
P.O. Box 26013
Kingston, ON K7M 4Y0
Phone: (613) 384-5564
Fax: (613) 384-0810
Website: www.cunninghamlindsey.com
After Hours/Emergencies –
1-800-235-8784
E-mail: agallagher@cl-na.com

KINGSTON–Continued

PCA ADJUSTERS LIMITED

234 Concession Street, Suite 201
Kingston, ON K7K 6W6
Phone: (613) 544-9771
Toll-free: 1-866-544-9771
Fax: (613) 544-3487
Phone and fax 24 hours
E-mail: claims@pca-adj.com
Website: www.pca-adj.com
Servicing all of the Eastern Ontario corridor.
Member: C.I.A.A., O.I.A.A., O.V.A.A., C.A.F.I.–A.M. Best Recommended 2018

KINGSTON–Forensic Accountants

MDD FORENSIC ACCOUNTANTS

Tracing its roots to 1933, MDD is an internationally recognized forensic accounting firm that focuses on economic damage quantification assessments. Our highly trained experienced professionals provide expert, consultant, and fact witness testimony. We have qualified as experts in courts around the world. Regardless of the nature of the assignment, MDD's exceptional dedication and demonstrated results have long been the hallmark of the firm.

See our Hamilton, Ontario, listing for a complete list of our practice areas.

KINGSTON–Continued

MDD FORENSIC ACCOUNTANTS–Continued

27 Princess Street
Suite 402
Kingston, ON K7L 1A3
Phone: (613) 389-3176
Fax: (613) 389-3590
Website: www.mdd.com
Esther A. Young, CPA, CMA, CFF, DIFA
Partner, Senior Vice President
E-mail: eyoung@mdd.com

KITCHENER/WATERLOO–Adjusters

CRAWFORD & COMPANY

General Insurance Adjusters
Head Office
539 Riverbend Drive
Kitchener, ON N2K 3S3
Phone: (519) 578-5540
E-mail: michael.mcleod@crawco.ca
Michael McLeod, Manager

KITCHENER/WATERLOO–Insurance Counsel

GIFFEN LLP

Lawyers
Donald C. Olson, B.A., LL.B.
Philip A. Garbutt, B.A., LL.B.
Graham M. Bennett, B.A. (Hons.), LL.B.*
John P. Murray, B.A., J.D.
Lorrie Stojni, B.A., M.A., LL.B.
Stephen T. Brogden, B.A. (Hons.), LL.B.
Kyle D. Cleaver, B.Comm. (Hons.), J.D.
Cynthia Davis, B.A. (Hons.), LL.B.
Nolan R. Downer, B.A., LL.B.
Gregory A. Carr, B.A., B.P.H.E., J.D.
Anamaria Maghetiu, B.A. (Hons.), J.D.
Nathan Spaling, B.A. (Hons.), J.D.
Jorden Gregory, B.A. (Hons.), J.D.
Derek K. Kim, B.A., J.D.
Simon J. Adler, LL.B., LL.M. – *Counsel*
J. Peter Giffen, Q.C.* – *Retired*
J. Scott Morley, B.Comm., LL.B. – *Retired*
David S. Whitfield, B.A., LL.B. – *Retired*
Gary E.J. Hauser, B.A., LL.B. – *Retired*
Brian R. Wagner, B.A., LL.B.* – *Retired*

Commerce House
50 Queen Street North, Suite 500
Kitchener, ON
Mailing address: P.O. Box 2396
Kitchener, ON N2H 6M3
Phone: (519) 578-4150
Fax: (519) 578-8740
E-mail: info@giffenlawyers.com
Website: www.giffenlawyers.com
Toronto Office:
330 Bay Street, Suite 1400
Toronto, ON M5H 2S8
Phone: (416) 628-5709
Fax: (416) 628-5692
*Certified by the Law Society as a Specialist in Civil Litigation.
Member: K-W Adjusters Association, Canadian Bar Association, Advocates' Society

KITCHENER/WATERLOO–Continued

MADORIN, SNYDER LLP

Barristers & Solicitors
W.H. Peter Madorin, Q.C.
pmadorin@kw-law.com
Frank D. Carere
fcarere@kw-law.com
Bruce Lackenbauer
blackenbauer@kw-law.com
James H. Bennett
jbennett@kw-law.com
Stephen R. Grant
sgrant@kw-law.com
Tim J. McGowan
tmcgowan@kw-law.com
Leanne E. Way
lway@kw-law.com
Edward J. Dreyer
edreyer@kw-law.com
Robert K. Bickle
rbickle@kw-law.com
Filipe A. Mendes
fmendes@kw-law.com
Dawn E. Phillips-Brown
dphillips-brown@kw-law.com
Christopher D. Clemmer
cclemmer@kw-law.com
Ross E. Weber
rweber@kw-law.com
Erin G. Kadwell
ekadwell@kw-law.com

Counsel
H. Wayne Snyder
wsnyder@kw-law.com
James R. Guy
jguy@kw-law.com
W. Charles Drewitz
Anthony T. Keller

Mailing address:
P.O. Box 1234
55 King Street West
6th Floor
Kitchener, ON N2G 4G9
Phone: (519) 744-4491
Fax: (519) 741-8060
E-mail: reception@kw-law.com
Website: www.kw-law.com

LONDON–Adjusters

CRAWFORD & COMPANY

General Insurance Adjusters
150 Kent Street, 1st Floor
London, ON N6A 1L3
Phone: (519) 432-3747
E-mail: london.claims@crawco.ca
Michael McLeod, Manager

CUNNINGHAM LINDSEY

1240 Commissioners Road West
Suite 206
London, ON N6K 1C7
Phone: (519) 432-8335
Fax: (519) 432-0054
Website: www.cunninghamlindsey.com
After Hours/Emergencies –
1-800-235-8784

DSB CLAIMS SOLUTIONS

General Insurance Adjusters
380 Wellington Street, Tower B
6th Floor
London, ON N6A 5B5
Phone: (519) 279-1978
Fax: 1-866-641-3151
E-mail: claims@dsbclaims.com
Website: www.dsbclaims.com
Brian Lloyd, Manager

LONDON–Forensic Accountants

MDD FORENSIC ACCOUNTANTS

Tracing its roots to 1933, MDD is an internationally recognized forensic accounting firm that focuses on economic damage quantification assessments. Our highly trained experienced professionals provide expert, consultant, and fact witness testimony. We have qualified as experts in courts around the world. Regardless of the nature of the assignment, MDD's exceptional dedication and demonstrated results have long been the hallmark of the firm.

LONDON–Continued

MDD FORENSIC ACCOUNTANTS–Continued

See our Hamilton, Ontario, listing for a complete list of our practice areas.

148 Fullarton Street, Suite 1704
London, ON N6A 5P3
Phone: (519) 432-1123
Fax: (519) 432-1503
Website: www.mdd.com
Sheri A. Gallant, CPA, CMA, CFF
Partner, Senior Vice President
E-mail: sgallant@mdd.com

LONDON–Insurance Loss Accountants

PRICEWATERHOUSECOOPERS LLP

Throughout Canada and around the world, PwC provides strategic assistance to insurance companies and legal counsel in investigating and resolving claims.

- *Business interruption losses*
- *Inventory assessment and valuation*
- *Economic loss quantification in liability claims, including product liability*
- *Product recall*
- *Assessment of financial motivation*
- *Personal injury tort claims for economic loss*
- *Valuation of fidelity and employee dishonesty claims*

465 Richmond Street, Suite 400
London, ON N6A 5P4
Phone: (519) 640-8000
Fax: (519) 460-8015
Website: www.pwc.com/ca/dai
PwC has over twenty offices across Canada.

MARKHAM–Adjusters

DSB CLAIMS SOLUTIONS

General Insurance Adjusters
8500 Leslie Street, Suite 101
Markham, ON L3T 7M8
Phone: (647) 545-4225
Fax: 1-866-641-3151
E-mail: claims@dsbclaims.com
Website: www.dsbclaims.com
Arwin Te, Manager

MILTON–Adjusters

CUNNINGHAM LINDSEY

50 Burnhamthorpe Road West
Suite 1102
Mississauga, ON L5B 3C2
Phone: (905) 896-8181
Fax: (905) 896-3485
Website: www.cunninghamlindsey.com
After Hours/Emergencies – 1-800-235-8784
E-mail: rgreyling@cl-na.com

MISSISSAUGA–Adjusters

CRAWFORD & COMPANY

General Insurance Adjusters
110 Matheson Boulevard West, Suite 301
Mississauga, ON L5R 4G7
Phone: (905) 568-7550
E-mail: torontowest.claims@crawco.ca
Kelly Stevens, Manager

CUNNINGHAM LINDSEY

Head Office
50 Burnhamthorpe Road West
Suite 1102
Mississauga, ON L5B 3C2
Phone: (905) 896-8181
Fax: (905) 896-3485
Website: www.cunninghamlindsey.com
After Hours/Emergencies – 1-800-235-8784
E-mail: rgreyling@cl-na.com

MISSISSAUGA–Environmental Consultants

PINCHIN LTD.

Head Office
2470 Milltower Court
Mississauga, ON L5N 7W5
Phone: (905) 363-0678
After hours: 1-800-577-2653
Fax: (905) 363-0681
E-mail: nbutler@pinchin.com
Website: www.pinchin.com
Contact: Neil Butler

MISSISSAUGA–Investigating Consultants and Forensics

KODSI ENGINEERING INC.

See Toronto, Ontario, listing for full details
Phone: (416) 977-0009
Fax: (416) 977-6622
Toll-free: 1-800-263-6351

NEW LISKEARD–Adjusters

ADJUSTERS SSA LIMITED

See North Bay, Ontario, listing for full details
Phone: (705) 476-1474
E-mail: ssanbay@vianet.on.ca

CRAWFORD & COMPANY

114 Whitewood Avenue
P.O. Box 280
New Liskeard, ON P0J 1P0
Phone: (705) 647-6781
E-mail: newliskeard.claims@crawco.ca

NEWMARKET–Adjusters

CRAWFORD & COMPANY

General Insurance Adjusters
120 Mulock Drive, Suite 1
Newmarket, ON L3Y 7C5
Phone: (905) 898-0008
E-mail: newmarket.claims@crawco.ca
Mary Charman, Manager

NIAGARA FALLS–Adjusters

LEADING EDGE CLAIMS SERVICES

See Niagara region, Ontario, listing for full details
Phone: (289) 897-8676
Fax: (289) 897-8677

NIAGARA FALLS–Insurance Counsel

SULLIVAN MAHONEY LLP

Lawyers
4781 Portage Road
Niagara Falls, ON L2E 6B1
Telephone: (905) 357-0500
Fax: (905) 357-0501
Head Office: St. Catharines, Ontario.

NIAGARA REGION–Adjusters

LEADING EDGE CLAIMS SERVICES

Property, Casualty, Transportation, Environmental, Agricultural, Marine, Superior Customer Service, Thoroughly Investigated Claims
78 Highway 20 West
P.O. Box 1399
Fonthill, ON L0S 1E0
Phone: (289) 897-8676
Fax: (289) 897-8677
Nights: (905) 704-9338
E-mail: jeff@leadingedgecs.ca
Website: www.leadingedgecs.ca
Jeff Edge, CIP, CFEI, President and Senior Technical Adjuster
Serving the Niagara Region, Hamilton, Burlington, Oakville, the Greater Toronto area, west to London.
Member: C.I.A.A., O.I.A.A.

NORTH BAY–Adjusters

ADJUSTERS SSA LIMITED

All Classes
1025 Cassells Street, P.O. Box 1436
North Bay, ON P1B 8K6
Phone: (705) 476-1474 (24 hours)
Fax: (705) 476-8285
Toll-free: 1-800 663-0355 (24 hours)
E-mail: ssanbay@vianet.on.ca
Servicing: North Bay, Mattawa, Powassan, Sundridge, Temiskaming Shores, Trout Creek, South River, Huntsville, New Liskeard, and Kirkland Lake.
Member: C.I.A.A., O.I.A.A., C.A.F.I., N.A.F.I.

CRAWFORD & COMPANY

General Insurance Adjusters
326 McIntyre Street West
North Bay, ON P1B 2Z1
Phone: (705) 476-2120
E-mail: northbay.claims@crawco.ca
Michael Bottan, Manager

CUNNINGHAM LINDSEY

66 Josephine Street
P.O. Box 24030
North Bay, ON P1B 0C7
Phone: (705) 474-7990
Fax: (705) 474-5434
Website: www.cunninghamlindsey.com
After Hours/Emergencies – 1-800-235-8784
E-mail: dfiloon@cl-na.com

SCS INSURANCE ADJUSTERS

General Insurance Adjusters
182 McIntyre Street East, Suite 1
North Bay, ON P1B 1C4
Phone: (705) 476-3700
Fax: (705) 476-8425
Marc R. Mantha, Branch Manager
E-mail: marcscs@vianet.ca
Other offices: Sault Ste. Marie, Sudbury, Timmins, and Thunder Bay.

NORTH BAY–Insurance Counsel

WEAVER, SIMMONS LLP

Barristers & Solicitors

116 McIntyre Street West
North Bay, ON P1B 2Y6
Phone: (705) 497-1900
Fax: (705) 497-1700
Website: www.weaversimmons.com

OAKVILLE–Adjusters

CRAWFORD & COMPANY

General Insurance Adjusters
110 Matheson Boulevard West, Suite 301
Mississauga, ON L5R 4G7
Phone: (905) 568-7550
E-mail: oakville.claims@crawco.ca
Michael McLeod, Manager

OAKVILLE–Insurance Loss Accountants

PRICEWATERHOUSECOOPERS LLP

Throughout Canada and around the world, PwC provides strategic assistance to insurance companies and legal counsel in investigating and resolving claims.

- *Business interruption losses*
- *Inventory assessment and valuation*
- *Economic loss quantification in liability claims, including product liability*
- *Product recall*
- *Assessment of financial motivation*
- *Personal injury tort claims for economic loss*
- *Valuation of fidelity and employee dishonesty claims*

PwC Centre
354 Davis Road, Suite 600
Oakville, ON L6J 0C5
Phone: (905) 815-6300
Fax: (905) 815-6499
Website: www.pwc.com/ca/dai
PwC has over twenty offices across Canada.

ORANGEVILLE–Adjusters

CRAWFORD & COMPANY

General Insurance Adjusters
75 First Street, Suite 243
Orangeville, ON L9W 5B6
Phone: (905) 898-0008
E-mail: orangeville.claims@crawco.ca
Mary Charman, Manager

OSHAWA–Adjusters

CUNNINGHAM LINDSEY

633 King Street East, Suite 202
Oshawa, ON L1H 1G3
Phone: (905) 723-8541
Fax: (905) 723-2065
Website: www.cunninghamlindsey.com
After Hours/Emergencies – 1-800-235-8784
E-mail: rgreyling@cl-na.com

DSB CLAIMS SOLUTIONS

General Insurance Adjusters
1288 Ritson Road North, Suite 357
Oshawa, ON L1G 8B2
Phone: (905) 233-2036
Fax: 1-866-641-3151
E-mail: claims@dsbclaims.com
Website: www.dsbclaims.com
Nesar Sadeque, Manager

KERNAGHAN ADJUSTERS

General Insurance Adjusters
27 – 1300 King Street East, Suite 282
Oshawa, ON L1H 8J4
Phone: (905) 260-3472
Fax: (905) 433-7045
E-mail: oshawa@kernaghan.com
Servicing: Clarington, Bowmanville, New Castle, Courtice, Whitby, Durham Region, Ajax, Lindsay, Uxbridge, Port Perry, Port Hope, Cobourg, Brighton, Trenton, and Kawartha Lakes.

OTTAWA–Adjusters

CUNNINGHAM LINDSEY

177 Colonnade Road South
Suite 100
Ottawa, ON K2E 7J4
Phone: (613) 728-9600
Fax: (613) 728-2922
Website: www.cunninghamlindsey.com
After Hours/Emergencies – 1-800-235-8784
E-mail: agallagher@cl-na.com

PCA ADJUSTERS LIMITED

The Chambers of Queensview
2725 Queensview Drive, Suite 100
Ottawa, ON K2B 0A1
Phone: (613) 726-9556
Toll-free: 1-800-722-9556
Fax: (613) 726-0000
Toll-free Fax: 1-800-722-7896
Phone and fax 24 hours
E-mail: claims@pca-adj.com
Website: www.pca-adj.com
Servicing all of the Eastern Ontario corridor.
Member: C.I.A.A., O.I.A.A., O.V.A.A., C.A.F.I.–A.M. Best Recommended 2018

OTTAWA–Continued

UPRIGHT CLAIMS SERVICES LTD.

General Insurance Adjusters specializing in large commercial and personal lines property and casualty losses, builders' risk, environmental losses, professional, product and general liability claims, business interruption, and title insurance claims

17 – 110 Didsbury Road
Ottawa, ON K2T 0C2
Phone: (613) 836-4660 (24/7)
Cell: (David Friesen) (613) 818-3593
Fax: (613) 482-4965
Nights: (613) 836-4660
E-mail: Dave.Friesen@uprightclaims.com
Website: www.uprightclaims.com
David Friesen, President
Covering Ottawa and Eastern Ontario.
Member: C.I.A.A., O.I.A.A.

OTTAWA–Insurance Loss Accountants

PRICEWATERHOUSECOOPERS LLP

Throughout Canada and around the world, PwC provides strategic assistance to insurance companies and legal counsel in investigating and resolving claims.

- *Business interruption losses*
- *Inventory assessment and valuation*
- *Economic loss quantification in liability claims, including product liability*
- *Product recall*
- *Assessment of financial motivation*
- *Personal injury tort claims for economic loss*
- *Valuation of fidelity and employee dishonesty claims*

99 Bank Street, Suite 800
Ottawa, ON K1P 1E4
Phone: (613) 237-3702
Fax: (613) 237-3963
Website: www.pwc.com/ca/dai
PwC has over twenty offices across Canada.

OWEN SOUND–Adjusters

CRAWFORD & COMPANY

General Insurance Adjusters
345 8th Street East, Suite 208
Owen Sound, ON N4K 1L3
Phone: (519) 371-2252
E-mail: owensound.claims@crawco.ca
Michael McLeod, Manager

CUNNINGHAM LINDSEY

1717 2nd Avenue East, Suite 103
Owen Sound, ON N4K 6V4
Phone: (519) 376-7590
Fax: (519) 376-7908
Website: www.cunninghamlindsey.com
After Hours/Emergencies – 1-800-235-8784
E-mail: hpalma@cl-na.com

PARRY SOUND–Insurance Counsel

WEAVER, SIMMONS LLP

Barristers & Solicitors

See Sudbury, Ontario, listing for full details
Phone: (705) 674-6421

PEMBROKE–Adjusters

D.R. SIEGEL INSURANCE ADJUSTERS LIMITED

Member of ClaimsPlus
129 Beckett View Drive
Pembroke, ON K8A 6W2
Phone: (613) 638-2400 (24 hours)
Fax: (613) 638-2402
E-mail: siegadj@nrtco.net
Don/Diane Siegel residence (613) 638-1236
Servicing the Upper Ottawa Valley including Pembroke, west to Rolphton, south to Bancroft, east to Arnprior and all points between.
Member: CIAA, OIAA, OVAA, CAFI

PEMBROKE/PETAWAWA–Adjusters

PCA ADJUSTERS LIMITED

The Chambers of Queensview
2725 Queensview Drive, Suite 100
Ottawa, ON K2B 0A1
Phone: (613) 726-9556
Toll-free: 1-800-722-9556
Fax: (613) 726-0000
Toll-free Fax: 1-800-722-7896
Phone and fax 24 hours
E-mail: claims@pca-adj.com
Website: www.pca-adj.com
Servicing all of the Eastern Ontario corridor.
Member: C.I.A.A., O.I.A.A., O.V.A.A., C.A.F.I.–A.M. Best Recommended 2018

PETERBOROUGH–Adjusters

CRAWFORD & COMPANY

General Insurance Adjusters
1600 Lansdowne Street West, Suite 9
Peterborough, ON K9J 7C7
Phone: (705) 876-1797
E-mail: peterborough.claims@crawco.ca
Brian Hambly, Manager

CUNNINGHAM LINDSEY

637 The Queensway, Unit 12
Peterborough, ON K9J 7J6
Phone: (705) 876-9620
Fax: (705) 876-7805
Website: www.cunninghamlindsey.com
After Hours/Emergencies – 1-800-235-8784
E-mail: agallagher@cl-na.com

DSB CLAIMS SOLUTIONS

General Insurance Adjusters
459 George Street North
Peterborough, ON K9H 3R6
Phone: (705)243-7238
Fax: 1-866-641-3151
E-mail: claims@dsbclaims.com
Website: www.dsbclaims.com
Balvinder Cheema, Manager

PICTON–Adjusters

PCA ADJUSTERS LIMITED

122 Parks Drive, Suite 4
Belleville, ON K8N 4Z5
Phone: (613) 962-9566 (24 hours)
Toll-free: 1-888-962-9556
Fax: (613) 962-9596
Toll-free Fax: 1-800-722-7896
Phone and fax 24 hours
E-mail: claims@pca-adj.com
Website: www.pca-adj.com
Servicing all of the Eastern Ontario corridor.
Member: C.I.A.A., O.I.A.A., O.V.A.A., C.A.F.I.–A.M. Best Recommended 2018

PORT HOPE–Adjusters

PCA ADJUSTERS LIMITED

122 Parks Drive, Suite 4
Belleville, ON K8N 4Z5
Phone: (613) 962-9566 (24 hours)
Toll-free: 1-888-962-9556
Fax: (613) 962-9596
Toll-free Fax: 1-800-722-7896
Phone and fax 24 hours
E-mail: claims@pca-adj.com
Website: www.pca-adj.com
Servicing all of the Eastern Ontario corridor.
Partners with The Adjusters Group International Ltd.
Member: C.I.A.A., O.I.A.A., O.V.A.A., C.A.F.I.–A.M. Best Recommended 2018

RENFREW–Adjusters

PCA ADJUSTERS LIMITED

The Chambers of Queensview
2725 Queensview Drive, Suite 100
Ottawa, ON K2B 0A1
Phone: (613) 726-9556
Toll-free: 1-800-722-9556
Fax: (613) 726-0000
Toll-free: 1-800-722-7896
Phone and fax 24 hours
E-mail: claims@pca-adj.com
Website: www.pca-adj.com
Servicing all of the Eastern Ontario corridor.
Member: C.I.A.A., O.I.A.A., O.V.A.A., C.A.F.I.–A.M. Best Recommended 2018

RICHMOND HILL–Adjusters

CUNNINGHAM LINDSEY

111 Granton Drive, Suite 220
Richmond Hill, ON L4B 1L5
Phone: (905) 707-5527
Fax: (905) 764-3398
Website: www.cunninghamlindsey.com
After Hours/Emergencies – 1-800-235-8784
E-mail: tcollins@cl-na.com

ST. CATHARINES–Adjusters

CRAWFORD & COMPANY

General Insurance Adjusters
55 King Street, Suite 300
St. Catharines, ON L2R 3H5
Phone: (905) 688-6391
E-mail: st.catharines.claims@crawco.ca
Kelly Stevens, Manager

CUNNINGHAM LINDSEY

235 Martindale Road
St. Catharines, ON L2W 1A5
Phone: (905) 688-6444
Fax: (905) 684-5033
Website: www.cunninghamlindsey.com
After Hours/Emergencies – 1-800-235-8784
E-mail: tblack@cl-na.com

KERNAGHAN ADJUSTERS

General Insurance Adjusters
602 – 1 St. Paul Street
St. Catharines, ON L2R 7L3
Phone: (289) 786-1074
Fax: (289) 723-1979
E-mail: stcatharines@kernaghan.com
Marie Gallagher, Branch Manager
Servicing: Beamsville, Niagara-on-the-Lake, Crystal Beach, Pelham, Dunnville, Port Colborne, Fenwick, Ridgeville, Fort Erie, Smithville, Grimsby, St. Catharines, Hamilton, Stoney Creek, Lincoln, Vineland, Lowbanks, Wainfleet, Niagara Falls, and Welland.

LEADING EDGE CLAIMS SERVICES

See Niagara region, Ontario, listing for full details
Phone: (289) 897-8676
Fax: (289) 897-8677

ST. CATHARINES–Insurance Counsel

SULLIVAN MAHONEY LLP

Lawyers
V.F. Muratori, Q.C.
P.B. Bedard
T.A. Richardson
P.M. Sheehan
W.B. McKaig
J. Dallal
D.A. Goslin
J.M. Gottli
R.B. Culliton
J.R. Bush
P.A. Mahoney
B.A. Macdonald
M.J. Bonomi
G.W. McCann
S.J. Premi
C. D'Angelo
R. Vacca
T. Wall
B.J. Troup
L.K. Parsons
J.P. Maloney
M.D. Atherton
D.M. Willer
D. Continenza
D.A. Maloney
L. Sgambelluri
P. Bush
C. Dilts
E. Bush
R. Corbett
Stefanie Anello

* * *

40 Queen Street, P.O. Box 1360
St. Catharines, ON L2R 6Z2
Telephone: (905) 688-6655
Fax: (905) 688-5814
E-mail: lawyers@sullivan-mahoney.com
Website: www.sullivan-mahoney.com
Branch Location:
4781 Portage Road
Niagara Falls, ON L2E 6B1
Telephone: (905) 357-0500
Fax: (905) 357-0501

SARNIA–Adjusters

CRAWFORD & COMPANY
General Insurance Adjusters
265 North Front Street, Suite 402
Sarnia, ON N7T 7X1
Phone: (519) 344-5277
E-mail: sarnia.claims@crawco.ca
David Bourke, Manager

SAULT STE. MARIE–Adjusters

CRAWFORD & COMPANY
General Insurance Adjusters
180 Bay Street, Suite 102A
Sault Ste. Marie, ON P6A 6S2
Phone: (705) 942-1300
E-mail: saultste.marie.claims@crawco.ca
David Marshall, Manager

CUNNINGHAM LINDSEY
369 Queen Street East, Suite 307
Sault Ste. Marie, ON P6A 1Z4
Phone: (705) 942-0324
Fax: (705) 942-8175
Website: www.cunninghamlindsey.com
After Hours/Emergencies – 1-800-235-8784
E-mail: dfiloon@cl-na.com

SCS INSURANCE ADJUSTERS
General Insurance Adjusters
369 Queen Street East, Suite 202
Sault Ste. Marie, ON P6A 1Z4
Phone: (705) 949-0961
Toll-free: 1-800-711-0311
Fax: (705) 949-2910
Ian Johnson, Branch Manager
E-mail: ianscs@vianet.ca
Other offices: North Bay, Sudbury, Timmins, and Thunder Bay.

SAULT STE. MARIE–Insurance Counsel

WEAVER, SIMMONS LLP
Barristers & Solicitors

See Sudbury, Ontario, listing for full details
Phone: (705) 674-6421

SEBRIGHT–Directory Services

DIRECTORIES NORTH
The Last Resort
R.R. #1
Sebright, ON L0K 1W0
Phone: (705) 833-2882
Gwen Peroni

STRATFORD–Adjusters

CUNNINGHAM LINDSEY
119 Albert Street
Stratford, ON N5A 3K5
Phone: (519) 271-8810
Fax: (519) 271-7951
Website: www.cunninghamlindsey.com
After Hours/Emergencies – 1-800-235-8784

STURGEON FALLS–Adjusters

ADJUSTERS SSA LIMITED
See North Bay, Ontario, listing for full details
Phone: (705) 476-1474
E-mail: ssanbay@vianet.on.ca

SUDBURY–Adjusters

CRAWFORD & COMPANY
General Insurance Adjusters
1177 Barrydowne Road
Sudbury, ON P3A 3V4
Phone: (705) 524-3611
E-mail: sudbury.claims@crawco.ca
Kenneth Graham, Manager

CUNNINGHAM LINDSEY
378 Whittaker Street
Sudbury, ON P3C 3X9
Phone: (705) 524-1661
Fax: (705) 524-2922
Website: www.cunninghamlindsey.com
After Hours/Emergencies – 1-800-235-8784
E-mail: dfiloon@cl-na.com

SCS INSURANCE ADJUSTERS
General Insurance Adjusters
Head Office
238 Cedar Street
Sudbury, ON P3B 1M7
Phone: (705) 674-2192
Toll-free: 1-800-461-4083
Fax: (705) 674-9947
Toll-free: 1-800-267-3289
Jennifer A. Gauthier, President
E-mail: jenscs@vianet.ca
Gary D. Gauthier, Director
E-mail: garyscs@vianet.ca
Other offices: North Bay, Sault Ste. Marie, Timmins, and Thunder Bay.

SUDBURY–Insurance Counsel

WEAVER, SIMMONS LLP
Barristers & Solicitors
James C. Simmons, Q.C.
P. Berk Keaney
Matti E. Mottonen
Stephen Vrbanac
Steve S. Moutsatsos
Geoff Jeffery
Marc A.J. Huneault
Daniel C. Sirois
R. Martin Bayer
R.W. Howard Lightle
Linda Laakso
Kathleen Stokes
Scott T. Croteau
Rose Muscolino
Michael J.N. Haraschuk
P. Peter Diavolitsis
Michael J. Venturi
Richard R.F. Nolin
Michel R. Carré
Sheena Alexander
Matthew Leef
Dhiren R. Chohan
Nicholas J. Kuchtaruk
Stephanie A. Farrell
Zachary T. Courtemanche
Scott M. Whalen

Associated as Counsel
Gerard E. McAndrew
Jack Braithwaite
Susan G. Larmer

233 Brady Street, Suite 400
P.O. Box 158
Sudbury, ON P3E 4N5
Telephone: (705) 674-6421
Fax: (705) 674-9948
E-mail: thefirm@weaversimmons.com
Website: www.weaversimmons.com

Serving Northern Ontario including Sudbury, Parry Sound, North Bay, New Liskeard, Haileybury, Cobalt, Timmins, Cochrane, Chapleau, Thunder Bay, Wawa, Sault Ste. Marie, Elliot Lake, Espanola, Little Current, Gore Bay, & Manitoulin.

TEMAGAMI–Adjusters

ADJUSTERS SSA LIMITED
See North Bay, Ontario, listing for full details
Phone: (705) 476-1474
E-mail: ssanbay@vianet.on.ca

THUNDER BAY–Adjusters

CRAWFORD & COMPANY
General Insurance Adjusters
395 Fort William Road, Suite 2
Thunder Bay, ON P7B 2Z5
Phone: (807) 344-1800
E-mail: thunderbay.claims@crawco.ca
Michael Bottan, Manager

CUNNINGHAM LINDSEY
920 Tungsten Street, Suite 101
Thunder Bay, ON P7B 5Z7
Phone: (807) 345-7676
Fax: (807) 345-7255
Website: www.cunninghamlindsey.com
After Hours/Emergencies –
1-800-235-8784
E-mail: dfiloon@cl-na.com

SCS INSURANCE ADJUSTERS
General Insurance Adjusters
200 Syndicate Avenue South, Suite 301
Thunder Bay, ON P7E 1C9
Phone: (807) 345-7730
Toll-free: 1-800-206-5068
Fax: (807) 345-8819
Wayne Picard, Branch Manager
E-mail: waynescsadj@tbaytel.net
Lou Pedron, Senior Adjuster
E-mail: louscsadj@tbaytel.net
Diane Savor, Adjuster
E-mail: dianescsadj@tbaytel.net
Other offices: North Bay, Sault Ste. Marie, Sudbury, and Timmins.

THUNDER BAY–Insurance Counsel

WEAVER, SIMMONS LLP
Barristers & Solicitors

See Sudbury, Ontario, listing for full details
Phone: (705) 674-6421

TIMMINS–Adjusters

CRAWFORD & COMPANY
General Insurance Adjusters
273 Third Avenue, Suite 401
Timmins, ON P4N 1E2
Phone: (705) 267-4040
E-mail: timmins.claims@crawco.ca
Michael Bottan, Manager

CUNNINGHAM LINDSEY
71 Balsam Street South, Unit 1
Timmins, ON P4N 2C9
Phone: (705) 264-1223
Fax: (705) 267-8057
Website: www.cunninghamlindsey.com
After Hours/Emergencies –
1-800-235-8784
E-mail: dfiloon@cl-na.com

SCS INSURANCE ADJUSTERS
General Insurance Adjusters
70C Mountjoy Street North, Suite 517
Timmins, ON P4N 4V7
Phone: (705) 267-1176
Fax: (705) 267-1684
Jennifer A. Gauthier, Branch Manager
E-mail: jenscs@vianet.ca
Other offices: North Bay, Sault Ste. Marie, Sudbury, and Thunder Bay.

TIMMINS–Insurance Counsel

WEAVER, SIMMONS LLP
Barristers & Solicitors

See Sudbury, Ontario, listing for full details
Phone: (705) 674-6421

TORONTO–Adjusters

BBCG CLAIM SERVICES a division of ClaimsPro
Specializing in Surety and Fidelity Bond Claims, E&O, D&O and Trade Credit Claims
3660 Hurontario Street, Suite 601
Mississauga, ON L5B 3C4
Phone: (905) 279-8880
Toll-free: 1-866-714-0001
Fax: (905) 279-5338
E-mail: agoguen@bbcg.ca
Arthur Goguen, Managing Director
Offices in British Columbia and Quebec.
Servicing all of Canada.
Member: C.I.A.A.

BDO CANADA LLP FINANCIAL ADVISORY SERVICES
See Toronto, Ontario–Insurance Loss Accountants

CUNNINGHAM LINDSEY
Head Office
50 Burnhamthorpe Road West
Suite 1102
Mississauga, ON L5B 3C2
Phone: (905) 896-8181
Fax: (905) 896-3485
Website: www.cunninghamlindsey.com
After Hours/Emergencies – 1-800-235-8784
E-mail: rgreyling@cl-na.com

TORONTO–Continued

DSB CLAIMS SOLUTIONS
General Insurance Adjusters
100 Consilium Place
Suite 200
Toronto, ON M1H 3E3
Phone: (416) 768-9837
Fax: 1-866-641-3151
E-mail: claims@dsbclaims.com
Website: www.dsbclaims.com
Yves Daniel Eleosida, Manager

KERNAGHAN ADJUSTERS
General Insurance Adjusters
202 – 310 North Queen Street
Toronto, ON M9C 5K4
Phone: (416) 251-2311
Toll-free: 1-800-247-4120
Fax: (416) 251-3819
E-mail: toronto@kernaghan.com
Servicing: Greater Toronto, Burlington, Mississauga, Brampton, Richmond Hill, Markham, Oshawa, Pickering, Newcastle, Bowmanville, Wasaga Beach, Barrie, Newmarket, Keswick, Orillia, and Gravenhurst.

MALTMAN GROUP INTERNATIONAL
Insurance adjusting and claims services
810 – 2001 Sheppard Avenue East
Toronto, ON M2J 4Z8
Phone: (416) 492-4411
Fax: (416) 492-5657
E-mail: claims@maltmans.com
Website: www.maltmans.com

TORONTO–Continued

SEDGWICK CMS CANADA INC.

General Insurance Adjusters,
Third Party Administrators
5915 Airport Road
Suite 201
Mississauga, ON L4V 1T1
Phone: (905) 671-7800
Toll-free: 1-866-278-0310
Fax: (905) 671-7819
E-mail: laurie.walker@sedgwickcms.ca
Website: www.sedgwickcms.ca
Contact: Laurie Walker, CIP, CRM

VERICLAIM

A Sedgwick company
5915 Airport Road
Suite 200
Mississauga, ON L4V 1T1
Phone: (905) 671-7830
Toll-free: 1-888-601-6228
Fax: (905) 671-7819
E-mail: rob.ginn@vericlaim.ca
Website: www.vericlaim.ca
Contact: Rob Ginn, B.Comm., CIP

TORONTO–Automobile Wreckers

See Toronto, Ontario–Salvage Factors

TORONTO–Environmental Consultants

PINCHIN LTD.

Branch Office
50 Wellington Street East, Suite 200
Toronto, ON M5E 1C8
Phone: (905) 363-0678
After hours: 1-800-577-2653
Fax: (416) 368-4120
E-mail: nbutler@pinchin.com
Website: www.pinchin.com
Contact: Neil Butler

TORONTO–Forensic Accountants

MDD FORENSIC ACCOUNTANTS

Tracing its roots to 1933, MDD is an internationally recognized forensic accounting firm that focuses on economic damage quantification assessments. Our highly trained experienced professionals provide expert, consultant, and fact witness testimony. We have qualified as experts in courts around the world.

Our practice areas include: Accident Benefits, Agriculture, Builders Risk, Business Disputes, Business Interruption, Business Valuation, Catastrophe Services, Class Actions, Construction, Contingency Entertainment, Disability, Matrimonial Disputes, Environmental Damages, Expropriation, Extra Expenses, Franchise, Fraud Investigations, Government Services, Intellectual Property, Liability Losses, Litigation, Lost Profits, Maritime, Mining & Refining, Oil & Gas, Personal Injury, Physical Damages, Power Generation, Product Liability, Reported Insurance, Stocks & Contents, Subrogation, Surety Funds, Toxic Tort, Transportation, and Valuable Papers.

4 King Street West, Suite 1010
Toronto, ON M5H 1B6
Phone: (416) 366-4968
Fax: (416) 366-4973
Website: www.mdd.com
Bradley J. Ebel, CPA, CA, CFE, CFF
Partner, President
E-mail: bebel@mdd.com
Gerry R. Bouwman, CPA, CMA, CFF
Partner, Senior Vice President
E-mail: gbouwman@mdd.com
Mark A. Gain, CPA, CA•IFA, CBV, CFF
Partner, Senior Vice President
E-mail: mgain@mdd.com
Matthew Mulholland, CPA, CMA, DIFA, CFF
Partner, Senior Vice President
E-mail: mmulholland@mdd.com
Ephraim Stulberg, CPA, CA, CBV, CFF
Partner, Senior Vice President
E-mail: estulberg@mdd.com

TORONTO–Insurance Counsel

AFFLECK GREENE McMURTRY LLP

Barristers and Solicitors
General insurance practice but specializing in surety defence, fidelity, dishonesty, performance, labour bonds claims, and E&O and directors liability claims

Suite 200, 365 Bay Street
Toronto, ON M5H 2V1
Phone: (416) 360-2800
Fax: (416) 360-5960
E-mail: info@agmlawyers.com
Website: www.agmlawyers.com
Senior Partner: Peter R. Greene
(416) 360-8767 (direct line)

BELL, TEMPLE

Barristers & Solicitors

Cameron C.R. Godden
cgodden@belltemple.com
David A. Tompkins
dtompkins@belltemple.com
Brian E. Lucas
blucas@belltemple.com
Hugh G. Brown
hbrown@belltemple.com
Lisa E. Hamilton
lhamilton@belltemple.com
Andrew K. Lee
alee@belltemple.com
Frank J. Kosturik
fkosturik@belltemple.com
Joseph A. Baldanza
jbaldanza@belltemple.com
Katherine Kolnhofer
kkolnhofer@belltemple.com
Derek V. Abreu
dabreu@belltemple.com
Lora Castellucci
lcastellucci@belltemple.com
Steven Carlstrom
scarlstrom@belltemple.com
Ryan J. Coughlin
rcoughlin@belltemple.com
J. Kendall Cumming
kcumming@belltemple.com

TORONTO–Continued

BELL, TEMPLE–Continued

Renata K. Laubman
rlaubman@belltemple.com
Frank D. Costantini
fcostantini@belltemple.com
Genevieve Durigon
gdurigon@belltemple.com
Sarah A. Deol
sdeol@belltemple.com
Trevor Tynan
ttynan@belltemple.com
Amanda Smallwood
asmallwood@belltemple.com
Dilraj Sandhu
dsandhu@belltemple.com
Jonathan Tatner
jtatner@belltemple.com
Ryan Truax
rtruax@belltemple.com
Damien Van Vroenhoven
dvanvroenhoven@belltemple.com
Ashleigh Martin
amartin@belltemple.com
Trevor Buckley
tbuckley@belltemple.com
Monika Korona
mkorona@belltemple.com
Madeleine Godard
mgodard@belltemple.com
Cassandra Thuen
cthuen@belltemple.com
Brenda Cuneo
bcuneo@belltemple.com
Adrian Serpa
aserpa@belltemple.com
Deema Elshourfa
delshourfa@belltemple.com
Mehran Wencho
mwench@belltemple.com
Ryan Everett
reverett@belltemple.com
Tal Letourneau
tletourneau@belltemple.com
Thamina Amiri
tamiri@belltemple.com

... continued on next page

TORONTO–Continued

BELL, TEMPLE–Continued

Rachel Floyd
rflyod@belltemple.com
Josh Marcus
jmarcus@belltemple.com
Suite 1300
393 University Avenue
Toronto, ON M5G 1E6
Telephone: (416) 581-8200
Fax: (416) 596-0952
Website: www.belltemple.com

BROWN & BURNES

Barristers-at-Law
Suite 1400, 390 Bay Street
Toronto, ON M5H 2Y2
Phone: (416) 366-7927
Fax: (416) 363-9602
E-mail: jmburnes@brownburnes.com
Website: www.brownburnes.com
Specializing in commercial, property, auto, and liability claims.

DUTTON BROCK LLP

Barristers and Solicitors
W. Graham Dutton, Q.C.*+
Brian J.E. Brock, Q.C.*
Philippa G. Samworth*
S. Wayne Morris*
Paul Tushinski*
Raymond A.D. Watt
Mark K. Donaldson
David H. Lauder*
Richard G. Hepner
Susan E. Gunter
Christopher R. Dunn†
Gillian B. Eckler
Stephen A. Mullings
Deanna M. Stea
David Raposo
Christopher R. Martyr
Eric J. Adams†•
Janet S. Young
Ryan St. Aubin
Dana R. Spadafina
Albert Wallrap†

TORONTO–Continued

DUTTON BROCK LLP–Continued

Shirline Apiou
Elizabeth A. DiQuattro
Jordan M. Black
Lisa Marie Buccella
Donna A. Polgar
Chad M. Leddy
Andrea R. Lim
Stephen N. Libin
Jocelyn Tatebe
Yusra Murad
Josiah MacQuarrie
Chris Cheung
Elie Goldberg
Teri Liu
Thomas R. Elliot
Shelby Chung
Jennifer Arduini
Rosalind Eastmond
Joanna Reznick
George J. Poirier
Lida Moazzam
Melissa J. Miles
Emily L. Densem
Michael E. Duboff
438 University Avenue
Suite 1700
Toronto, ON M5G 2L9
Telephone: (416) 593-4411
Fax: (416) 593-5922
E-mail: info@duttonbrock.com
Website: www.duttonbrock.com
* Certified as a Specialist in Civil Litigation by the Law Society of Upper Canada.
† Also of the British Columbia Bar.
• Also of the Alberta Bar.
+ Retired.

GIFFEN LLP

See Kitchener-Waterloo, Ontario, listing for full details
330 Bay Street, Suite 1400
Toronto, ON M5H 2S8
Phone: (416) 628-5709
Fax: (416) 628-5692

TORONTO–Continued

O'DONNELL, ROBERTSON & PARTNERS

Barristers & Solicitors
Mark M. O'Donnell
Stuart M. Robertson
Mark W. Barrett
Douglas C. Richardson
Jennifer A. Guy
Antonios T. Antoniou
Steven G. Canto
Brendan J. Hughes
Frank C. Caruso
Kiri F. McDermott-Berryman
Cameron L. Foster
Victoria Dale
36 King Street East
Suite 800
Toronto, ON M5C 1E5
Phone: (416) 214-0606
Fax: (416) 214-0605
E-mail: info@orplawyers.com
Website: www.orplawyers.com

Practice focussed on providing insurance-related litigation services and coverage advice to insurers; plaintiff retainers adverse to our insurer clients are never accepted.

Defence of Errors and Omissions Claims against Professionals, Commercial and Personal Property Claims, Liability Defence Matters, Personal Injury Claims, Motor Vehicle Defence, Defamation, Libel and Slander Claims, Toxic Tort and Environmental Litigation, Sexual Abuse Claims, General Liability Coverage Matters and providing counsel on insurance-related issues.

ZUBER & COMPANY LLP

Insurance Defence Litigation
David Zuber
100 Simcoe Street, Suite 500
Toronto, ON M5H 3G2
Phone: (416) 362-5005
Fax: (416) 362-5289
E-mail: dzuber@zubco.com
Website: www.zubco.com

TORONTO–Insurance Loss Accountants

BDO CANADA LLP FINANCIAL ADVISORY SERVICES

Financial & Investigative Accountants

At BDO we are dedicated to understanding the complexities our clients face every day. Insurance Claims are often complex and require a professional, analytical approach to assist in an ultimate resolution. Relying on external vendors with extensive experience to fairly and objectively quantify losses across industry lines benefits insurance companies – Insurance claim professionals working seamlessly as part of a loss adjusting team allows for timely, objective reporting.

How we help:.

- Accident Benefits
- Financial Dependency
- Tort Claims
- Commercial Losses
- Business Interruption
- Inventory Loss Assessment
- Litigation Support
- Extra Expense Claims
- Expert Testimony
- Forensic Accounting

2680 Matheson Boulevard East
Suite 204
Mississauga, ON L4W 0A5
Phone: (416) 233-5577
Toll-free: 1-866-233-5577
Website: www.bdo.ca

Contact:
Janet L. Olsen, CPA, CA, CFE, CFF
Partner, Mississauga
jolsen@bdo.ca
Chetan Segal, CPA, CA•IFA, CFF, CFI, CAMS
Partner, Toronto
csegal@bdo.ca
Crystal Hawryluk, CPA, CGA, CBV, CFE
Partner, Calgary
chawryluk@bdo.ca

... continued on next page

TORONTO–Continued

BDO CANADA LLP
FINANCIAL ADVISORY SERVICES–Continued

Dan Jennings, CPA, CA, CBV, CF
Partner, Halifax
djennings@bdo.ca

BDO Canada LLP, a limited liability partnership, is a member of BDO International Limited, a UK company limited by guarantee.

TORONTO–Continued

PRICEWATERHOUSECOOPERS LLP

Throughout Canada and around the world, PwC provides strategic assistance to insurance companies and legal counsel in investigating and resolving claims.

- *Business interruption losses*
- *Inventory assessment and valuation*
- *Economic loss quantification in liability claims, including product liability*
- *Product recall*
- *Assessment of financial motivation*
- *Personal injury tort claims for economic loss*
- *Valuation of fidelity and employee dishonesty claims*

PwC Tower, 18 York Street, Suite 2600
Toronto, ON M5J 0B2
Phone: (416) 863-1133
Fax: (416) 365-8215
Website: www.pwc.com/ca/dai
PwC has over twenty offices across Canada.

TORONTO–Investigating Consultants and Forensics

ACSEM ENGINEERING GROUP INC.

Forensic Engineers, Architect and Code Advisors

207 Edgeley Boulevard
Suite 17
Toronto (Concord), ON L4K 4B5
Phone: (905) 660-8877
Fax: (905) 660-5947

George Paolantonio, P.Eng.
Civil Engineer
Rosairo Fernando, P.Eng.
Structural Engineer
Nelson Tong, P.Eng.
Mechanical Engineer
Raul M. Knoll, P.Eng.
Electrical Engineer
Knoll Engineering Inc.
Ricardo Lopez, M.Eng.
Forensic Investigator
Anthony C. Battaglia, O.A.A.
Battaglia Associates Inc., Architects
Louis Vlahakis, B.Tech.Arch.
Architectural Designer
Adamo Caputo, Dip.Arch.Tech.
Architectural Technologist

BROSZ FORENSIC SERVICES INC.

Consulting Forensic Electrical Engineers and Fire Investigators

64 Bullock Drive
Markham, ON L3P 3P2
Phone: (905) 472-6660 (24 hours)
Fax: (905) 472-6665
E-mail: info@brosz.net
Website: www.brosz.net

TORONTO–Continued

KODSI ENGINEERING INC.

Providing nation-wide engineering expertise from claim to settlement

We specialize in:

- *Accident Reconstruction*
- *Biomechanical Injury Assessments*
- *Mechanical Assessments*
- *Personal Injury – Slip/Trip and Fall Assessments*
- *Forensic Structural Engineering (ON, BC, AB)*
- *Evidence Preservation*
- *Critiques of Opposing Expert Reports*
- *Expert Witness Testimony*

1 – 225 Traders Boulevard East
Mississauga, ON L4Z 3L8
Phone (GTA): (416) 977-0009
Fax: (416) 977-6622
Toll-free: 1-800-263-6351
E-mail: info@kodsiengineering.com
Website: www.kodsiengineering.com

Sam Kodsi, P.Eng.
Shady Attalla, P.Eng.
Karla Cassidy, M.A.Sc., P.Eng.
Richard W. Robertson, P.Eng.
Cristin McCarty, Ph.D.
Sarah Selesnic, B.Sc., M.A.Sc.
Dwayne Toscano, B.A.Sc.
Sami Shaker, B.Sc.
Russ Heslop
Avery Chakravarty, M.A.Sc.
Cheryl Fookes, B.A.Sc.
Kenneth Cowie, B.Sc.E.

WALTERS FORENSIC ENGINEERING INC.

Consulting Professional Engineers to the Insurance Industry

800 – 277 Wellington Street West
Toronto, ON M5V 3E4
Toll-free: 1-800-387-1950
Phone: (416) 971-8900
Fax: (416) 971-6319
E-mail: engineer@waltersforensic.com
Website: www.waltersforensic.com

TORONTO–Salvage Factors

HOLCO SALVAGE SALES

Insurance Salvors
514 Yonge Street
Toronto, ON M4Y 1X9
Phone: (416) 922-5842
Fax: (416) 922-1085
E-mail:
jhsltd@hollanderandsons.com
Website:
www.hollanderandsons.com
Jack Hollander, residence:
(416) 226-0615
Cellular: (416) 520-7922
Gary Hollander
Services include on-site inventories.
Operates coast-to-coast.
Professional experience for one half century.

STANDARD AUTO WRECKERS

Automobile Wreckers
1216 Sewells Road
Toronto, ON M1X 1S1
Phone: (416) 286-8686, ext. 232
Fax: (416) 286-4501
Website:
www.standardautowreckers.com
Standard Auto Wreckers has been Canada's most prolific and environmentally friendly auto recycler since 1979 and is a founding company of Fenix Parts – a leading recycler and reseller of OEM automotive products in the United States and Canada. We process approximately 400 to 500 vehicles every week and have more than 100,000+ parts in stock throughout our locations at any given time. We also provide the highest-quality recycling services for all salvage vehicles. We are ARA Gold Seal Certified and have been providing excellent service to our customers for 39 years. In addition, we have a well-trained, experienced and qualified shipping department to ensure parts arrive safely and on time. Standard Auto Wreckers has 4 locations to serve you better: Toronto, Ottawa, Port Hope, and Niagara Falls, New York, USA.

TRENTON–Adjusters

PCA ADJUSTERS LIMITED

122 Parks Drive, Suite 4
Belleville, ON K8N 4Z5
Phone: (613) 962-9566 (24 hours)
Toll-free: 1-888-962-9556
Fax: (613) 962-9596
Toll-free Fax: 1-800-722-7896
Phone and fax 24 hours
E-mail: claims@pca-adj.com
Website: www.pca-adj.com
Servicing all of the Eastern Ontario corridor.
Member: C.I.A.A., O.I.A.A., O.V.A.A., C.A.F.I.–A.M. Best Recommended 2018

WELLAND–Adjusters

LEADING EDGE CLAIMS SERVICES

See Niagara region, Ontario, listing for full details
Phone: (289) 897-8676
Fax: (289) 897-8677

WINDSOR–Adjusters

CUNNINGHAM LINDSEY

242 Lauzon Road
Windsor, ON N8S 3L6
Phone: (519) 944-1811
Fax: (519) 944-6988
Website: www.cunninghamlindsey.com
After Hours/Emergencies –
1-800-235-8784

WOODSTOCK–Adjusters

CUNNINGHAM LINDSEY

594 Dundas Street
Woodstock, ON N4S 1C8
Phone: (519) 537-5571
Fax: (519) 537-8781
Website: www.cunninghamlindsey.com
After Hours/Emergencies –
1-800-235-8784

Prince Edward Island

CHARLOTTETOWN–Adjusters

CUNNINGHAM LINDSEY
See Halifax, Nova Scotia, listing for full details
After Hours/Emergencies – 1-800-235-8784

CHARLOTTETOWN–Investigating Consultants and Forensics

KODSI ENGINEERING INC.
See Halifax, Nova Scotia, listing for full details
Phone: 1-800-263-6351

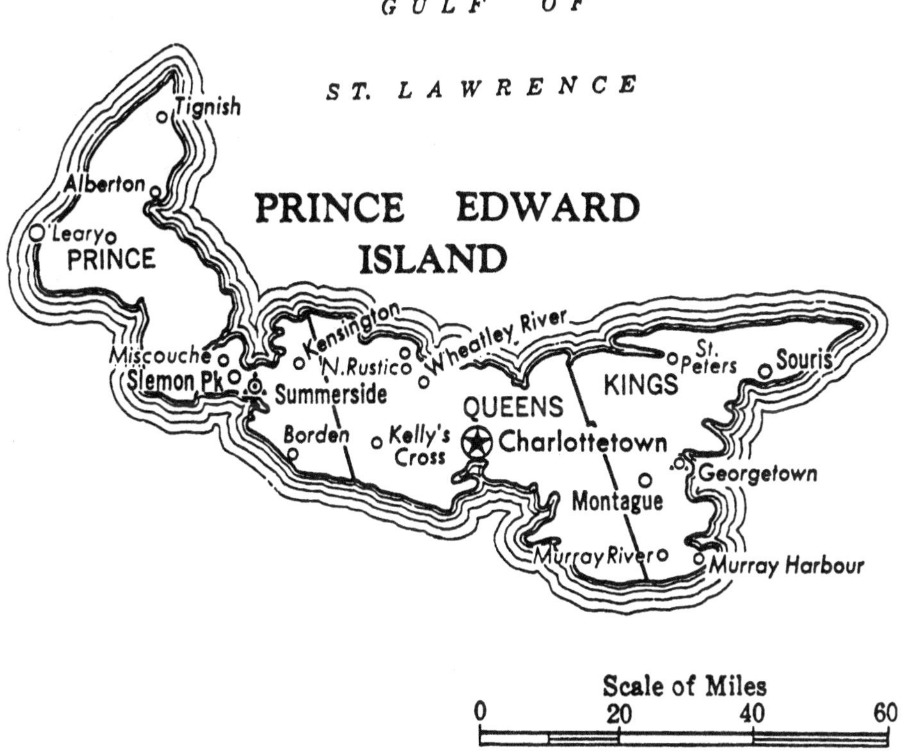

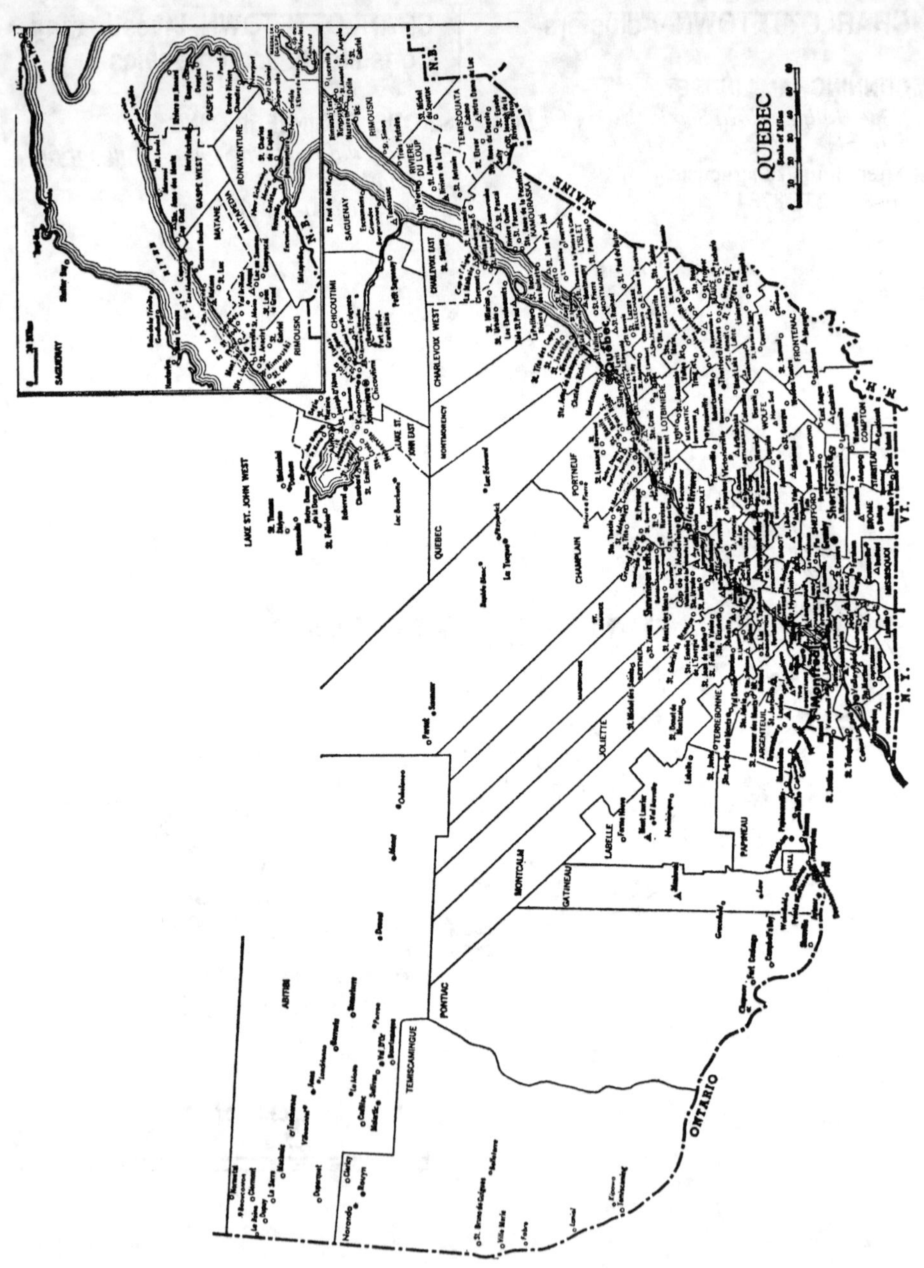
QUEBEC
Scale of Miles
ONTARIO
MAINE
N.B.
N.Y.
VT.
N.H.
Montreal
Quebec
Sherbrooke
ABITIBI
PONTIAC
TEMISCAMINGUE
MONTCALM
GATINEAU
LABELLE
PAPINEAU
HULL
JOLIETTE
CHAMPLAIN
PORTNEUF
QUEBEC
CHICOUTIMI
RIMOUSKI
MATANE
BONAVENTURE
GASPE EAST
GASPE WEST
KAMOURASKA
TEMISCOUATA
FRONTENAC
COMPTON
LOTBINIERE
WOLFE
SHEFFORD
BROME
MISSISQUOI
ARGENTEUIL
TERREBONNE
LAKE ST. JOHN WEST
CHARLEVOIX WEST
CHARLEVOIX EAST
SAGUENAY

Quebec

AMQUI–Adjusters

CUNNINGHAM LINDSEY
C.P. 1299
Amqui, QC G0J 1J0
Phone: (418) 756-1312
Fax: (418) 756-1315
Website: www.cunninghamlindsey.com
Emergency/After Hours –
1-800-235-8784

BLAINVILLE–Adjusters

CUNNINGHAM LINDSEY
10 boulevard de la Seigneurie est
Bureau 206
Blainville, QC J7C 3V5
Phone: (450) 420-8100
Fax: (450) 420-8129
Website: www.cunninghamlindsey.com
Emergency/After Hours –
1-800-235-8784
E-mail: rcuende@cl-na.com

CAUSAPSCAL–Adjusters

CUNNINGHAM LINDSEY
C.P. 1299
Causapscal, QC G0J 1J0
Phone: (418) 756-1312
Fax: (418) 756-1315
Website: www.cunninghamlindsey.com
Emergency/After Hours –
1-800-235-8784

CHICOUTIMI–Insurance Counsel

ROBINSON SHEPPARD SHAPIRO
S.E.N.C.R.L. • L.L.P.
Avocats • Barristers & Solicitors
Marcel-Olivier Nadeau
Annie Packwood
Rachel Guénette-Lemieux
255 Racine Street East, Suite 530
Chicoutimi, QC G7H 7L2
Telephone: (418) 579-3113
Fax: (418) 579-3114
Head Office:
Tour de la Bourse
800 Place Victoria, Bureau 4700
Montréal, QC H4Z 1H6
Telephone: (514) 878-2631
Fax: (514) 878-1865
E-mail: info@rsslex.com
Website: www.rsslex.com

CHICOUTIMI/SAGUENAY/LAC ST-JEAN–Adjusters

CUNNINGHAM LINDSEY
C.P. 31012, Place Davis
Jonquière, QC G7S 6C2
Phone: (418) 412-3420
Fax: (418) 412-6105
Website: www.cunninghamlindsey.com
Emergency/After Hours –
1-800-235-8784
E-mail: rcuende@cl-na.com

GATINEAU–Adjusters

CRAWFORD & COMPANY
General Insurance Adjusters
5100 rue Sherbrooke est, Bureau 702
Montreal, QC H1V 3R9
Phone: 1-888-776-5511
E-mail: montreal.claims@crawco.ca
France Paul, Manager

GATINEAU–Continued

CUNNINGHAM LINDSEY
15 Buteau Street, Bureau 210
Gatineau, QC J8Z 1V4
Phone: (819) 776-3171
Fax: (819) 776-6075
Website: www.cunninghamlindsey.com
Emergency/After Hours – 1-800-235-8784

JOLIETTE–Adjusters

CUNNINGHAM LINDSEY
10 boulevard de la Seigneurie est
Bureau 206
Blainville, QC J7C 3V5
Phone: (450) 729-0191
Website: www.cunninghamlindsey.com
Emergency/After Hours – 1-800-235-8784
E-mail: rcuende@cl-na.com

LA SARRE–Adjusters

CUNNINGHAM LINDSEY
C.P. 241
La Sarre, QC J9Z 2X5
Phone: (819) 333-4090
Fax: (819) 333-4091
Website: www.cunninghamlindsey.com
Emergency/After Hours – 1-800-235-8784

MONT-LAURIER–Adjusters

CRAWFORD & COMPANY
General Insurance Adjusters
5100 rue Sherbrooke est, Bureau 702
Montreal, QC H1V 3R9
Phone: 1-877-823-4153
E-mail: patrice.janes@crawco.ca
Patrice Janes, Manager

MONTREAL–Adjusters

BBCG CLAIM SERVICES
a division of ClaimsPro
Specializing in surety and fidelity bond claims, E&O, D&O and trade credit claims
1200 Chomedey Boulevard
Suite 700
Laval, QC H7V 3Z3
Phone: (450) 688-3113
Sans Frais: 1-866-714-0003
Fax: (450) 688-6996
Michael Prud'homme
E-mail: mprudhomme@bbcg.ca
Luc-André Girard
E-mail: lagirard@bbcg.ca
Offices in Ontario and British Columbia.
Servicing all of Canada.
Member: C.I.A.A.

CRAWFORD & COMPANY
General Insurance Adjusters
5100 rue Sherbrooke est, Bureau 702
Montreal, QC H1V 3R9
Phone: (514) 748-7300
E-mail: montreal.claims@crawco.ca
Luc Gnocchini, Manager

CUNNINGHAM LINDSEY
Head Office for Quebec Division
1250, rue Guy, Bureau 1000
Montréal, QC H3H 2T4
Phone: (514) 938-5400
Fax: (514) 938-5445
Website: www.cunninghamlindsey.com
Emergency/After Hours – 1-800-235-8784
E-mail: kcorreia@cl-na.com

MONTREAL–Forensic Accountants

MDD FORENSIC ACCOUNTANTS

Tracing its roots to 1933, MDD is an internationally recognized forensic accounting firm that focuses on economic damage quantification assessments. Our highly trained experienced professionals provide expert, consultant, and fact witness testimony. We have qualified as experts in courts around the world. Regardless of the nature of the assignment, MDD's exceptional dedication and demonstrated results have long been the hallmark of the firm.

Our practice areas include: Agriculture, Builders Risk, Business Disputes, Business Interruption, Business Valuation, Catastrophe Services, Class Actions, Construction, Contingency Entertainment, Disability, Matrimonial Disputes, Environmental Damages, Expropriation, Extra Expenses, Franchise, Fraud Investigations, Government Services, Intellectual Property, Liability Losses, Litigation, Lost Profits, Maritime, Mining & Refining, Oil & Gas, Personal Injury, Physical Damages, Power Generation, Product Liability, Reported Insurance, Stocks & Contents, Subrogation, Surety Funds, Toxic Tort, Transportation, and Valuable Papers.

625 President Kennedy Avenue, Suite 1015
Montreal, QC H3A 1K2
Phone: (514) 288-4852
Fax: (514) 288-0742
Website: www.mdd.com
Martin Pavelic, CPA, CMA, CFF
Partner, Senior Vice President
E-mail: mpavelic@mdd.com
Philippe Couture,CPA, CA, CFF
Senior Manager, Vice President
E-mail: pcouture@mdd.com

MONTREAL–Insurance Counsel

ROBINSON SHEPPARD SHAPIRO

S.E.N.C.R.L. • L.L.P.
Avocats • Barristers & Solicitors
Jonathan J. Robinson
Claude-Armand Sheppard
Barry H. Shapiro
Charles E. Flam
Michel J. Green
Richard Uditsky
Jean E. Clerk
Jean-Marc Fortier
Jean-Yves Fortin
Herbert Z. Pinchuk
Theodore Goloff
Yves Cousineau
Patrick Henry
Louise Baillargeon
Éric Boulva
Jean-Denis Boucher
Luc Fleurant
Peter S. Martin
Lynne Kassie
Benoît G. Bourgon
Jean-François Lamoureux
Jacques Bélanger
Marilyn Piccini Roy
Martin Lord
Sharon G. Druker
Nicholas J. Krnjevic
Jean-Pierre Sheppard
Jean-François Bilodeau
Fabienne Beauvais
François A. Raymond
Pierre Brossoit
Dominique Poulin
Normand Laurendeau
Julie Forest
Mariella De Stefano
Rhona Luger
Chantal Noël
Brigitte Garceau
Élisabeth Laroche
Gilbert A. Hourani
Pierre Visockis
Pierre Bazinet
Hughes Duguay

... continued on next page

MONTREAL–Continued

ROBINSON SHEPPARD SHAPIRO–Continued

Rachel Clément
Geneviève Goulet
Katherine Delage
David Alexander Genest
Benoît Chartier
Benoît Byette
Frédéric Savard-Scott
Martin Coté
Annie Claude Beauchemin
Doree Levine
Marika Douville
Natacha Calixte
Ariane Légère-Bordeleau
Carly Flam
Matthew McLaughlin
Yaël Lachkar
Ann-Julie Auclair
Jonathan Feingold
Jennifer L. Hansen
Stewart Litvack
Louis Dessureault
Jeanine Guindi
Alexandra Kallos
Stéphanie-Alexandra Lo Vasco
Justin Beeby
Julien Robidoux
Benjamin Prud'homme
Marc-André McCann

MONTREAL–Continued

ROBINSON SHEPPARD SHAPIRO–Continued

Zachary Ouimet
Véronique Pagé
Patricia Baram
David Paradis
Nicolas Drolet
Geneviève M. Griffin
Jordi Montblanch
Maude Léveillé
Trent Helms
Sandrine Bédard
Jasmine Guilbault
Xavier Morand-Bock
Tasy Bacolias
Médgine Gourdet

Tour de la Bourse
800 Place Victoria, Bureau 4700
Montréal, QC H4Z 1H6 Telephone: (514) 878-2631
Fax: (514) 878-1865
E-mail: info@rsslex.com
Website: www.rsslex.com
Saguenay Office:
255 Racine Street East, Suite 530
Chicoutimi, QC G7H 7L2
Telephone: (418) 579-3113
Fax: (418) 579-3114

MONTREAL–Salvage Factors

CONTINENTAL SALVAGE & AUCTIONEERS

Insurance Underwriters Salvors
Operating from Coast-to-Coast
1493 rue Bégin
St. Laurent, QC H4R 1V8
Phone: (514) 875-6661
Fax: (514) 875-6662
E-mail: info@cntcap.com
Website:
www.continentalauctioneers.com
Canada's leaders in salvage recovery & commercial auctioneering.

CRESCENT SALVAGE

Servicing the insurance industry for over 50 years
5430 Royalmount Avenue
Montreal, QC H4P 1H7
Phone: (514) 739-3355 (Montreal)
(416) 283-2221 (Toronto)
Fax: (514) 342-7874
Emergency: (514) 234-0664
Contact: Cosimo La Rosa
E-mail: clarosa@c3.com
Website: www.c3.com
Servicing Canada and the United States. Full Service: Salvage – Appraisals – Commercial auctioneers – Sales arrangement of merchandise, equipment – Warehousing – Inventory services.

QUEBEC CITY–Adjusters

CRAWFORD & COMPANY

General Insurance Adjusters
1305 boulevard Lebourgneuf
Bureau 303
Quebec, QC G2K 2E4
Phone: (418) 872-7050
E-mail: quebeccity.claims@crawco.ca
Jacques Beland, Manager

QUEBEC CITY–Insurance Loss Accountants

PRICEWATERHOUSECOOPERS LLP

Throughout Canada and around the world, PwC provides strategic assistance to insurance companies and legal counsel in investigating and resolving claims.

- *Business interruption losses*
- *Inventory assessment and valuation*
- *Economic loss quantification in liability claims, including product liability*
- *Product recall*
- *Assessment of financial motivation*
- *Personal injury tort claims for economic loss*
- *Valuation of fidelity and employee dishonesty claims*

Place de la Cité, Tour Cominar
2640 Laurier Boulevard, Bureau 1700
Sainte-Foy, QC G1V 5C2
Phone: (418) 522-7001
Fax: (418) 522-5663
Website: www.pwc.com/ca/dai
PwC has over twenty offices across Canada.

RIVIÈRE DU LOUP–Adjusters

CUNNINGHAM LINDSEY

502 boulevard Hébert
Rivière du Loup, QC G6G 5S5
Phone: (418) 300-0597
Fax: (418) 300-0596
Website: www.cunninghamlindsey.com
After Hours/Emergencies –
1-800-235-8784
E-mail: rcuende@cl-na.com

ROUYN-NORANDA–Adjusters

CUNNINGHAM LINDSEY

C.P. 37 Rouyn
Rouyn-Noranda, QC J9X 5C1
Phone: (819) 797-2441
Fax: (819) 797-2449
Website: www.cunninghamlindsey.com
Emergency/After Hours –
1-800-235-8784

SAGUENAY–Adjusters

CRAWFORD & COMPANY
General Insurance Adjusters
2321 du chemin de la Montagne
Alma, QC G8B 5V2
Phone: (418) 480-1944
E-mail: jacques.beland@crawco.ca
Jacques Beland, Manager

ST. JEROME–Adjusters

CRAWFORD & COMPANY
General Insurance Adjusters
5100 rue Sherbrooke est, Bureau 702
Montreal, QC H1V 3R9
Phone: 1-800-407-3507
E-mail: st.jerome.claims@crawco.ca
France Paul, Manager

SENNETERRE–Adjusters

CUNNINGHAM LINDSEY
281 rue Principale
Senneterre, QC J0Y 2M0
Phone: (819) 737-4090
Fax: (819) 737-4091
Website: www.cunninghamlindsey.com

SHERBROOKE–Adjusters

CRAWFORD & COMPANY
General Insurance Adjusters
P.O. Box 566
Sherbrooke, QC J1C 1A1
Phone: (514) 748-7300
E-mail: jacques.beland@crawco.ca
Jacques Beland, Manager

CUNNINGHAM LINDSEY
C.P. 36009
Sherbrooke, QC J1L 2L3
Phone: (819) 575-0626
Fax: (819) 575-0627
Website: www.cunninghamlindsey.com
Emergency/After Hours –
1-800-235-8784
E-mail: rcuende@cl-na.com

TROIS-RIVIÈRES–Adjusters

CRAWFORD & COMPANY
General Insurance Adjusters
5100 rue Sherbrooke est, Bureau 702
Trois-Rivières, QC H1V 3R9
Phone: (514) 748-7300
E-mail: trois-rivieres.claims@crawco.ca
France Paul, Manager

CUNNINGHAM LINDSEY
C.P. 22010, C.P. du Carrefour
Trois-Rivières, QC G9A 4N0
Phone: (819) 694-0530
Fax: (819) 694-1016
Website: www.cunninghamlindsey.com
Emergency/After Hours –
1-800-235-8784

VAL D'OR–Adjusters

CUNNINGHAM LINDSEY
C.P. 561
Val D'Or, QC J9P 4P5
Phone: (819) 737-4090
Fax: (819) 737-4091
Website: www.cunninghamlindsey.com
Emergency/After Hours –
1-800-235-8784

VICTORIAVILLE–Adjusters

CUNNINGHAM LINDSEY
268 boulevard Bois-Francs Nord
Victoriaville, QC G6P 1G5
Phone: (819) 751-0393
Fax: (819) 751-2770
Website: www.cunninghamlindsey.com
Emergency/After Hours –
1-800-235-8784
E-mail: rcuende@cl-na.com

VILLE DE QUÉBEC–Adjusters

See Quebec City listings

Saskatchewan

REGINA–Adjusters

A.C. ALL CLAIMS GENERAL INSURANCE ADJUSTERS INC.

All lines of insurance adjusting including Property, Liability, Agricultural, Farm Equipment, Heavy Equipment, Boiler and Machinery, Watercraft, ATV and Recreational Vchicles.
We are locally owned and operated and take pride in our rapid response to claims across the province on a 24/7 basis with afterhours service.
36 – 395 Park Street
Regina, SK S4N 5B2
Phone: (306) 790-5840
Fax: (306) 790-5849
Nights: (306) 790-5840 (24 hours)
E-mail: allclaims@accesscomm.ca
Website: www.allclaims.ca
Dale Wolkowski
Randy Duran, CIP
Al Trainor
Don Jeannotte
Paul Duran, B.A., C.M.A.
Mark Trainor
Wanda Hildebrand
Serving southern and central Saskatchewan.
Member: I.A.A.I., S.A.I.A., C.C.A.I.F., and Honourable Order of Blue Goose

CRAWFORD & COMPANY

General Insurance Adjusters
2150 Scarth Street, Suite 120
Regina, SK S4P 2H7
Phone: (306) 586-4994
E-mail: regina.claims@crawco.ca
Bruce Toma, Manager

REGINA–Continued

FRONTIER ADJUSTERS OF REGINA, SASKATCHEWAN

Multiple Lines
Phone: (306) 545-7730 (24 hours)
Fax: (306) 545-7731
E-mail: regina@frontieradjusters.com
Stefan Arnason, Owner-Operator

MIDWEST CLAIMS SERVICES

All Lines including Property and Casualty, Heavy Equipment, Farm Machinery, Specialty and Complex Loss
2 – 2072 McIntyre Street
Regina, SK S4P 2R6
Phone: (306) 522-1656
Facsimile: (306) 569-1256
E-mail: admin@midwestclaims.ca
Website: www.midwestclaims.ca
After hours 24/7 call: (306) 533-0732
Garrett Schous, C.I.P.
Shari Mosthaf, C.I.P.
Darren Kuznitsoff, C.I.P.
Colin Warnecke, C.I.P.
Rob Johnston, C.I.P.
Jordan Demarsh
Curtis Horwath
Amy Woods
Also serving Moose Jaw, Yorkton, Estevan, and Weyburn.

SASKATCHEWAN
Scale of Miles
MACKENZIE
ALBERTA
MANITOBA
MONT.
N. DAK.
DIV. NO. 18
DIV. NO. 17
DIV. NO. 16
DIV. NO. 15
DIV. NO. 14
DIV. NO. 13
DIV. NO. 12
DIV. NO. 11
DIV. NO. 10
DIV. NO. 9
DIV. NO. 8
DIV. NO. 7
DIV. NO. 6
DIV. NO. 5
DIV. NO. 4
DIV. NO. 3
DIV. NO. 2
DIV. NO. 1
Uranium City
L. Athabaska
Fond du Lac
Stony Rapids
Wollaston Lake
Reindeer
L. Frobisher
Peter Pond Lake
Ile a la Crosse L.
Stanley Mission
La Ronge
L. La Ronge
Creighton
Lake Deschambault
Montreal L.
Waskesiu
L. Cumberland
Cumberland House
Meadow Lake
Big River
St. Walburg
Leoville
Turtleford
Lloydminster
Spiritwood
Maidstone
Shellbrook
Prince Albert
Garrick
Nipawin
Carrot River
Arborfield
Birch Hills
Kinistino
Star City
Melfort
Tisdale
Hudson Bay
Blaine Lake
Duck Lake
North Battleford
Battleford
Rosthern
Wakaw
Unity
Macklin
Wilkie
Radisson
Cudworth
Naicam
Weekes
Saskatoon
Bruno
Humboldt
Kelvington
Luseland
Kerrobert
Biggar
Delisle
Watson
Wadena
Preeceville
Sturgis
Lanigan
Wynyard
Watrous
Nokomis
Foam Lake
Canora
Kamsack
Ebenezer
Kindersley
Rosetown
Outlook
Alsask
Imperial
Davidson
Yorkton
Wroxton
Ituna
Eatonia
Eston
Elrose
Dunblane
Craik
Strasbourg
Langenburg
Melville
Leader
Prelate
Lucky Lake
Riverhurst
Demaine
Mawer
Fort Qu'Appelle
Balcarres
Lemberg
Cabri
Lumsden
Qu'Appelle
Indian Head
Grenfell
Fox Valley
Swift Current
Herbert
Morse
Moose Jaw
Regina
Wolseley
Broadview
Whitewood
Gull Lake
Pense
Rouleau
Moosomin
Kipling
Maple Creek
Gravelbourg
Yellowgrass
Shaunavon
Ponteix
La Fleche
Assiniboia
Ogema
Weyburn
Arcola
Carlyle
Redvers
Eastend
Hardy
Radville
Alida
Lampman
Willow Bunch
Bengough
Val Marie
Oxbow
Carnduff
Rockglen
Minton
Estevan
Bienfait

REGINA–Insurance Counsel

McKERCHER LLP
Insurance Practice Group
Richard B. Morris, Q.C.
Alan G. McIntyre, Q.C.
Gregory A. Thompson, Q.C.*
David E. Thera, Q.C.
Sheila E. Caston*
Kaylea M. Dunn*
Nicholas M. Cann
Dean C. Stanley*
Anita G. Fraser*
Brittnee J. Holliday
Robert J. Affleck*
Jeremy N. Ellergodt
Kit McGuinness*
Caroline J. Smith*
Kamara Q. Willett
Andrew W. Restall*
C. Kelsey O'Brien*
Richika J. Bodani
Connor M. Clyde

REGINA–Continued

McKERCHER LLP–Continued
Katherine S. Melnychuk
Matthew J. Bennett*
Amelia A. Lowe-Muller*
*Resident in Saskatoon Office
800 – 1801 Hamilton Street
Regina, SK S4P 4B4
Telephone: (306) 565-6500
Fax: (306) 565-6565
E-mail: info@mckercher.ca
Website: www.mckercher.ca
Saskatoon Office:
374 Third Avenue South
Saskatoon, SK S7K 1M5
Telephone: (306) 653-2000
Fax: (306) 653-2669
E-mail: info@mckercher.ca
Website: www.mckercher.ca
Member: Risk Management Counsel of Canada

SASKATOON–Adjusters

CUNNINGHAM LINDSEY
2911B Cleveland Avenue
Saskatoon, SK S7L 8A9
Phone: (306) 652-1611
Fax: (306) 665-6115
Website: www.cunninghamlindsey.com
After Hours/Emergencies – 1-800-235-8784
E-mail: jjory@cl-na.com

MIDWEST CLAIMS SERVICES
All Lines including Property and Casualty, Heavy Equipment, Farm Machinery, Specialty and Complex Loss
7 – 1622 Ontario Avenue
Saskatoon, SK S7K 1S8
Phone: (306) 668-0870
Facsimile: (306) 249-4114
E-mail: saskatoon@midwestclaims.ca
Website: www.midwestclaims.ca
Lee Dixon, B.Comm., C.I.P.
Jamie Birns
Nathan Rivard, C.I.P., CFEI, CRM
Don Zazula, C.I.P.
Kevin Bucholz, B.A.
Serving central and northern Saskatchewan including Prince Albert, North Battleford, Meadow Lake, and the remote north.

SASKATOON–Insurance Counsel

McKERCHER LLP
Insurance Practice Group
Richard B. Morris, Q.C.*
Alan G. McIntyre, Q.C.*
Gregory A. Thompson, Q.C.
David E. Thera, Q.C.*
Sheila E. Caston
Kaylea M. Dunn
Nicholas M. Cann*
Dean C. Stanley
Anita G. Fraser
Brittnee J. Holliday*
Robert J. Affleck

SASKATOON–Continued

McKERCHER LLP–Continued
Jeremy N. Ellergodt*
Kit McGuinness
Caroline J. Smith
Kamara Q. Willett*
Andrew W. Restall
C. Kelsey O'Brien
Richika J. Bodani*
Connor M. Clyde*
Katherine S. Melnychuk*
Matthew J. Bennett
Amelia A. Lowe-Muller
*Resident in Regina Office
374 Third Avenue South
Saskatoon, SK S7K 1M5
Telephone: (306) 653-2000
Fax: (306) 653-2669
E-mail: info@mckercher.ca
Website: www.mckercher.ca
Regina Office:
800 – 1801 Hamilton Street
Regina, SK S4P 4B4
Telephone: (306) 565-6500
Fax: (306) 565-6565
Member: Risk Management Counsel of Canada

SWIFT CURRENT–Adjusters

MIDWEST CLAIMS SERVICES
All Lines including Property and Casualty, Heavy Equipment, Farm Machinery, Specialty and Complex Loss
317 – 12 Cheadle Street West
Swift Current, SK S9H 0A9
Phone: (306) 773-8848
Facsimile: (306) 773-8849
E-mail: nicole@midwestclaims.ca
Website: www.midwestclaims.ca
Nicole McClelland, C.I.P.
Serving southwest Saskatchewan including Kindersley.

ADJUSTERS AND INSURANCE COUNSEL IN THE UNITED STATES

This supplement is published to meet a demand in Canada for a list of United States Adjusters and Insurance Counsel to whom all classes of Insurance Claims may be referred with every confidence.

Alabama

ANNISTON–Adjusters

CUSTARD INSURANCE ADJUSTERS, INC.

Automobile, Trucking Liability, Property, Casualty, Fire & Allied Lines, Workers' Compensation, Heavy Equipment, Product Liability, Bonds, and Appraisals.

P.O. Box 1814
Anniston, AL 36202
Phone: (256) 236-5933
Fax: (256) 237-9751
Custard Hotline Center (24 hours)
1-800-457-3390
Head Office: Atlanta, Georgia
Rick Linville, Chairman of the Board
Charlie Peek, Chief Executive Officer
Serving the U.S. and Canada with 24 hour service through 250 offices in 48 states.
Visit us on the Web at www.custard.com
Covering 75 mile radius of Anniston.

BIRMINGHAM–Adjusters

CUSTARD INSURANCE ADJUSTERS, INC.

Automobile, Trucking Liability, Property, Casualty, Fire & Allied Lines, Workers' Compensation, Heavy Equipment, Product Liability, Bonds, and Appraisals.

600 Vestavia Parkway, Suite 291
Birmingham, AL 35216
Phone: (205) 823-1230
Fax: (205) 823-4688
Custard Hotline Center (24 hours)
1-800-457-3390
Head Office: Atlanta, Georgia
Rick Linville, Chairman of the Board
Charlie Peek, Chief Executive Officer
Serving the U.S. and Canada with 24 hour service through 250 offices in 48 states.
Visit us on the Web at www.custard.com
Covering 75 mile radius of Birmingham.

BIRMINGHAM–Continued

SPECIALTY GROUP, INC.

Auto Liability, Auto Physical Damage, Cargo, Casualty, Construction Defect Liability, Construction Defect Mediation, E&O, Fidelity Bonds, Inter-Company Arbitration, Liquor Liability, Long Haul Trucking, Longshore & Harborworkers, Malpractice, OLT, Products Liability, Workers' Compensation, Surveillance, Full Service SIU and Data Services.

4000 Eagle Point Corporate Drive
Birmingham, AL 35242
Phone: 1-888-888-9989
Fax: 1-866-537-3097
Toll-free: 1-888-888-9989
Nights: 1-888-888-9989
E-mail:
alsales@specialtygroupinc.com
Website: www.specialtygroupinc.com
Jeffrey A. Kaiser, President

HUNTSVILLE–Adjusters

CUSTARD INSURANCE ADJUSTERS, INC.

Automobile, Trucking Liability, Property, Casualty, Fire & Allied Lines, Workers' Compensation, Heavy Equipment, Product Liability, Bonds, and Appraisals.

5959 Shallowford Road
Suite 209-5
Huntsville, AL 37421
Phone: (256) 882-5052
Fax: (256) 882-5053
Custard Hotline Center (24 hours)
1-800-457-3390
Head Office: Atlanta, Georgia
Rick Linville, Chairman of the Board
Charlie Peek, Chief Executive Officer
Serving the U.S. and Canada with 24 hour service through 250 offices in 48 states.
Visit us on the Web at www.custard.com
Covering 75 mile radius of Huntsville.

MOBILE–Adjusters

CUSTARD INSURANCE ADJUSTERS, INC.

Automobile, Trucking Liability, Property, Casualty, Fire & Allied Lines, Workers' Compensation, Heavy Equipment, Product Liability, Bonds, and Appraisals.
2614 Dauphin Street
Mobile, AL 36606
Phone: (251) 471-3356
Fax: (251) 471-3358
Custard Hotline Center (24 hours)
1-800-457-3390
Head Office: Atlanta, Georgia
Rick Linville, Chairman of the Board
Charlie Peek, Chief Executive Officer
Serving the U.S. and Canada with 24 hour service through 250 offices in 48 states.
Visit us on the Web at www.custard.com
Covering 75 mile radius of Mobile.

MONTGOMERY–Adjusters

CUSTARD INSURANCE ADJUSTERS, INC.

Automobile, Trucking Liability, Property, Casualty, Fire & Allied Lines, Workers' Compensation, Heavy Equipment, Product Liability, Bonds, and Appraisals.
640 South McDonough Street, Suite 2
Montgomery, AL 36104
Phone: (334) 263-4814
Fax: (334) 263-4817
Custard Hotline Center (24 hours)
1-800-457-3390
Head Office: Atlanta, Georgia
Rick Linville, Chairman of the Board
Charlie Peek, Chief Executive Officer
Serving the U.S. and Canada with 24 hour service through 250 offices in 48 states.
Visit us on the Web at www.custard.com
Covering 75 mile radius of Montgomery.

TUSCALOOSA–Adjusters

CUSTARD INSURANCE ADJUSTERS, INC.

Automobile, Trucking Liability, Property, Casualty, Fire & Allied Lines, Workers' Compensation, Heavy Equipment, Product Liability, Bonds, and Appraisals.
P.O. Box 2407
Tuscaloosa, AL 35403
Phone: (205) 210-3636
Fax: (205) 210-3637
Custard Hotline Center (24 hours)
1-800-457-3390
Head Office: Atlanta, Georgia
Rick Linville, Chairman of the Board
Charlie Peek, Chief Executive Officer
Serving the U.S. and Canada with 24 hour service through 250 offices in 48 states.
Visit us on the Web at www.custard.com
Covering 75 mile radius of Tuscaloosa.

Alaska

ANCHORAGE–Adjusters

NORTHERN ADJUSTERS, INC.

Multi-line including property, casualty, transportation, appraisals, underwriting inspections and workers' compensation
1401 Rudakof Circle
Anchorage, AK 99508
Phone: (907) 338-7484
Fax: (907) 338-6364
Susan R. Daniels, President/CEO
E-mail: sdaniels@nadj.com
Website: www.nadj.com
Servicing the entire state of Alaska.
Member: N.A.I.I.A., Affiliated Adjusters, Inc., National Claims Professionals, Inc., Alaska Independent Agents and Brokers, Inc.

Arizona

FLAGSTAFF–Adjusters

CUSTARD INSURANCE ADJUSTERS, INC.

Automobile, Trucking Liability, Property, Casualty, Fire & Allied Lines, Workers' Compensation, Heavy Equipment, Product Liability, Bonds, and Appraisals.

P.O. Box 21031
Sedona, AZ 86341
Phone: (928) 284-0757
Fax: (928) 527-0311
Custard Hotline Center (24 hours)
1-800-457-3390
Head Office: Atlanta, Georgia
Rick Linville, Chairman of the Board
Charlie Peek, Chief Executive Officer
Serving the U.S. and Canada with 24 hour service through 250 offices in 48 states.
Visit us on the Web at www.custard.com
Covering 75 mile radius of Flagstaff.

CUSTARD INSURANCE ADJUSTERS, INC. – TPA OFFICE

Automobile, Trucking Liability, Property, Casualty, Fire & Allied Lines, Workers' Compensation, Heavy Equipment, Product Liability, Bonds, and Appraisals.

P.O. Box 21031
Sedona, AZ 86341
Phone: (928) 284-0757
Fax: (928) 527-0311
Custard Hotline Center (24 hours)
1-800-457-3390
Head Office: Atlanta, Georgia
Rick Linville, Chairman of the Board
Charlie Peek, Chief Executive Officer
Serving the U.S. and Canada with 24 hour service through 250 offices in 48 states.
Visit us on the Web at www.custard.com
Covering 75 mile radius of Flagstaff.

PHOENIX–Adjusters

CUSTARD INSURANCE ADJUSTERS, INC.

Automobile, Trucking Liability, Property, Casualty, Fire & Allied Lines, Workers' Compensation, Heavy Equipment, Product Liability, Bonds, and Appraisals.

3519 E. Shea Boulevard, Suite 125
Phoenix, AZ 85028
Phone: (602) 274-1606
Fax: (602) 274-6736
Custard Hotline Center (24 hours)
1-800-457-3390
Head Office: Atlanta, Georgia
Rick Linville, Chairman of the Board
Charlie Peek, Chief Executive Officer
Serving the U.S. and Canada with 24 hour service through 250 offices in 48 states.
Visit us on the Web at www.custard.com
Covering 75 mile radius of Phoenix.

FRONTIER ADJUSTERS – PHOENIX HOME & CLAIMS OFFICE

Multiple Lines

4745 N. 7th Street, Suite 320
Phoenix, AZ 85014
P.O. Box 7610
Phoenix, AZ 85011
Phone: (602) 264-1061
1-800-528-1187 Toll-free (Nat.)
Fax: (602) 279-5813 or
1-800-553-4799 Toll-free (Nat.)
Emergency Hotline (24 Hr.)
(800) 426-7228 Toll-free (Nat.)
E-mail:
newclaim@frontieradjusters.com
Website:
www.frontieradjusters.com

TUCSON–Adjusters

CUSTARD INSURANCE ADJUSTERS, INC.
Automobile, Trucking Liability, Property, Casualty, Fire & Allied Lines, Workers' Compensation, Heavy Equipment, Product Liability, Bonds, and Appraisals.
7090 N. Oracle Road
Suite 178-155
Tucson, AZ 85704
Phone: (520) 204-1558
Fax: (520) 733-3849
Custard Hotline Center (24 hours)
1-800-457-3390
Head Office: Atlanta, Georgia
Rick Linville, Chairman of the Board
Charlie Peek, Chief Executive Officer
Serving the U.S. and Canada with 24 hour service through 250 offices in 48 states.
Visit us on the Web at www.custard.com
Covering 75 mile radius of Tucson.

Arkansas

FAYETTEVILLE–Adjusters

CUSTARD INSURANCE ADJUSTERS, INC.
Automobile, Trucking Liability, Property, Casualty, Fire & Allied Lines, Workers' Compensation, Heavy Equipment, Product Liability, Bonds, and Appraisals.
P.O. Box 1664
Fayetteville, AR 72702
Phone: (479) 521-1049
Fax: (479) 444-6102
Custard Hotline Center (24 hours)
1-800-457-3390
Head Office: Atlanta, Georgia
Rick Linville, Chairman of the Board
Charlie Peek, Chief Executive Officer
Serving the U.S. and Canada with 24 hour service through 250 offices in 48 states.
Visit us on the Web at www.custard.com
Covering 75 mile radius of Fayetteville.

LITTLE ROCK–Adjusters

CUSTARD INSURANCE ADJUSTERS, INC.
Automobile, Trucking Liability, Property, Casualty, Fire & Allied Lines, Workers' Compensation, Heavy Equipment, Product Liability, Bonds, and Appraisals.
10201 West Markham
Suite 204
Little Rock, AR 72205
Phone: (501) 223-8073
Fax: (501) 223-2066
Custard Hotline Center (24 hours)
1-800-457-3390
Head Office: Atlanta, Georgia
Rick Linville, Chairman of the Board
Charlie Peek, Chief Executive Officer
Serving the U.S. and Canada with 24 hour service through 250 offices in 48 states.
Visit us on the Web at www.custard.com
Covering 75 mile radius of Little Rock.

California

ANAHEIM–Adjusters

CUSTARD INSURANCE ADJUSTERS, INC.
Automobile, Trucking Liability, Property, Casualty, Fire & Allied Lines, Workers' Compensation, Heavy Equipment, Product Liability, Bonds, and Appraisals.
P.O. Box 4566
Anaheim, CA 92803
Phone: (714) 254-0400
Fax: (714) 254-0444
Custard Hotline Center (24 hours)
1-800-457-3390
Head Office: Atlanta, Georgia
Rick Linville, Chairman of the Board
Charlie Peek, Chief Executive Officer
Serving the U.S. and Canada with 24 hour service through 250 offices in 48 states.
Visit us on the Web at www.custard.com
Covering 75 mile radius of Anaheim.

FRESNO–Adjusters

CUSTARD INSURANCE ADJUSTERS, INC.

Automobile, Trucking Liability, Property, Casualty, Fire & Allied Lines, Workers' Compensation, Heavy Equipment, Product Liability, Bonds, and Appraisals.

2037 W. Bullard Avenue
PMB 160
Fresno, CA 93711
Phone: (559) 592-5064
Fax: (559) 592-5229
Custard Hotline Center (24 hours)
1-800-457-3390
Head Office: Atlanta, Georgia
Rick Linville, Chairman of the Board
Charlie Peek, Chief Executive Officer
Serving the U.S. and Canada with 24 hour service through 250 offices in 48 states.
Visit us on the Web at www.custard.com
Covering 75 mile radius of Fresno.

LOS ANGELES–Adjusters

CUSTARD INSURANCE ADJUSTERS, INC.

Automobile, Trucking Liability, Property, Casualty, Fire & Allied Lines, Workers' Compensation, Heavy Equipment, Product Liability, Bonds, and Appraisals.

1901 West Pacific Avenue
Suite 100
West Covina, CA 91790
Phone: (626) 962-6841
Fax: (626) 962-7246
Custard Hotline Center (24 hours)
1-800-457-3390
Head Office: Atlanta, Georgia
Rick Linville, Chairman of the Board
Charlie Peek, Chief Executive Officer
Serving the U.S. and Canada with 24 hour service through 250 offices in 48 states.
Visit us on the Web at www.custard.com
Covering 75 mile radius of Los Angeles.

LOS ANGELES–Continued

CUSTARD INSURANCE ADJUSTERS, INC. – TPA OFFICE

Automobile, Trucking Liability, Property, Casualty, Fire & Allied Lines, Workers' Compensation, Heavy Equipment, Product Liability, Bonds, and Appraisals.

1901 W. Pacific Avenue, Suite 100
West Covina, CA 91790
Phone: (626) 962-6841
Fax: (626) 962-7246
Custard Hotline Center (24 hours)
1-800-457-3390
Head Office: Atlanta, Georgia
Rick Linville, Chairman of the Board
Charlie Peek, Chief Executive Officer
Serving the U.S. and Canada with 24 hour service through 250 offices in 48 states.
Visit us on the Web at www.custard.com
Covering 75 mile radius of Los Angeles.

OAKLAND–Adjusters

CUSTARD INSURANCE ADJUSTERS, INC.

Automobile, Trucking Liability, Property, Casualty, Fire & Allied Lines, Workers' Compensation, Heavy Equipment, Product Liability, Bonds, and Appraisals.

22693 Hesperian Boulevard, Suite 270
Hayward, CA 94541
Phone: (510) 785-2900
Fax: (510) 785-2930
Custard Hotline Center (24 hours)
1-800-457-3390
Head Office: Atlanta, Georgia
Rick Linville, Chairman of the Board
Charlie Peek, Chief Executive Officer
Serving the U.S. and Canada with 24 hour service through 250 offices in 48 states.
Visit us on the Web at www.custard.com
Covering 75 mile radius of Oakland.

PALM SPRINGS–Adjusters

CUSTARD INSURANCE ADJUSTERS, INC.

Automobile, Trucking Liability, Property, Casualty, Fire & Allied Lines, Workers' Compensation, Heavy Equipment, Product Liability, Bonds, and Appraisals.

611 South Palm Canyon Drive
Suite 7 – 130
Palm Springs, CA 92264
Phone: (760) 365-9030
Fax: (760) 365-9060
Custard Hotline Center (24 hours)
1-800-457-3390
Head Office: Atlanta, Georgia
Rick Linville, Chairman of the Board
Charlie Peek, Chief Executive Officer
Serving the U.S. and Canada with 24 hour service through 250 offices in 48 states.
Visit us on the Web at www.custard.com
Covering 75 mile radius of Palm Springs.

SACRAMENTO–Adjusters

CUSTARD INSURANCE ADJUSTERS, INC.

Automobile, Trucking Liability, Property, Casualty, Fire & Allied Lines, Workers' Compensation, Heavy Equipment, Product Liability, Bonds, and Appraisals.

7625 Sunrise Boulevard, Suite 212
Citrus Heights, CA 95610
Phone: (916) 721-6211
Fax: (916) 721-6214
Custard Hotline Center (24 hours)
1-800-457-3390
Head Office: Atlanta, Georgia
Rick Linville, Chairman of the Board
Charlie Peek, Chief Executive Officer
Serving the U.S. and Canada with 24 hour service through 250 offices in 48 states.
Visit us on the Web at www.custard.com
Covering 75 mile radius of Sacramento.

SAN DIEGO–Adjusters

CUSTARD INSURANCE ADJUSTERS, INC.

Automobile, Trucking Liability, Property, Casualty, Fire & Allied Lines, Workers' Compensation, Heavy Equipment, Product Liability, Bonds, and Appraisals.

6977 Navajo Road, Suite 116
San Diego, CA 92119
Phone: (619) 298-7494
Fax: (619) 298-9711
Custard Hotline Center (24 hours)
1-800-457-3390
Head Office: Atlanta, Georgia
Rick Linville, Chairman of the Board
Charlie Peek, Chief Executive Officer
Serving the U.S. and Canada with 24 hour service through 250 offices in 48 states.
Visit us on the Web at www.custard.com
Covering 75 mile radius of San Diego.

SAN FRANCISCO–Adjusters

CUSTARD INSURANCE ADJUSTERS, INC.

Automobile, Trucking Liability, Property, Casualty, Fire & Allied Lines, Workers' Compensation, Heavy Equipment, Product Liability, Bonds, and Appraisals.

601 Van Ness Avenue
Suite E-3, No. 980
San Francisco, CA 94102
Phone: (415) 673-3399
Fax: (415) 673-4443
Custard Hotline Center (24 hours)
1-800-457-3390
Head Office: Atlanta, Georgia
Rick Linville, Chairman of the Board
Charlie Peek, Chief Executive Officer
Serving the U.S. and Canada with 24 hour service through 250 offices in 48 states.
Visit us on the Web at www.custard.com
Covering 75 mile radius of San Francisco.

SAN JOSE–Adjusters

CUSTARD INSURANCE ADJUSTERS, INC.

Automobile, Trucking Liability, Property, Casualty, Fire & Allied Lines, Workers' Compensation, Heavy Equipment, Product Liability, Bonds, and Appraisals.

4960 Almaden Expressway, Suite 161
San Jose, CA 95118
Phone: (408) 287-6891
Fax: (408) 287-6893
Custard Hotline Center (24 hours)
1-800-457-3390
Head Office: Atlanta, Georgia
Rick Linville, Chairman of the Board
Charlie Peek, Chief Executive Officer
Serving the U.S. and Canada with 24 hour service through 250 offices in 48 states.
Visit us on the Web at www.custard.com
Covering 75 mile radius of San Jose.

Colorado

COLORADO SPRINGS–Adjusters

CUSTARD INSURANCE ADJUSTERS, INC.

Automobile, Trucking Liability, Property, Casualty, Fire & Allied Lines, Workers' Compensation, Heavy Equipment, Product Liability, Bonds, and Appraisals.

13900 E. Harvard Avenue, Suite 206
Aurora, CO 80014
Phone: (719) 634-3330
Fax: (719) 634-0553
Custard Hotline Center (24 hours)
1-800-457-3390
Head Office: Atlanta, Georgia
Rick Linville, Chairman of the Board
Charlie Peek, Chief Executive Officer
Serving the U.S. and Canada with 24 hour service through 250 offices in 48 states.
Visit us on the Web at www.custard.com
Covering 75 mile radius of Colorado Springs.

DENVER–Adjusters

CUSTARD INSURANCE ADJUSTERS, INC.

Automobile, Trucking Liability, Property, Casualty, Fire & Allied Lines, Workers' Compensation, Heavy Equipment, Product Liability, Bonds, and Appraisals.

3091 South Jamaica Court, Suite 140
Aurora, CO 80014
Phone: (303) 338-1015
Fax: (303) 338-1018
Custard Hotline Center (24 hours)
1-800-457-3390
Head Office: Atlanta, Georgia
Rick Linville, Chairman of the Board
Charlie Peek, Chief Executive Officer
Serving the U.S. and Canada with 24 hour service through 250 offices in 48 states.
Visit us on the Web at www.custard.com
Covering 75 mile radius of Denver.

GLENWOOD SPRINGS–Adjusters

CUSTARD INSURANCE ADJUSTERS, INC.

Automobile, Trucking Liability, Property, Casualty, Fire & Allied Lines, Workers' Compensation, Heavy Equipment, Product Liability, Bonds, and Appraisals.

1338 Grand Avenue
PMB 174
Glenwood Springs, CO 81601
Phone: (970) 945-1177
Fax: (970) 945-1597
Custard Hotline Center (24 hours)
1-800-457-3390
Head Office: Atlanta, Georgia
Rick Linville, Chairman of the Board
Charlie Peek, Chief Executive Officer
Serving the U.S. and Canada with 24 hour service through 250 offices in 48 states.
Visit us on the Web at www.custard.com
Covering 75 mile radius of Glenwood Springs.

GRAND JUNCTION–Adjusters

CUSTARD INSURANCE ADJUSTERS, INC.

Automobile, Trucking Liability, Property, Casualty, Fire & Allied Lines, Workers' Compensation, Heavy Equipment, Product Liability, Bonds, and Appraisals.

1338 Grand Avenue
PMB 174
Glenwood Springs, CO 81601
Phone: (970) 945-1177
Fax: (970) 945-1597
Custard Hotline Center (24 hours)
1-800-457-3390
Head Office: Atlanta, Georgia
Rick Linville, Chairman of the Board
Charlie Peek, Chief Executive Officer
Serving the U.S. and Canada with 24 hour service through 250 offices in 48 states.
Visit us on the Web at www.custard.com
Covering 75 mile radius of Grand Junction.

Connecticut

HARTFORD–Adjusters

CUSTARD INSURANCE ADJUSTERS, INC.

Automobile, Trucking Liability, Property, Casualty, Fire & Allied Lines, Workers' Compensation, Heavy Equipment, Product Liability, Bonds, and Appraisals.

854 Farmington Avenue
West Hartford, CT 06119
Phone: (860) 523-4266
Fax: (860) 231-1477
Custard Hotline Center (24 hours)
1-800-457-3390
Head Office: Atlanta, Georgia
Rick Linville, Chairman of the Board
Charlie Peek, Chief Executive Officer
Serving the U.S. and Canada with 24 hour service through 250 offices in 48 states.
Visit us on the Web at www.custard.com
Covering 75 mile radius of Hartford.

NEW HAVEN–Adjusters

CUSTARD INSURANCE ADJUSTERS, INC.

Automobile, Trucking Liability, Property, Casualty, Fire & Allied Lines, Workers' Compensation, Heavy Equipment, Product Liability, Bonds, and Appraisals.

854 Farmington Avenue
West Hartford, CT 06119
Phone: (203) 795-0300
Fax: (203) 795-0702
Custard Hotline Center (24 hours)
1-800-457-3390
Head Office: Atlanta, Georgia
Rick Linville, Chairman of the Board
Charlie Peek, Chief Executive Officer
Serving the U.S. and Canada with 24 hour service through 250 offices in 48 states.
Visit us on the Web at www.custard.com
Covering 75 mile radius of New Haven.

Delaware

DOVER–Adjusters

CUSTARD INSURANCE ADJUSTERS, INC.

Automobile, Trucking Liability, Property, Casualty, Fire & Allied Lines, Workers' Compensation, Heavy Equipment, Product Liability, Bonds, and Appraisals.

P.O. Box 0481
Dover, DE 19903
Phone: (302) 736-1297
Fax: (302) 736-1298
Custard Hotline Center (24 hours)
1-800-457-3390
Head Office: Atlanta, Georgia
Rick Linville, Chairman of the Board
Charlie Peek, Chief Executive Officer
Serving the U.S. and Canada with 24 hour service through 250 offices in 48 states.
Visit us on the Web at www.custard.com
Covering 75 mile radius of Dover.

WILMINGTON–Adjusters

CUSTARD INSURANCE ADJUSTERS, INC.
Automobile, Trucking Liability, Property, Casualty, Fire & Allied Lines, Workers' Compensation, Heavy Equipment, Product Liability, Bonds, and Appraisals.
4023 Kennett Pike, Suite 882
Wilmington, DE 19807
Phone: (302) 778-0778
Fax: (302) 778-5989
Custard Hotline Center (24 hours)
1-800-457-3390
Head Office: Atlanta, Georgia
Rick Linville, Chairman of the Board
Charlie Peek, Chief Executive Officer
Serving the U.S. and Canada with 24 hour service through 250 offices in 48 states.
Visit us on the Web at www.custard.com
Covering 75 mile radius of Wilmington.

District of Columbia

WASHINGTON–Adjusters

CUSTARD INSURANCE ADJUSTERS, INC.
Automobile, Trucking Liability, Property, Casualty, Fire & Allied Lines, Workers' Compensation, Heavy Equipment, Product Liability, Bonds, and Appraisals.
5614 Connecticut Avenue N.W.
Suite 101
Washington, DC 20015
Phone: (301) 345-7766
Fax: (301) 474-6816
Custard Hotline Center (24 hours)
1-800-457-3390
Head Office: Atlanta, Georgia
Rick Linville, Chairman of the Board
Charlie Peek, Chief Executive Officer
Serving the U.S. and Canada with 24 hour service through 250 offices in 48 states.
Visit us on the Web at www.custard.com
Throughout Washington, DC and the Baltimore area.

Florida

DAYTONA BEACH–Adjusters

CUSTARD INSURANCE ADJUSTERS, INC.
Automobile, Trucking Liability, Property, Casualty, Fire & Allied Lines, Workers' Compensation, Heavy Equipment, Product Liability, Bonds, and Appraisals.
P.O. Box 5023
Deltona, FL 32738
Phone: (386) 323-7455
Fax: (386) 323-7456
Custard Hotline Center (24 hours)
1-800-457-3390
Head Office: Atlanta, Georgia
Rick Linville, Chairman of the Board
Charlie Peek, Chief Executive Officer
Serving the U.S. and Canada with 24 hour service through 250 offices in 48 states.
Visit us on the Web at www.custard.com
Covering 75 mile radius of Daytona Beach.

DESTIN–Adjusters

CUSTARD INSURANCE ADJUSTERS, INC.
Automobile, Trucking Liability, Property, Casualty, Fire & Allied Lines, Workers' Compensation, Heavy Equipment, Product Liability, Bonds, and Appraisals.
P.O. Box 419
Freeport, FL 32439
Phone: (850) 588-3539
Fax: (850) 269-0089
Custard Hotline Center (24 hours)
1-800-457-3390
Head Office: Atlanta, Georgia
Rick Linville, Chairman of the Board
Charlie Peek, Chief Executive Officer
Serving the U.S. and Canada with 24 hour service through 250 offices in 48 states.
Visit us on the Web at www.custard.com
Covering 75 mile radius of Destin.

FLORIDA
Scale of Miles
0
20
40
60
GA.
ALA.
NASSAU
DUVAL
Jacksonville
BAKER
HAMILTON
COLUMBIA
SUWANNEE
LAFAYETTE
UNION
BRADFORD
CLAY
ST. JOHNS
PUTNAM
FLAGLER
ALACHUA
Gainesville
GILCHRIST
LEVY
DIXIE
MARION
Ocala
VOLUSIA
Daytona Beach
LAKE
SEMINOLE
Orlando
ORANGE
CITRUS
SUMTER
HERNANDO
PASCO
POLK
Lakeland
HILLSBOROUGH
Tampa
Clearwater
St. Petersburg
MANATEE
HARDEE
DE SOTO
SARASOTA
CHARLOTTE
LEE
Fort Myers
HENDRY
COLLIER
MONROE
Key West
DADE
Miami
BROWARD
Fort Lauderdale
PALM BEACH
West Palm Beach
MARTIN
ST. LUCIE
Fort Pierce
INDIAN RIVER
BREVARD
OSCEOLA
OKEECHOBEE
HIGHLANDS
GLADES
LEON
Tallahassee
JEFFERSON
MADISON
TAYLOR
WAKULLA
GADSDEN
FRANKLIN
ESCAMBIA
SANTA ROSA
OKALOOSA
WALTON
HOLMES
JACKSON
WASHINGTON
CALHOUN
BAY
Panama City
GULF
LIBERTY
Pensacola

FORT LAUDERDALE–Adjusters

BURTON CLAIM SERVICE, INC.

Multi-Line Insurance Adjusters
2941 West Cypress Creek Road
Suite 101
Fort Lauderdale, FL 33309
Phone: (954) 972-4820
Fax: (954) 972-4879
Toll-free : 1-800-330-2524
Website: www.burtonclaimservice.com
E-mail: info@burtonclaimservice.com

CUSTARD INSURANCE ADJUSTERS, INC.

Automobile, Trucking Liability, Property, Casualty, Fire & Allied Lines, Workers' Compensation, Heavy Equipment, Product Liability, Bonds, and Appraisals.
Maitland City Plaza
9000 Regency Square Boulevard
Suite 203
Jacksonville, FL 32211
Phone: (850) 588-3539
Fax: (850) 269-0089
Custard Hotline Center (24 hours)
1-800-457-3390
Head Office: Atlanta, Georgia
Rick Linville, Chairman of the Board
Charlie Peek, Chief Executive Officer
Serving the U.S. and Canada with 24 hour service through 250 offices in 48 states.
Visit us on the Web at www.custard.com
Covering 75 mile radius of Fort Lauderdale.

FORT LAUDERDALE–Continued

SPECIALTY GROUP, INC.

Auto Liability, Auto Physical Damage, Cargo, Casualty, Construction Defect Liability, Construction Defect Mediation, E&O, Workers' Compensation, Fidelity Bonds, Inter-Company Arbitration, Liquor Liability, Long Haul Trucking, Longshore & Harborworkers, Malpractice, OLT, Products Liability, Surveillance, Full Service SIU and Data Services.
6750 North Andrews Avenue
Suite 200
Fort Lauderdale, FL 33309
Phone: (954) 485-9664
Fax: (954) 485-9522
Toll-free: 1-888-748-8648
Nights: (954) 485-9664
E-mail: ftlsales@specialtygroupinc.com
Website: www.specialtygroupinc.com
Jeffrey A. Kaiser, President
Servicing the entire state of Florida.

FORT MYERS–Adjusters

CRITTENDEN ADJUSTMENT COMPANY (FLORIDA), INC.

Multi-line Adjustment Services
5700 Halifax Avenue, Suite 1
Fort Myers, FL 33912
Phone: (239) 415-1700
Toll-free Assignment Hot Line:
1-800-283-5515
Fax: (239) 415-1701
Nights: Same as above
E-mail: operations@cacadjfla.com
Website: www.cacadjfla.com
Edward R. Crittenden, President
Providing independent adjustment services throughout the entire State of Florida.
Member: N.A.I.I.A., ProNet International, International Assn. of Arson Investigators, Inc.

CUSTARD INSURANCE ADJUSTERS, INC.

Automobile, Trucking Liability, Property, Casualty, Fire & Allied Lines, Workers' Compensation, Heavy Equipment, Product Liability, Bonds, and Appraisals.
125 South Swoope Avenue
Suite 106
Maitland, FL 32751
Phone: (239) 277-9966
Fax: (239) 277-9989
Custard Hotline Center (24 hours)
1-800-457-3390
Head Office: Atlanta, Georgia
Rick Linville, Chairman of the Board
Charlie Peek, Chief Executive Officer
Serving the U.S. and Canada with 24 hour service through 250 offices in 48 states.
Visit us on the Web at www.custard.com
Covering 75 mile radius of Fort Myers.

FORT PIERCE/STUART–Adjusters

CUSTARD INSURANCE ADJUSTERS, INC.

Automobile, Trucking Liability, Property, Casualty, Fire & Allied Lines, Workers' Compensation, Heavy Equipment, Product Liability, Bonds, and Appraisals.
P.O. Box 881782
Port St. Lucie, FL 34988-1782
Phone: (772) 464-5972
Fax: (772) 464-6480
Custard Hotline Center (24 hours)
1-800-457-3390
Head Office: Atlanta, Georgia
Rick Linville, Chairman of the Board
Charlie Peek, Chief Executive Officer
Serving the U.S. and Canada with 24 hour service through 250 offices in 48 states.
Visit us on the Web at www.custard.com
Covering 75 mile radius of Fort Pierce/ Stuart.

JACKSONVILLE–Adjusters

CUSTARD INSURANCE ADJUSTERS, INC.

Automobile, Trucking Liability, Property, Casualty, Fire & Allied Lines, Workers' Compensation, Heavy Equipment, Product Liability, Bonds, and Appraisals.
9000 Regency Square Boulevard
Suite 203
Jacksonville, FL 32211
Phone: (904) 724-1937
Fax: (904) 724-2768
Custard Hotline Center (24 hours)
1-800-457-3390
Head Office: Atlanta, Georgia
Rick Linville, Chairman of the Board
Charlie Peek, Chief Executive Officer
Serving the U.S. and Canada with 24 hour service through 250 offices in 48 states.
Visit us on the Web at www.custard.com
Covering 75 mile radius of Jacksonville.

JACKSONVILLE–Continued

SPECIALTY GROUP, INC.

Auto Liability, Auto Physical Damage, Cargo, Casualty, Construction Defect Liability, Construction Defect Mediation, E&O, Fidelity Bonds, Inter-Company Arbitration, Liquor Liability, Long Haul Trucking, Longshore & Harborworkers, Malpractice, OLT, Products Liability, Workers' Compensation, Surveillance, Full Service SIU and Data Services.
4720 Salisbury Road
Jacksonville, FL 32256
Phone: (904) 396-1144
Fax: (904) 396-1148
Toll-free: 1-888-678-6800
Nights: (904) 396-1144
E-mail:
jaxsales@specialtygroupinc.com
Website: www.specialtygroupinc.com
Jeffrey A. Kaiser, President
Servicing the entire state of Florida.
Member: Jacksonville Claims Assn.

LAKELAND–Adjusters

CRITTENDEN ADJUSTMENT COMPANY (FLORIDA), INC.

Multi-line Adjustment Services
2000 S. Florida Avenue
Lakeland, FL 33803
Phone: (863) 577-1465
Toll-free Assignment Hot Line:
1-800-283-5515
Fax: (863) 682-2797
Nights: Same as above
E-mail: operations@cacadjfla.com
Website: www.cacadjfla.com
Edward R. Crittenden, President
Providing independent adjustment services throughout the entire State of Florida.
Member: N.A.I.I.A., ProNet International, International Assn. of Arson Investigators, Inc.

MELBOURNE–Adjusters

CUSTARD INSURANCE ADJUSTERS, INC.

Automobile, Trucking Liability, Property, Casualty, Fire & Allied Lines, Workers' Compensation, Heavy Equipment, Product Liability, Bonds, and Appraisals.
P.O. Box 361893
Melbourne, FL 32936
Phone: (321) 752-7334
Fax: (321) 752-7337
Custard Hotline Center (24 hours)
1-800-457-3390
Head Office: Atlanta, Georgia
Rick Linville, Chairman of the Board
Charlie Peek, Chief Executive Officer
Serving the U.S. and Canada with 24 hour service through 250 offices in 48 states.
Visit us on the Web at www.custard.com
Covering 75 mile radius of Melbourne.

MIAMI–Adjusters

CRITTENDEN ADJUSTMENT COMPANY (FLORIDA), INC.

Multi-line Adjustment Services
17801 N.W. 14 Court
Miami, FL 33169
Phone: (305) 471-9655
Toll-free Assignment Hot Line:
1-800-283-5515
Fax: (305) 471-9653
Nights: Same as above
E-mail: operations@cacadjfla.com
Website: www.cacadjfla.com
Johnny McGee, Adjuster
Providing independent adjustment services throughout the entire State of Florida.
Member: N.A.I.I.A., ProNet International, International Assn. of Arson Investigators, Inc.

MIAMI–Continued

CUSTARD INSURANCE ADJUSTERS, INC.

Automobile, Trucking Liability, Property, Casualty, Fire & Allied Lines, Workers' Compensation, Heavy Equipment, Product Liability, Bonds, and Appraisals.
P.O. Box 66-9263
Miami, FL 33166
Phone: (305) 424-1952
Fax: (305) 207-9989
Custard Hotline Center (24 hours)
1-800-457-3390
Head Office: Atlanta, Georgia
Rick Linville, Chairman of the Board
Charlie Peek, Chief Executive Officer
Serving the U.S. and Canada with 24 hour service through 250 offices in 48 states.
Visit us on the Web at www.custard.com
Covering 75 mile radius of Miami and Florida Keys to Key West.

NAPLES–Adjusters

CRITTENDEN ADJUSTMENT COMPANY (FLORIDA), INC.

Multi-line Adjustment Services
5700 Halifax Avenue
Suite One
Fort Myers, FL 33912
Phone: (239) 262-4226
Toll-free Assignment Hot Line:
1-800-283-5515
Fax: (239) 262-4222
Nights: Same as above
E-mail: operations@cacadjfla.com
Website: www.cacadjfla.com
John Prestigiovanni,
Senior Adjuster
Providing independent adjustment services throughout the entire State of Florida.
Member: N.A.I.I.A., ProNet International, International Assn. of Arson Investigators, Inc.

OCALA/GAINESVILLE–Adjusters

CUSTARD INSURANCE ADJUSTERS, INC.

Automobile, Trucking Liability, Property, Casualty, Fire & Allied Lines, Workers' Compensation, Heavy Equipment, Product Liability, Bonds, and Appraisals.
P.O. Box 606
Summerfield, FL 34492
Phone: (352) 314-2546
Fax: (352) 314-2576
Custard Hotline Center (24 hours)
1-800-457-3390
Head Office: Atlanta, Georgia
Rick Linville, Chairman of the Board
Charlie Peek, Chief Executive Officer
Serving the U.S. and Canada with 24 hour service through 250 offices in 48 states.
Visit us on the Web at www.custard.com
Covering 75 mile radius of Ocala/Gainesville area.

ORLANDO–Adjusters

CRITTENDEN ADJUSTMENT COMPANY (FLORIDA), INC.

Multi-line Adjustment Services
2000 S. Florida Avenue
Lakeland, FL 33803
Phone: (407) 671-3004
Toll-free Assignment Hot Line:
1-800-283-5515
Fax: (407) 671-3009
Nights: Same as above
E-mail: operations@cacadjfla.com
Website: www.cacadjfla.com
Edward R. Crittenden, President
Providing independent adjustment services throughout the entire State of Florida.
Member: N.A.I.I.A., ProNet International, International Assn. of Arson Investigators, Inc.

ORLANDO–Continued

CUSTARD INSURANCE ADJUSTERS, INC.

Automobile, Trucking Liability, Property, Casualty, Fire & Allied Lines, Workers' Compensation, Heavy Equipment, Product Liability, Bonds, and Appraisals.

Maitland City Plaza
125 S. Swoope Avenue, Suite 106
Maitland, FL 32751
Phone: (407) 539-2632
Fax: (407) 539-2531
Custard Hotline Center (24 hours)
1-800-457-3390
Head Office: Atlanta, Georgia
Rick Linville, Chairman of the Board
Charlie Peek, Chief Executive Officer
Serving the U.S. and Canada with 24 hour service through 250 offices in 48 states.
Visit us on the Web at www.custard.com
Covering 75 mile radius of Orlando.

SPECIALTY GROUP, INC.

Auto Liability, Auto Physical Damage, Cargo, Casualty, Construction Defect Liability, Construction Defect Mediation, E&O, Fidelity Bonds, Inter-Company Arbitration, Liquor Liability, Long Haul Trucking, Longshore & Harborworkers, Malpractice, OLT, Products Liability, Workers' Compensation, Surveillance, Full Service SIU and Data Services.

4100 Metric Drive
Suite 700
Winter Park, FL 32792
Phone: (407) 678-0204
Fax: (407) 678-7210
Toll-free: 1-888-888-9989
E-mail:
orlsales@specialtygroupinc.com
Website: www.specialtygroupinc.com
Jeffrey A. Kaiser, President
Serving the entire state of Florida.
Member: Orlando Claims Assn., Sarasota-Bradenton Claims Assn.

PANAMA CITY BEACH–Adjusters

CUSTARD INSURANCE ADJUSTERS, INC.

Automobile, Trucking Liability, Property, Casualty, Fire & Allied Lines, Workers' Compensation, Heavy Equipment, Product Liability, Bonds, and Appraisals.

9000 Regency Square Boulevard
Suite 201
Jacksonville, FL 32211
Phone: (850) 588-3539
Fax: (850) 230-1375
Custard Hotline Center (24 hours)
1-800-457-3390
Head Office: Atlanta, Georgia
Rick Linville, Chairman of the Board
Charlie Peek, Chief Executive Officer
Serving the U.S. and Canada with 24 hour service through 250 offices in 48 states.
Visit us on the Web at www.custard.com
Covering 75 mile radius of Panama City Beach.

PINE ISLAND–Adjusters

CRITTENDEN ADJUSTMENT COMPANY (FLORIDA), INC.

Multi-line Adjustment Services

4985 Curlew Drive
St. James City, FL 33956
Phone: (239) 707-8181
Toll-free Assignment Hot Line:
1-800-283-5515
Fax: 1-800-329-4287
Nights: Same as above
E-mail: operations@cacadjfla.com
Website: www.cacadjfla.com
Edward R. Crittenden, ACA
Adam M. Crittenden, ACA
Providing independent adjustment services throughout the entire State of Florida.
Member: N.A.I.I.A., ProNet International, International Assn. of Arson Investigators, Inc.

ST. PETERSBURG–Adjusters

CUSTARD INSURANCE ADJUSTERS, INC.

Automobile, Trucking Liability, Property, Casualty, Fire & Allied Lines, Workers' Compensation, Heavy Equipment, Product Liability, Bonds, and Appraisals.
5601 Mariner Street, Suite 240
Tampa, FL 33609
Phone: (813) 286-1984
Fax: (813) 286-8513
Custard Hotline Center (24 hours)
1-800-457-3390
Head Office: Atlanta, Georgia
Rick Linville, Chairman of the Board
Charlie Peek, Chief Executive Officer
Serving the U.S. and Canada with 24 hour service through 250 offices in 48 states.
Visit us on the Web at www.custard.com
Covering 75 mile radius of St. Petersburg.

TALLAHASSEE–Adjusters

CUSTARD INSURANCE ADJUSTERS, INC.

Automobile, Trucking Liability, Property, Casualty, Fire & Allied Lines, Workers' Compensation, Heavy Equipment, Product Liability, Bonds, and Appraisals.
9000 Regency Square Boulevard
Suite 203
Jacksonville, FL 32211
Phone: (850) 383-1828
Fax: (850) 383-1848
Custard Hotline Center (24 hours)
1-800-457-3390
Head Office: Atlanta, Georgia
Rick Linville, Chairman of the Board
Charlie Peek, Chief Executive Officer
Serving the U.S. and Canada with 24 hour service through 250 offices in 48 states.
Visit us on the Web at www.custard.com
Covering 75 mile radius of Tallahassee.

TAMPA–Adjusters

CRITTENDEN ADJUSTMENT COMPANY (FLORIDA), INC.

Multi-line Adjustment Services
2000 S. Florida Avenue
Lakeland, FL 33803
Phone: (813) 910-8900
Toll-free Assignment Hot Line:
1-800-283-5515
Fax: (813) 910-8989
Nights: Same as above
E-mail: operations@cacadjfla.com
Website: www.cacadjfla.com
Edward R. Crittenden, President
Providing independent adjustment services throughout the entire State of Florida.
Member: N.A.I.I.A., ProNet International, International Assn. of Arson Investigators, Inc.

CUSTARD INSURANCE ADJUSTERS, INC.

Auto Liability, General Liability, Trucking, Workers' Compensation, Public Entities, Product Liability, Commercial Property, and Non-trucking.
5601 Mariner Street, Suite 240
Tampa, FL 33609
Phone: (813) 286-1984
Fax: (813) 286-8513
Custard Hotline Center (24 hours)
1-800-457-3390
Head Office: Atlanta, Georgia
Rick Linville, Chairman of the Board
Charlie Peek, Chief Executive Officer
Serving the U.S. and Canada with 24 hour service through 250 offices in 48 states.
Visit us on the Web at www.custard.com
Covering 75 mile radius of Tampa.

TAMPA–Continued

CUSTARD INSURANCE ADJUSTERS, INC.

Auto Liability, General Liability, Trucking, Workers' Compensation, Public Entities, Product Liability, Commercial Property, and Non-trucking.
FSM
19532 Leland Avenue
Spring Hill, FL 34610
Phone: (727) 378-9742
Fax: (727) 857-2376
Custard Hotline Center (24 hours)
1-800-457-3390
Head Office: Atlanta, Georgia
Rick Linville, Chairman of the Board
Charlie Peek, Chief Executive Officer
Serving the U.S. and Canada with 24 hour service through 250 offices in 48 states.
Visit us on the Web at www.custard.com
Covering 75 mile radius of Tampa.

SPECIALTY GROUP, INC.

Auto Liability, Auto Physical Damage, Cargo, Casualty, Construction Defect Liability, Construction Defect Mediation, E&O, Fidelity Bonds, Inter-Company Arbitration, Liquor Liability, Long Haul Trucking, Longshore & Harborworkers, Malpractice, OLT, Products Liability, Workers' Compensation, Surveillance, Full Service SIU and Data Services.
8270 Woodland Center Boulevard
Tampa, FL 33614
Phone: (813) 282-0602
Fax: (813) 282-0604
Toll-free: 1-866-683-4662
E-mail:
tampasales@specialtygroupinc.com
Website: www.specialtygroupinc.com
Jeffrey A. Kaiser, President
Member: Property & Casualty Claims Professionals (PCCP) and Workers' Compensation Claims Professionals (WCCP).

WEST PALM BEACH–Adjusters

CUSTARD INSURANCE ADJUSTERS, INC.

Automobile, Trucking Liability, Property, Casualty, Fire & Allied Lines, Workers' Compensation, Heavy Equipment, Product Liability, Bonds, and Appraisals.
P.O. Box 7251
Delray Beach, FL 33482
Phone: (561) 776-5651
Fax: (561) 776-1569
Custard Hotline Center (24 hours)
1-800-457-3390
Head Office: Atlanta, Georgia
Rick Linville, Chairman of the Board
Charlie Peek, Chief Executive Officer
Serving the U.S. and Canada with 24 hour service through 250 offices in 48 states.
Visit us on the Web at www.custard.com
Covering 75 mile radius of West Palm Beach.

Georgia

ALBANY–Adjusters

CUSTARD INSURANCE ADJUSTERS, INC.

Automobile, Trucking Liability, Property, Casualty, Fire & Allied Lines, Workers' Compensation, Heavy Equipment, Product Liability, Bonds, and Appraisals.
P.O. Box 70726
Albany, GA 31708
Phone: (229) 759-9567
Fax: (229) 435-0935
Custard Hotline Center (24 hours)
1-800-457-3390
Head Office: Atlanta, Georgia
Rick Linville, Chairman of the Board
Charlie Peek, Chief Executive Officer
Serving the U.S. and Canada with 24 hour service through 250 offices in 48 states.
Visit us on the Web at www.custard.com
Covering 75 mile radius of Albany.

ATHENS–Adjusters

CUSTARD INSURANCE ADJUSTERS, INC.

Automobile, Trucking Liability, Property, Casualty, Fire & Allied Lines, Workers' Compensation, Heavy Equipment, Product Liability, Bonds, and Appraisals.

196 Alps Road, Suite 2
Athens, GA 30606
Phone: (706) 548-1368
Fax: (706) 548-8962
Custard Hotline Center (24 hours)
1-800-457-3390
Head Office: Atlanta, Georgia
Rick Linville, Chairman of the Board
Charlie Peek, Chief Executive Officer
Serving the U.S. and Canada with 24 hour service through 250 offices in 48 states.
Visit us on the Web at www.custard.com
Covering 75 mile radius of Athens.

ATLANTA–Adjusters

CUSTARD INSURANCE ADJUSTERS, INC. - CORPORATE OFFICE

Automobile, Trucking Liability, Property, Casualty, Fire & Allied Lines, Workers' Compensation, Heavy Equipment, Product Liability, Bonds, and Appraisals.

Corporate Office:
4875 Avalon Ridge Parkway
Norcross, GA 30071
Phone: (770) 263-6800
Fax: (770) 368-3375
Custard Hotline Center (24 hours)
1-800-457-3390
Head Office: Atlanta, Georgia
Rick Linville, Chairman of the Board
Charlie Peek, Chief Executive Officer
Serving the U.S. and Canada with 24 hour service through 250 offices in 48 states.
Visit us on the Web at www.custard.com
Covering 75 mile radius of Atlanta.

ATLANTA–Continued

SPECIALTY GROUP, INC.

Auto Liability, Auto Physical Damage, Cargo, Casualty, Construction Defect Liability, Construction Defect Mediation, E&O, Fidelity Bonds, Inter-Company Arbitration, Liquor Liability, Long Haul Trucking, Longshore & Harborworkers, Malpractice, OLT, Products Liability, Workers' Compensation, Surveillance, Full Service SIU and Data Services.

303 Perimeter Center North
Suite 300
Atlanta, GA 30346
Phone: (770) 814-4211
Fax: 1-866-537-3097
Toll-free: 1-888-888-9989
Nights: (770) 814-4211
E-mail:
atlsales@specialtygroupinc.com
Website: www.specialtygroupinc.com
Jeffrey A. Kaiser, President
Servicing the entire state of Georgia.
Member: Atlanta Claims Association.

AUGUSTA–Adjusters

CUSTARD INSURANCE ADJUSTERS, INC.

Automobile, Trucking Liability, Property, Casualty, Fire & Allied Lines, Workers' Compensation, Heavy Equipment, Product Liability, Bonds, and Appraisals.

119 Davis Road, Suite 5-A
Augusta, GA 30907
Phone: (706) 860-2066
Fax: (706) 860-2068
Custard Hotline Center (24 hours)
1-800-457-3390
Head Office: Atlanta, Georgia
Rick Linville, Chairman of the Board
Charlie Peek, Chief Executive Officer
Serving the U.S. and Canada with 24 hour service through 250 offices in 48 states.
Visit us on the Web at www.custard.com
Covering 75 mile radius of Augusta.

CARTERSVILLE–Adjusters

CUSTARD INSURANCE ADJUSTERS, INC.

Automobile, Trucking Liability, Property, Casualty, Fire & Allied Lines, Workers' Compensation, Heavy Equipment, Product Liability, Bonds, and Appraisals.

P.O. Box 2424
Cartersville, GA 30120
Phone: (770) 387-0043
Fax: (770) 387-1308
Custard Hotline Center (24 hours)
1-800-457-3390
Head Office: Atlanta, Georgia
Rick Linville, Chairman of the Board
Charlie Peek, Chief Executive Officer
Serving the U.S. and Canada with 24 hour service through 250 offices in 48 states.
Visit us on the Web at www.custard.com
Covering 75 mile radius of Cartersville.

COLUMBUS–Adjusters

CUSTARD INSURANCE ADJUSTERS, INC.

Automobile, Trucking Liability, Property, Casualty, Fire & Allied Lines, Workers' Compensation, Heavy Equipment, Product Liability, Bonds, and Appraisals.

P.O. Box 8133
Columbus, GA 31908
Phone: (706) 561-5590
Fax: (706) 561-5592
Custard Hotline Center (24 hours)
1-800-457-3390
Head Office: Atlanta, Georgia
Rick Linville, Chairman of the Board
Charlie Peek, Chief Executive Officer
Serving the U.S. and Canada with 24 hour service through 250 offices in 48 states.
Visit us on the Web at www.custard.com
Covering 75 mile radius of Columbus.

MACON–Adjusters

CUSTARD INSURANCE ADJUSTERS, INC.

Automobile, Trucking Liability, Property, Casualty, Fire & Allied Lines, Workers' Compensation, Heavy Equipment, Product Liability, Bonds, and Appraisals.

P.O. Box 6433
Macon, GA 31208
Phone: (478) 745-1449
Fax: (478) 745-1446
Custard Hotline Center (24 hours)
1-800-457-3390
Head Office: Atlanta, Georgia
Rick Linville, Chairman of the Board
Charlie Peek, Chief Executive Officer
Serving the U.S. and Canada with 24 hour service through 250 offices in 48 states.
Visit us on the Web at www.custard.com
Covering 75 mile radius of Macon.

PEACHTREE CITY–Adjusters

CUSTARD INSURANCE ADJUSTERS, INC.

Automobile, Trucking Liability, Property, Casualty, Fire & Allied Lines, Workers' Compensation, Heavy Equipment, Product Liability, Bonds, and Appraisals.

123 Nicki Court
Hampton, GA 30228
Phone: (770) 897-2201
Fax: (770) 897-2202
Custard Hotline Center (24 hours)
1-800-457-3390
Head Office: Atlanta, Georgia
Rick Linville, Chairman of the Board
Charlie Peek, Chief Executive Officer
Serving the U.S. and Canada with 24 hour service through 250 offices in 48 states.
Visit us on the Web at www.custard.com
Covering 75 mile radius of Peachtree City.

ROME–Adjusters

CUSTARD INSURANCE ADJUSTERS, INC.

Automobile, Trucking Liability, Property, Casualty, Fire & Allied Lines, Workers' Compensation, Heavy Equipment, Product Liability, Bonds, and Appraisals.
3135 Avalon Ridge Place, Suite 200
Norcross, GA 30071
Phone: (706) 291-2802
Fax: (706) 235-8906
Custard Hotline Center (24 hours)
1-800-457-3390
Head Office: Atlanta, Georgia
Rick Linville, Chairman of the Board
Charlie Peek, Chief Executive Officer
Serving the U.S. and Canada with 24 hour service through 250 offices in 48 states.
Visit us on the Web at www.custard.com
Covering 75 mile radius of Rome.

SAVANNAH–Adjusters

CUSTARD INSURANCE ADJUSTERS, INC.

Automobile, Trucking Liability, Property, Casualty, Fire & Allied Lines, Workers' Compensation, Heavy Equipment, Product Liability, Bonds, and Appraisals.
P.O. Box 7162
Tifton, GA 31793
Phone: (912) 897-2120
Fax: (912) 898-9260
Custard Hotline Center (24 hours)
1-800-457-3390
Head Office: Atlanta, Georgia
Rick Linville, Chairman of the Board
Charlie Peek, Chief Executive Officer
Serving the U.S. and Canada with 24 hour service through 250 offices in 48 states.
Visit us on the Web at www.custard.com
Covering 75 mile radius of Savannah.

TIFTON–Adjusters

CUSTARD INSURANCE ADJUSTERS, INC.

Automobile, Trucking Liability, Property, Casualty, Fire & Allied Lines, Workers' Compensation, Heavy Equipment, Product Liability, Bonds, and Appraisals.
P.O. Box 7162
Tifton, GA 31793-7162
Phone: (229) 382-6162
Fax: (229) 382-7802
Custard Hotline Center (24 hours)
1-800-457-3390
Head Office: Atlanta, Georgia
Rick Linville, Chairman of the Board
Charlie Peek, Chief Executive Officer
Serving the U.S. and Canada with 24 hour service through 250 offices in 48 states.
Visit us on the Web at www.custard.com
Covering 75 mile radius of Tifton.

Idaho

BOISE–Adjusters

CUSTARD INSURANCE ADJUSTERS, INC.

Automobile, Trucking Liability, Property, Casualty, Fire & Allied Lines, Workers' Compensation, Heavy Equipment, Product Liability, Bonds, and Appraisals.
13601 W. McMillan Road
PMB 105, Suite 102
Boise, ID 83713
Phone: (208) 938-4166
Fax: (208) 392-1585
Custard Hotline Center (24 hours)
1-800-457-3390
Head Office: Atlanta, Georgia
Rick Linville, Chairman of the Board
Charlie Peek, Chief Executive Officer
Serving the U.S. and Canada with 24 hour service through 250 offices in 48 states.
Visit us on the Web at www.custard.com
Covering 75 mile radius of Boise.

COEUR D'ALENE–Adjusters

CUSTARD INSURANCE ADJUSTERS, INC.

Automobile, Trucking Liability, Property, Casualty, Fire & Allied Lines, Workers' Compensation, Heavy Equipment, Product Liability, Bonds, and Appraisals.

2900 North Government Way
PMB 227
Coeur D'Alene, ID 83815
Phone: (208) 676-0975
Fax: (208) 666-1059
Custard Hotline Center (24 hours)
1-800-457-3390
Head Office: Atlanta, Georgia
Rick Linville, Chairman of the Board
Charlie Peek, Chief Executive Officer
Serving the U.S. and Canada with 24 hour service through 250 offices in 48 states.
Visit us on the Web at www.custard.com
Covering 75 mile radius of Coeur D'Alene.

IDAHO FALLS–Adjusters

CUSTARD INSURANCE ADJUSTERS, INC.

Automobile, Trucking Liability, Property, Casualty, Fire & Allied Lines, Workers' Compensation, Heavy Equipment, Product Liability, Bonds, and Appraisals.

2184 Channing Way
PMB 446
Idaho Falls, ID 83404
Phone: (208) 356-7079
Fax: (208) 417-0791
Custard Hotline Center (24 hours)
1-800-457-3390
Head Office: Atlanta, Georgia
Rick Linville, Chairman of the Board
Charlie Peek, Chief Executive Officer
Serving the U.S. and Canada with 24 hour service through 250 offices in 48 states.
Visit us on the Web at www.custard.com
Covering 75 mile radius of Idaho Falls.

Illinois

BELLEVILLE–Adjusters

CUSTARD INSURANCE ADJUSTERS, INC.

Automobile, Trucking Liability, Property, Casualty, Fire & Allied Lines, Workers' Compensation, Heavy Equipment, Product Liability, Bonds, and Appraisals.

P.O. Box 23514
Belleville, IL 62223
Phone: (618) 277-1440
Fax: (618) 277-5336
Custard Hotline Center (24 hours)
1-800-457-3390
Head Office: Atlanta, Georgia
Rick Linville, Chairman of the Board
Charlie Peek, Chief Executive Officer
Serving the U.S. and Canada with 24 hour service through 250 offices in 48 states.
Visit us on the Web at www.custard.com
Covering 75 mile radius of Belleville.

CHICAGO–Adjusters

CUSTARD INSURANCE ADJUSTERS, INC.

Automobile, Trucking Liability, Property, Casualty, Fire & Allied Lines, Workers' Compensation, Heavy Equipment, Product Liability, Bonds, and Appraisals.

1701 E. Woodfield Road, Suite 423
Schaumburg, IL 60173
Phone: (847) 240-9622
Fax: (847) 240-9699
Custard Hotline Center (24 hours)
1-800-457-3390
Head Office: Atlanta, Georgia
Rick Linville, Chairman of the Board
Charlie Peek, Chief Executive Officer
Serving the U.S. and Canada with 24 hour service through 250 offices in 48 states.
Visit us on the Web at www.custard.com
Throughout Chicago Metropolitan Area.

PEORIA–Adjusters

CUSTARD INSURANCE ADJUSTERS, INC.

Automobile, Trucking Liability, Property, Casualty, Fire & Allied Lines, Workers' Compensation, Heavy Equipment, Product Liability, Bonds, and Appraisals.
P.O. Box 530
Tremont, IL 61568
Phone: (309) 688-9065
Fax: (309) 688-9085
Custard Hotline Center (24 hours)
1-800-457-3390
Head Office: Atlanta, Georgia
Rick Linville, Chairman of the Board
Charlie Peek, Chief Executive Officer
Serving the U.S. and Canada with 24 hour service through 250 offices in 48 states.
Visit us on the Web at www.custard.com
Covering 75 mile radius of Peoria.

ROCKFORD–Adjusters

CUSTARD INSURANCE ADJUSTERS, INC.

Automobile, Trucking Liability, Property, Casualty, Fire & Allied Lines, Workers' Compensation, Heavy Equipment, Product Liability, Bonds, and Appraisals.
P.O. Box 562
Freeport, IL 61032
Phone: (847) 240-9622
Fax: (847) 240-9699
Custard Hotline Center (24 hours)
1-800-457-3390
Head Office: Atlanta, Georgia
Rick Linville, Chairman of the Board
Charlie Peek, Chief Executive Officer
Serving the U.S. and Canada with 24 hour service through 250 offices in 48 states.
Visit us on the Web at www.custard.com
Covering 75 mile radius of Rockford.

SPRINGFIELD–Adjusters

MICHEL & CULLY CLAIMS SERVICE

All Lines
1525 S. MacArthur Boulevard
P.O. Box 1114
Springfield, IL 62705
Phone: (217) 787-5780
Fax: (217) 787-7653
E-mail: michelandcully@gmail.com
Website: www.michelandcully.com
Nights: (217) 546-2405
(217) 652-1310
C. Edward Cully, Casualty & WC
Peter Vangieson, CPCU, AIC,
Property, General Adjuster
Covering a 150 mile radius of Springfield, Illinois.
Member: C.I.A.A., I.A.I.I.A.

Indiana

BLOOMINGTON–Adjusters

CUSTARD INSURANCE ADJUSTERS, INC.

Automobile, Trucking Liability, Property, Casualty, Fire & Allied Lines, Workers' Compensation, Heavy Equipment, Product Liability, Bonds, and Appraisals.
P.O. Box 1845
Bloomington, IN 47402
Phone: (812) 287-9466
Fax: (812) 558-0374
Custard Hotline Center (24 hours)
1-800-457-3390
Head Office: Atlanta, Georgia
Rick Linville, Chairman of the Board
Charlie Peek, Chief Executive Officer
Serving the U.S. and Canada with 24 hour service through 250 offices in 48 states.
Visit us on the Web at www.custard.com
Covering 75 mile radius of Bloomington.

ELKHART–Adjusters

CUSTARD INSURANCE ADJUSTERS, INC.

Automobile, Trucking Liability, Property, Casualty, Fire & Allied Lines, Workers' Compensation, Heavy Equipment, Product Liability, Bonds, and Appraisals.

P.O. Box 808
South Bend, IN 46624
Phone: (574) 295-1318
Fax: (574) 287-0422
Custard Hotline Center (24 hours)
1-800-457-3390
Head Office: Atlanta, Georgia
Rick Linville, Chairman of the Board
Charlie Peek, Chief Executive Officer
Serving the U.S. and Canada with 24 hour service through 250 offices in 48 states.
Visit us on the Web at www.custard.com
Covering 75 mile radius of Elkhart.

EVANSVILLE–Adjusters

CUSTARD INSURANCE ADJUSTERS, INC.

Automobile, Trucking Liability, Property, Casualty, Fire & Allied Lines, Workers' Compensation, Heavy Equipment, Product Liability, Bonds, and Appraisals.

P.O. Box 15801
Evansville, IN 47716-0801
Phone: (812) 476-5980
Fax: (812) 476-5983
Custard Hotline Center (24 hours)
1-800-457-3390
Head Office: Atlanta, Georgia
Rick Linville, Chairman of the Board
Charlie Peek, Chief Executive Officer
Serving the U.S. and Canada with 24 hour service through 250 offices in 48 states.
Visit us on the Web at www.custard.com
Covering 75 mile radius of Evansville including Upper Kentucky and South-western Illinois.

FORT WAYNE–Adjusters

CUSTARD INSURANCE ADJUSTERS, INC.

Automobile, Trucking Liability, Property, Casualty, Fire & Allied Lines, Workers' Compensation, Heavy Equipment, Product Liability, Bonds, and Appraisals.

6343 Constitution Drive
Fort Wayne, IN 46804
Phone: (260) 459-9194
Fax: (260) 459-9160
Custard Hotline Center (24 hours)
1-800-457-3390
Head Office: Atlanta, Georgia
Rick Linville, Chairman of the Board
Charlie Peek, Chief Executive Officer
Serving the U.S. and Canada with 24 hour service through 250 offices in 48 states.
Visit us on the Web at www.custard.com
Covering 75 mile radius of Ft. Wayne.

GARY–Adjusters

CUSTARD INSURANCE ADJUSTERS, INC.

Automobile, Trucking Liability, Property, Casualty, Fire & Allied Lines, Workers' Compensation, Heavy Equipment, Product Liability, Bonds, and Appraisals.

1255 Erie Court
Suite D
Crown Point, IN 46307
Phone: (219) 663-5130
Fax: (219) 738-1707
Custard Hotline Center (24 hours)
1-800-457-3390
Head Office: Atlanta, Georgia
Rick Linville, Chairman of the Board
Charlie Peek, Chief Executive Officer
Serving the U.S. and Canada with 24 hour service through 250 offices in 48 states.
Visit us on the Web at www.custard.com
Covering 75 mile radius of Gary.

INDIANAPOLIS–Adjusters

CUSTARD INSURANCE ADJUSTERS, INC.
Automobile, Trucking Liability, Property, Casualty, Fire & Allied Lines, Workers' Compensation, Heavy Equipment, Product Liability, Bonds, and Appraisals.
7168 Graham Road, Suite 100
Indianapolis, IN 46250
Phone: (317) 598-6242
Fax: (317) 598-6244
Custard Hotline Center (24 hours)
1-800-457-3390
Head Office: Atlanta, Georgia
Rick Linville, Chairman of the Board
Charlie Peek, Chief Executive Officer
Serving the U.S. and Canada with 24 hour service through 250 offices in 48 states.
Visit us on the Web at www.custard.com
Covering 75 mile radius of Indianapolis.

KOKOMO–Adjusters

CUSTARD INSURANCE ADJUSTERS, INC.
Automobile, Trucking Liability, Property, Casualty, Fire & Allied Lines, Workers' Compensation, Heavy Equipment, Product Liability, Bonds, and Appraisals.
P.O. Box 2145
Kokomo, IN 46904-2145
Phone: (765) 453-4545
Fax: (765) 455-0174
Custard Hotline Center (24 hours)
1-800-457-3390
Head Office: Atlanta, Georgia
Rick Linville, Chairman of the Board
Charlie Peek, Chief Executive Officer
Serving the U.S. and Canada with 24 hour service through 250 offices in 48 states.
Visit us on the Web at www.custard.com
Covering 75 mile radius of Kokomo.

LAFAYETTE–Adjusters

CUSTARD INSURANCE ADJUSTERS, INC.
Automobile, Trucking Liability, Property, Casualty, Fire & Allied Lines, Workers' Compensation, Heavy Equipment, Product Liability, Bonds, and Appraisals.
4315 Commerce Drive, Suite 440-167
Lafayette, IN 47905
Phone: (765) 447-5002
Fax: (765) 447-1580
Custard Hotline Center (24 hours)
1-800-457-3390
Head Office: Atlanta, Georgia
Rick Linville, Chairman of the Board
Charlie Peek, Chief Executive Officer
Serving the U.S. and Canada with 24 hour service through 250 offices in 48 states.
Visit us on the Web at www.custard.com
Covering 75 mile radius of Lafayette.

LAWRENCEBURG–Adjusters

METRO ADJUSTING SERVICE/ AmeriClaim of KY
See Cincinnati, Ohio, listing
Phone: (859) 491-6333

MADISON–Adjusters

METRO ADJUSTING SERVICE/ AmeriClaim of KY
See Cincinnati, Ohio, listing
Phone: (859) 491-6333

MUNCIE–Adjusters

CUSTARD INSURANCE ADJUSTERS, INC.

Automobile, Trucking Liability, Property, Casualty, Fire & Allied Lines, Workers' Compensation, Heavy Equipment, Product Liability, Bonds, and Appraisals.

4319 West Clara Lane, Suite 311
Muncie, IN 47304
Phone: (765) 289-8023
Fax: (765) 455-0174
Custard Hotline Center (24 hours)
1-800-457-3390
Head Office: Atlanta, Georgia
Rick Linville, Chairman of the Board
Charlie Peek, Chief Executive Officer
Serving the U.S. and Canada with 24 hour service through 250 offices in 48 states.
Visit us on the Web at www.custard.com
Covering 75 mile radius of Muncie and Western Ohio.

NEW ALBANY–Adjusters

CUSTARD INSURANCE ADJUSTERS, INC.

Automobile, Trucking Liability, Property, Casualty, Fire & Allied Lines, Workers' Compensation, Heavy Equipment, Product Liability, Bonds, and Appraisals.

P.O. Box 528
New Albany, IN 47151-0528
Phone: (812) 945-2596
Fax: (502) 459-9621
Custard Hotline Center (24 hours)
1-800-457-3390
Head Office: Atlanta, Georgia
Rick Linville, Chairman of the Board
Charlie Peek, Chief Executive Officer
Serving the U.S. and Canada with 24 hour service through 250 offices in 48 states.
Visit us on the Web at www.custard.com
Covering 75 mile radius of New Albany including all Southeastern Indiana.

SOUTH BEND–Adjusters

CUSTARD INSURANCE ADJUSTERS, INC.

Automobile, Trucking Liability, Property, Casualty, Fire & Allied Lines, Workers' Compensation, Heavy Equipment, Product Liability, Bonds, and Appraisals.

1112 North Clay Street
Mishawaka, IN 46545
Phone: (574) 252-5513
Fax: (574) 287-0422
Custard Hotline Center (24 hours)
1-800-457-3390
Head Office: Atlanta, Georgia
Rick Linville, Chairman of the Board
Charlie Peek, Chief Executive Officer
Serving the U.S. and Canada with 24 hour service through 250 offices in 48 states.
Visit us on the Web at www.custard.com
Covering 75 mile radius of South Bend including Lower Michigan.

TERRE HAUTE–Adjusters

CUSTARD INSURANCE ADJUSTERS, INC.

Automobile, Trucking Liability, Property, Casualty, Fire & Allied Lines, Workers' Compensation, Heavy Equipment, Product Liability, Bonds, and Appraisals.

P.O. Box 3002
Terre Haute, IN 47803
Phone: (812) 238-1557
Fax: (812) 232-8950
Custard Hotline Center (24 hours)
1-800-457-3390
Head Office: Atlanta, Georgia
Rick Linville, Chairman of the Board
Charlie Peek, Chief Executive Officer
Serving the U.S. and Canada with 24 hour service through 250 offices in 48 states.
Visit us on the Web at www.custard.com
Covering 75 mile radius of Terre Haute.

Iowa

DAVENPORT–Adjusters

CUSTARD INSURANCE ADJUSTERS, INC.

Auto Liability, General Liability, Trucking, Workers' Compensation, Public Entities, Product Liability, Commercial Property, and Non-trucking.

PMB 112
102 E. Kimberly Road, Suite 1
Davenport, IA 52806
Phone: (563) 355-7898
Fax: (563) 355-8012
Custard Hotline Center (24 hours)
1-800-457-3390
Head Office: Atlanta, Georgia
Rick Linville, Chairman of the Board
Charlie Peek, Chief Executive Officer
Serving the U.S. and Canada with 24 hour service through 250 offices in 48 states.
Visit us on the Web at www.custard.com
Covering 75 mile radius of Davenport.

DES MOINES–Adjusters

CUSTARD INSURANCE ADJUSTERS, INC.

Automobile, Trucking Liability, Property, Casualty, Fire & Allied Lines, Workers' Compensation, Heavy Equipment, Product Liability, Bonds, and Appraisals.

8450 Hickman Road, Suite 21
Des Moines, IA 50325
Phone: (515) 276-2561
Fax: (515) 276-0620
Custard Hotline Center (24 hours)
1-800-457-3390
Head Office: Atlanta, Georgia
Rick Linville, Chairman of the Board
Charlie Peek, Chief Executive Officer
Serving the U.S. and Canada with 24 hour service through 250 offices in 48 states.
Visit us on the Web at www.custard.com
Covering 75 mile radius of Des Moines.

SIOUX CITY–Adjusters

CUSTARD INSURANCE ADJUSTERS, INC.

Automobile, Trucking Liability, Property, Casualty, Fire & Allied Lines, Workers' Compensation, Heavy Equipment, Product Liability, Bonds, and Appraisals.

P.O. Box 1826
Sioux City, IA 51102
Phone: (712) 277-5994
Fax: (712) 277-0183
Custard Hotline Center (24 hours)
1-800-457-3390
Head Office: Atlanta, Georgia
Rick Linville, Chairman of the Board
Charlie Peek, Chief Executive Officer
Serving the U.S. and Canada with 24 hour service through 250 offices in 48 states.
Visit us on the Web at www.custard.com
Covering 75 mile radius of Sioux City.

Kansas

WICHITA–Adjusters

CUSTARD INSURANCE ADJUSTERS, INC.

Automobile, Trucking Liability, Property, Casualty, Fire & Allied Lines, Workers' Compensation, Heavy Equipment, Product Liability, Bonds, and Appraisals.

1405A S. Hydraulic Street
Wichita, KS 67211
Phone: (316) 265-2611
Fax: (316) 265-2263
Custard Hotline Center (24 hours)
1-800-457-3390
Head Office: Atlanta, Georgia
Rick Linville, Chairman of the Board
Charlie Peek, Chief Executive Officer
Serving the U.S. and Canada with 24 hour service through 250 offices in 48 states.
Visit us on the Web at www.custard.com
Covering 75 mile radius of Wichita.

Kentucky

BOWLING GREEN–Adjusters

CUSTARD INSURANCE ADJUSTERS, INC.

Automobile, Trucking Liability, Property, Casualty, Fire & Allied Lines, Workers' Compensation, Heavy Equipment, Product Liability, Bonds, and Appraisals.

P.O. Box 50738
Bowling Green, KY 42102
Phone: (270) 393-2388
Fax: (270) 393-4845
Custard Hotline Center (24 hours)
1-800-457-3390
Head Office: Atlanta, Georgia
Rick Linville, Chairman of the Board
Charlie Peek, Chief Executive Officer
Serving the U.S. and Canada with 24 hour service through 250 offices in 48 states.
Visit us on the Web at www.custard.com
Covering 75 mile radius of Bowling Green.

COVINGTON–Adjusters

METRO ADJUSTING SERVICE/ AmeriClaim of KY

Automobile (all lines); Fire & Allied Lines; General Liability (bodily injury, physical damage, Workers' Compensation).

34 West 6th Street
Covington, KY 41011
Phone: (859) 491-6333
Toll-free: 1-800-685-4567
Fax: (859) 491-2520
Nights: (859) 491-6333
E-mail: info@metroadjusting.com
Website: www.metroadjusting.com
David P. Meisner, President
Serving Cincinnati, Dayton and Columbus, Ohio metropolitan areas; Northern & Central KY including Louisville and Lexington, KY; Southeastern Indiana.
Member: N.A.I.I.A., N.S.P.I.I., Dayton and Cincinnati, Ohio Claims Associations, Bluegrass Claims Assn., and Columbus, Ohio Claims Assn., Northern Kentucky Claims Assn., Kentucky Claims Assn.

FLORENCE–Adjusters

CUSTARD INSURANCE ADJUSTERS, INC.

Automobile, Trucking Liability, Property, Casualty, Fire & Allied Lines, Workers' Compensation, Heavy Equipment, Product Liability, Bonds, and Appraisals.

P.O. Box 1324
Florence, KY 41022
Phone: (859) 525-0101
Fax: (859) 525-0111
Custard Hotline Center (24 hours)
1-800-457-3390
Head Office: Atlanta, Georgia
Rick Linville, Chairman of the Board
Charlie Peek, Chief Executive Officer
Serving the U.S. and Canada with 24 hour service through 250 offices in 48 states.
Visit us on the Web at www.custard.com
Covering 75 mile radius of Florence.

METRO ADJUSTING SERVICE/ AmeriClaim of KY

See Covington, Kentucky, listing

Phone: (859) 491-6333

LEXINGTON–Adjusters

CUSTARD INSURANCE ADJUSTERS, INC.

Automobile, Trucking Liability, Property, Casualty, Fire & Allied Lines, Workers' Compensation, Heavy Equipment, Product Liability, Bonds, and Appraisals.

P.O. Box 13653
Lexington, KY 40583
Phone: (859) 253-9499
Fax: (859) 309-6791
Custard Hotline Center (24 hours)
1-800-457-3390
Head Office: Atlanta, Georgia
Rick Linville, Chairman of the Board
Charlie Peek, Chief Executive Officer
Serving the U.S. and Canada with 24 hour service through 250 offices in 48 states.
Visit us on the Web at www.custard.com
Covering 75 mile radius of Lexington.

LOUISVILLE–Adjusters

CUSTARD INSURANCE ADJUSTERS, INC.

Automobile, Trucking Liability, Property, Casualty, Fire & Allied Lines, Workers' Compensation, Heavy Equipment, Product Liability, Bonds, and Appraisals.
3000 Breckenridge Lane
Second Floor
Louisville, KY 40220
Phone: (502) 451-9401
Fax: (502) 459-9621
Custard Hotline Center (24 hours)
1-800-457-3390
Head Office: Atlanta, Georgia
Rick Linville, Chairman of the Board
Charlie Peek, Chief Executive Officer
Serving the U.S. and Canada with 24 hour service through 250 offices in 48 states.
Visit us on the Web at www.custard.com
Covering 75 mile radius of Louisville.

PADUCAH–Adjusters

CUSTARD INSURANCE ADJUSTERS, INC.

Automobile, Trucking Liability, Property, Casualty, Fire & Allied Lines, Workers' Compensation, Heavy Equipment, Product Liability, Bonds, and Appraisals.
P.O. Box 8354
Paducah, KY 42002
Phone: (270) 442-1343
Fax: (270) 442-1344
Custard Hotline Center (24 hours)
1-800-457-3390
Head Office: Atlanta, Georgia
Rick Linville, Chairman of the Board
Charlie Peek, Chief Executive Officer
Serving the U.S. and Canada with 24 hour service through 250 offices in 48 states.
Visit us on the Web at www.custard.com
Covering 75 mile radius of Paducah.

Louisiana

BATON ROUGE–Adjusters

CUSTARD INSURANCE ADJUSTERS, INC.

Automobile, Trucking Liability, Property, Casualty, Fire & Allied Lines, Workers' Compensation, Heavy Equipment, Product Liability, Bonds, and Appraisals.
17534 Old Jefferson Highway
Suite A-2
Prairieville, LA 70769
Phone: (225) 673-5403
Fax: (225) 677-9618
Custard Hotline Center (24 hours)
1-800-457-3390
Head Office: Atlanta, Georgia
Rick Linville, Chairman of the Board
Charlie Peek, Chief Executive Officer
Serving the U.S. and Canada with 24 hour service through 250 offices in 48 states.
Visit us on the Web at www.custard.com
Covering 75 mile radius of Baton Rouge.

LAKE CHARLES–Adjusters

CUSTARD INSURANCE ADJUSTERS, INC.

Automobile, Trucking Liability, Property, Casualty, Fire & Allied Lines, Workers' Compensation, Heavy Equipment, Product Liability, Bonds, and Appraisals.
10333 Northwest Freeway
Suite 201
Houston, TX 77092
Phone: (337) 433-6577
Fax: (337) 433-6578
Custard Hotline Center (24 hours)
1-800-457-3390
Head Office: Atlanta, Georgia
Rick Linville, Chairman of the Board
Charlie Peek, Chief Executive Officer
Serving the U.S. and Canada with 24 hour service through 250 offices in 48 states.
Visit us on the Web at www.custard.com
Covering 75 mile radius of Lake Charles.

NEW ORLEANS–Adjusters

CUSTARD INSURANCE ADJUSTERS, INC.

Automobile, Trucking Liability, Property, Casualty, Fire & Allied Lines, Workers' Compensation, Heavy Equipment, Product Liability, Bonds, and Appraisals.

2439 Manhattan Boulevard
Suite 206
Harvey, LA 70058
Phone: (504) 365-5536
Fax: (504) 455-7460
Custard Hotline Center (24 hours)
1-800-457-3390
Head Office: Atlanta, Georgia
Rick Linville, Chairman of the Board
Charlie Peek, Chief Executive Officer
Serving the U.S. and Canada with 24 hour service through 250 offices in 48 states.
Visit us on the Web at www.custard.com
Covering 75 mile radius of New Orleans.

SHREVEPORT–Adjusters

CUSTARD INSURANCE ADJUSTERS, INC.

Automobile, Trucking Liability, Property, Casualty, Fire & Allied Lines, Workers' Compensation, Heavy Equipment, Product Liability, Bonds, and Appraisals.

P.O. Box 4617
Shreveport, LA 71134
Phone: (318) 861-4244
Fax: (318) 861-3591
Custard Hotline Center (24 hours)
1-800-457-3390
Head Office: Atlanta, Georgia
Rick Linville, Chairman of the Board
Charlie Peek, Chief Executive Officer
Serving the U.S. and Canada with 24 hour service through 250 offices in 48 states.
Visit us on the Web at www.custard.com
Covering 75 mile radius of Shreveport.

Maine

PORTLAND–Adjusters

CUSTARD INSURANCE ADJUSTERS, INC.

Automobile, Trucking Liability, Property, Casualty, Fire & Allied Lines, Workers' Compensation, Heavy Equipment, Product Liability, Bonds, and Appraisals.

P.O. Box 912
Portland, ME 04104
Phone: (207) 774-2000
Fax: (207) 873-1462
Custard Hotline Center (24 hours)
1-800-457-3390
Head Office: Atlanta, Georgia
Rick Linville, Chairman of the Board
Charlie Peek, Chief Executive Officer
Serving the U.S. and Canada with 24 hour service through 250 offices in 48 states.
Visit us on the Web at www.custard.com
Covering 75 mile radius of Portland.

WATERVILLE–Adjusters

CUSTARD INSURANCE ADJUSTERS, INC.

Automobile, Trucking Liability, Property, Casualty, Fire & Allied Lines, Workers' Compensation, Heavy Equipment, Product Liability, Bonds, and Appraisals.

100 A Pleasant St.
Waterville, ME 04901
Phone: (207) 873-7127
Fax: (207) 873-1462
Custard Hotline Center (24 hours)
1-800-457-3390
Head Office: Atlanta, Georgia
Rick Linville, Chairman of the Board
Charlie Peek, Chief Executive Officer
Serving the U.S. and Canada with 24 hour service through 250 offices in 48 states.
Visit us on the Web at www.custard.com
Covering 75 mile radius of Waterville.

Maryland

BALTIMORE–Adjusters

CUSTARD INSURANCE ADJUSTERS, INC.
Automobile, Trucking Liability, Property, Casualty, Fire & Allied Lines, Workers' Compensation, Heavy Equipment, Product Liability, Bonds, and Appraisals.
5004 Honeygo Center Drive
Suite 102, PMB 234
Perry Hall, MD 21128
Phone: (410) 882-4185
Fax: (410) 882-3761
Custard Hotline Center (24 hours)
1-800-457-3390
Head Office: Atlanta, Georgia
Rick Linville, Chairman of the Board
Charlie Peek, Chief Executive Officer
Serving the U.S. and Canada with 24 hour service through 250 offices in 48 states.
Visit us on the Web at www.custard.com
Throughout Baltimore and the Washington, DC area.

HAGERSTOWN–Adjusters

CUSTARD INSURANCE ADJUSTERS, INC.
Automobile, Trucking Liability, Property, Casualty, Fire & Allied Lines, Workers' Compensation, Heavy Equipment, Product Liability, Bonds, and Appraisals.
19813 Leitersburg Pike
Hagerstown, MD 21742
Phone: (301) 791-6148
Fax: (301) 791-6149
Custard Hotline Center (24 hours)
1-800-457-3390
Head Office: Atlanta, Georgia
Rick Linville, Chairman of the Board
Charlie Peek, Chief Executive Officer
Serving the U.S. and Canada with 24 hour service through 250 offices in 48 states.
Visit us on the Web at www.custard.com
Covering 75 mile radius of Hagerstown.

SALISBURY–Adjusters

CUSTARD INSURANCE ADJUSTERS, INC.
Automobile, Trucking Liability, Property, Casualty, Fire & Allied Lines, Workers' Compensation, Heavy Equipment, Product Liability, Bonds, and Appraisals.
1147 Salisbury Boulevard
Suite 8, PMB 361
Salisbury, MD 21801
Phone: (410) 548-5383
Fax: (410) 548-1391
Custard Hotline Center (24 hours)
1-800-457-3390
Head Office: Atlanta, Georgia
Rick Linville, Chairman of the Board
Charlie Peek, Chief Executive Officer
Serving the U.S. and Canada with 24 hour service through 250 offices in 48 states.
Visit us on the Web at www.custard.com
Covering 75 mile radius of Salisbury.

Massachusetts

BOSTON–Adjusters

CUSTARD INSURANCE ADJUSTERS, INC.
Automobile, Trucking Liability, Property, Casualty, Fire & Allied Lines, Workers' Compensation, Heavy Equipment, Product Liability, Bonds, and Appraisals.
280 Hillside Avenue
Needham, MA 02494
Phone: (781) 449-2300
Fax: (781) 444-9498
Custard Hotline Center (24 hours)
1-800-457-3390
Head Office: Atlanta, Georgia
Rick Linville, Chairman of the Board
Charlie Peek, Chief Executive Officer
Serving the U.S. and Canada with 24 hour service through 250 offices in 48 states.
Visit us on the Web at www.custard.com
Covering 75 mile radius of Boston.

BOSTON–Continued

CUSTARD INSURANCE ADJUSTERS, INC. - TPA OFFICE

Automobile, Trucking Liability, Property, Casualty, Fire & Allied Lines, Workers' Compensation, Heavy Equipment, Product Liability, Bonds, and Appraisals.

280 Hillside Avenue
Needham, MA 02494
Phone: (781) 449-2300
Fax: (781) 444-9498
Custard Hotline Center (24 hours)
1-800-457-3390
Head Office: Atlanta, Georgia
Rick Linville, Chairman of the Board
Charlie Peek, Chief Executive Officer
Serving the U.S. and Canada with 24 hour service through 250 offices in 48 states.
Visit us on the Web at www.custard.com
Covering 75 mile radius of Boston.

CAPE COD–Adjusters

CUSTARD INSURANCE ADJUSTERS, INC.

Automobile, Trucking Liability, Property, Casualty, Fire & Allied Lines, Workers' Compensation, Heavy Equipment, Product Liability, Bonds, and Appraisals.

P.O. Box 503
Buzzards Bay, MA 02532
Phone: (508) 295-0300
Fax: (508) 295-0400
Custard Hotline Center (24 hours)
1-800-457-3390
Head Office: Atlanta, Georgia
Rick Linville, Chairman of the Board
Charlie Peek, Chief Executive Officer
Serving the U.S. and Canada with 24 hour service through 250 offices in 48 states.
Visit us on the Web at www.custard.com
Covering 75 mile radius of Cape Cod.

LEOMINSTER–Adjusters

CUSTARD INSURANCE ADJUSTERS, INC.

Automobile, Trucking Liability, Property, Casualty, Fire & Allied Lines, Workers' Compensation, Heavy Equipment, Product Liability, Bonds, and Appraisals.

280 Hillside Avenue
Needham, MA 02494
Phone: (978) 840-8222
Fax: (978) 840-3637
Custard Hotline Center (24 hours)
1-800-457-3390
Head Office: Atlanta, Georgia
Rick Linville, Chairman of the Board
Charlie Peek, Chief Executive Officer
Serving the U.S. and Canada with 24 hour service through 250 offices in 48 states.
Visit us on the Web at www.custard.com
Covering 75 mile radius of Worcester/ Leominster.

LYNNFIELD–Adjusters

CUSTARD INSURANCE ADJUSTERS, INC.

Automobile, Trucking Liability, Property, Casualty, Fire & Allied Lines, Workers' Compensation, Heavy Equipment, Product Liability, Bonds, and Appraisals.

280 Hillside Avenue
Needham, MA 02494
Phone: (781) 581-6466
Fax: (781) 599-9674
Custard Hotline Center (24 hours)
1-800-457-3390
Head Office: Atlanta, Georgia
Rick Linville, Chairman of the Board
Charlie Peek, Chief Executive Officer
Serving the U.S. and Canada with 24 hour service through 250 offices in 48 states.
Visit us on the Web at www.custard.com
Covering 75 mile radius of Lynnfield.

SPRINGFIELD–Adjusters

CUSTARD INSURANCE ADJUSTERS, INC.

Automobile, Trucking Liability, Property, Casualty, Fire & Allied Lines, Workers' Compensation, Heavy Equipment, Product Liability, Bonds, and Appraisals.

P.O. Box 60901
Longmeadow, MA 01116
Phone: (413) 737-3547
Fax: (413) 737-6389
Custard Hotline Center (24 hours)
1-800-457-3390
Head Office: Atlanta, Georgia
Rick Linville, Chairman of the Board
Charlie Peek, Chief Executive Officer
Serving the U.S. and Canada with 24 hour service through 250 offices in 48 states.
Visit us on the Web at www.custard.com
Covering 75 mile radius of Springfield.

Michigan

DETROIT–Adjusters

CUSTARD INSURANCE ADJUSTERS, INC.

Automobile, Trucking Liability, Property, Casualty, Fire & Allied Lines, Workers' Compensation, Heavy Equipment, Product Liability, Bonds, and Appraisals.

17250 W. 12 Mile Road, Suite 115
Southfield, MI 48076
Phone: (248) 557-0088
Fax: (248) 557-6334
Custard Hotline Center (24 hours)
1-800-457-3390
Head Office: Atlanta, Georgia
Rick Linville, Chairman of the Board
Charlie Peek, Chief Executive Officer
Serving the U.S. and Canada with 24 hour service through 250 offices in 48 states.
Visit us on the Web at www.custard.com
Covering 75 mile radius of Detroit.

FLINT–Adjusters

CUSTARD INSURANCE ADJUSTERS, INC.

Automobile, Trucking Liability, Property, Casualty, Fire & Allied Lines, Workers' Compensation, Heavy Equipment, Product Liability, Bonds, and Appraisals.

P.O. Box 310060
Flint, MI 48531
Phone: (810) 785-9268
Fax: (810) 785-9269
Custard Hotline Center (24 hours)
1-800-457-3390
Head Office: Atlanta, Georgia
Rick Linville, Chairman of the Board
Charlie Peek, Chief Executive Officer
Serving the U.S. and Canada with 24 hour service through 250 offices in 48 states.
Visit us on the Web at www.custard.com
Covering 75 mile radius of Flint.

GRAND RAPIDS–Adjusters

CUSTARD INSURANCE ADJUSTERS, INC.

Automobile, Trucking Liability, Property, Casualty, Fire & Allied Lines, Workers' Compensation, Heavy Equipment, Product Liability, Bonds, and Appraisals.

6026 Kalamazoo Avenue
P.O. Box 118
Kentwood, MI 49508
Phone: (616) 662-1241
Fax: (616) 538-5569
Custard Hotline Center (24 hours)
1-800-457-3390
Head Office: Atlanta, Georgia
Rick Linville, Chairman of the Board
Charlie Peek, Chief Executive Officer
Serving the U.S. and Canada with 24 hour service through 250 offices in 48 states.
Visit us on the Web at www.custard.com
Covering 75 mile radius of Grand Rapids.

JACKSON–Adjusters

CUSTARD INSURANCE ADJUSTERS, INC.

Automobile, Trucking Liability, Property, Casualty, Fire & Allied Lines, Workers' Compensation, Heavy Equipment, Product Liability, Bonds, and Appraisals.

1163 S. Main Street, Suite 271
Chelsea, MI 48118
Phone: (517) 796-4610
Fax: (517) 796-4614
Custard Hotline Center (24 hours)
1-800-457-3390
Head Office: Atlanta, Georgia
Rick Linville, Chairman of the Board
Charlie Peek, Chief Executive Officer
Serving the U.S. and Canada with 24 hour service through 250 offices in 48 states.
Visit us on the Web at www.custard.com
Covering 75 mile radius of Jackson.

LANSING–Adjusters

CUSTARD INSURANCE ADJUSTERS, INC.

Automobile, Trucking Liability, Property, Casualty, Fire & Allied Lines, Workers' Compensation, Heavy Equipment, Product Liability, Bonds, and Appraisals.

P.O. Box 4306
East Lansing, MI 48826
Phone: (517) 485-7450
Fax: (517) 485-7458
Custard Hotline Center (24 hours)
1-800-457-3390
Head Office: Atlanta, Georgia
Rick Linville, Chairman of the Board
Charlie Peek, Chief Executive Officer
Serving the U.S. and Canada with 24 hour service through 250 offices in 48 states.
Visit us on the Web at www.custard.com
Covering 75 mile radius of Lansing.

SAGINAW–Adjusters

CUSTARD INSURANCE ADJUSTERS, INC.

Automobile, Trucking Liability, Property, Casualty, Fire & Allied Lines, Workers' Compensation, Heavy Equipment, Product Liability, Bonds, and Appraisals.

4352 Bay Road, Suite 157
Saginaw, MI 48603
Phone: (989) 799-1169
Fax: (989) 799-1829
Custard Hotline Center (24 hours)
1-800-457-3390
Head Office: Atlanta, Georgia
Rick Linville, Chairman of the Board
Charlie Peek, Chief Executive Officer
Serving the U.S. and Canada with 24 hour service through 250 offices in 48 states.
Visit us on the Web at www.custard.com
Covering 75 mile radius of Saginaw.

Minnesota

BRAINERD–Adjusters

CUSTARD INSURANCE ADJUSTERS, INC.

Automobile, Trucking Liability, Property, Casualty, Fire & Allied Lines, Workers' Compensation, Heavy Equipment, Product Liability, Bonds, and Appraisals.

P.O. Box 8
Brainerd, MN 56401
Phone: (218) 829-2486
Fax: (218) 829-2535
Custard Hotline Center (24 hours)
1-800-457-3390
Head Office: Atlanta, Georgia
Rick Linville, Chairman of the Board
Charlie Peek, Chief Executive Officer
Serving the U.S. and Canada with 24 hour service through 250 offices in 48 states.
Visit us on the Web at www.custard.com
Covering 75 mile radius of Brainerd.

MINNEAPOLIS–Adjusters

CUSTARD INSURANCE ADJUSTERS, INC.

Automobile, Trucking Liability, Property, Casualty, Fire & Allied Lines, Workers' Compensation, Heavy Equipment, Product Liability, Bonds, and Appraisals.
3300 County Road 10, Suite 101
Brooklyn Center, MN 55429
Phone: (763) 566-4485
Fax: (651) 631-1515
Custard Hotline Center (24 hours)
1-800-457-3390
Head Office: Atlanta, Georgia
Rick Linville, Chairman of the Board
Charlie Peek, Chief Executive Officer
Serving the U.S. and Canada with 24 hour service through 250 offices in 48 states.
Visit us on the Web at www.custard.com
Covering 75 mile radius of Minneapolis/St. Paul.

ROCHESTER–Adjusters

CUSTARD INSURANCE ADJUSTERS, INC.

Automobile, Trucking Liability, Property, Casualty, Fire & Allied Lines, Workers' Compensation, Heavy Equipment, Product Liability, Bonds, and Appraisals.
P.O. Box 533
Owatonna, MN 55060
Phone: (507) 288-3123
Fax: (507) 288-5445
Custard Hotline Center (24 hours)
1-800-457-3390
Head Office: Atlanta, Georgia
Rick Linville, Chairman of the Board
Charlie Peek, Chief Executive Officer
Serving the U.S. and Canada with 24 hour service through 250 offices in 48 states.
Visit us on the Web at www.custard.com
Covering 75 mile radius of Rochester.

Mississippi

JACKSON–Adjusters

CUSTARD INSURANCE ADJUSTERS, INC.

Automobile, Trucking Liability, Property, Casualty, Fire & Allied Lines, Workers' Compensation, Heavy Equipment, Product Liability, Bonds, and Appraisals.
110-C Southpointe Drive
Byram, MS 39272
Phone: (601) 502-1023
Fax: (601) 824-9933
Custard Hotline Center (24 hours)
1-800-457-3390
Head Office: Atlanta, Georgia
Rick Linville, Chairman of the Board
Charlie Peek, Chief Executive Officer
Serving the U.S. and Canada with 24 hour service through 250 offices in 48 states.
Visit us on the Web at www.custard.com
Covering 75 mile radius of Jackson.

Missouri

JEFFERSON CITY–Adjusters

CUSTARD INSURANCE ADJUSTERS, INC.

Automobile, Trucking Liability, Property, Casualty, Fire & Allied Lines, Workers' Compensation, Heavy Equipment, Product Liability, Bonds, and Appraisals.
P.O. Box 986
Linn, MO 65051
Phone: (573) 897-2958
Fax: (573) 303-5966
Custard Hotline Center (24 hours)
1-800-457-3390
Head Office: Atlanta, Georgia
Rick Linville, Chairman of the Board
Charlie Peek, Chief Executive Officer
Serving the U.S. and Canada with 24 hour service through 250 offices in 48 states.
Visit us on the Web at www.custard.com
Covering 75 mile radius of Jefferson City.

JOPLIN–Adjusters

CUSTARD INSURANCE ADJUSTERS, INC. – TPA OFFICE

Automobile, Trucking Liability, Property, Casualty, Fire & Allied Lines, Workers' Compensation, Heavy Equipment, Product Liability, Bonds, and Appraisals.

2401 E. 32nd Street, Suite 10-359
Joplin, MO 64804
Phone: (417) 624-4332
Fax: (417) 624-4623
Custard Hotline Center (24 hours)
1-800-457-3390
Head Office: Atlanta, Georgia
Rick Linville, Chairman of the Board
Charlie Peek, Chief Executive Officer
Serving the U.S. and Canada with 24 hour service through 250 offices in 48 states.
Visit us on the Web at www.custard.com
Covering 75 mile radius of Joplin.

KANSAS CITY–Adjusters

CUSTARD INSURANCE ADJUSTERS, INC. – TPA OFFICE

Automobile, Trucking Liability, Property, Casualty, Fire & Allied Lines, Workers' Compensation, Heavy Equipment, Product Liability, Bonds, and Appraisals.

200 N.E. Missouri Road, Suite 305
Lees Summit, MO 64086
Phone: (816) 943-1779
Fax: (816) 943-1149
Custard Hotline Center (24 hours)
1-800-457-3390
Head Office: Atlanta, Georgia
Rick Linville, Chairman of the Board
Charlie Peek, Chief Executive Officer
Serving the U.S. and Canada with 24 hour service through 250 offices in 48 states.
Visit us on the Web at www.custard.com
Covering 75 mile radius of Kansas City.

KANSAS CITY AREA–Adjusters

CUSTARD INSURANCE ADJUSTERS, INC.

Automobile, Trucking Liability, Property, Casualty, Fire & Allied Lines, Workers' Compensation, Heavy Equipment, Product Liability, Bonds, and Appraisals.

202 E. 18th Avenue
North Kansas City, MO 64116
Phone: (816) 221-0689
Fax: (816) 221-1985
Custard Hotline Center (24 hours)
1-800-457-3390
Head Office: Atlanta, Georgia
Rick Linville, Chairman of the Board
Charlie Peek, Chief Executive Officer
Serving the U.S. and Canada with 24 hour service through 250 offices in 48 states.
Visit us on the Web at www.custard.com
Covering 75 mile radius of Kansas City.

SAINT LOUIS–Adjusters

CUSTARD INSURANCE ADJUSTERS, INC.

Automobile, Trucking Liability, Property, Casualty, Fire & Allied Lines, Workers' Compensation, Heavy Equipment, Product Liability, Bonds, and Appraisals.

50 Crestwood Executive Center
Suite 201
St. Louis, MO 63126
Phone: (314) 729-7744
Fax: (314) 729-7755
Custard Hotline Center (24 hours)
1-800-457-3390
Head Office: Atlanta, Georgia
Rick Linville, Chairman of the Board
Charlie Peek, Chief Executive Officer
Serving the U.S. and Canada with 24 hour service through 250 offices in 48 states.
Visit us on the Web at www.custard.com
Covering 75 mile radius of St. Louis.

SPRINGFIELD–Adjusters

CUSTARD INSURANCE ADJUSTERS, INC.

Automobile, Trucking Liability, Property, Casualty, Fire & Allied Lines, Workers' Compensation, Heavy Equipment, Product Liability, Bonds, and Appraisals.

P.O. Box 10425
Springfield, MO 65808
Phone: (417) 882-9651
Fax: (417) 882-9761
Custard Hotline Center (24 hours)
1-800-457-3390
Head Office: Atlanta, Georgia
Rick Linville, Chairman of the Board
Charlie Peek, Chief Executive Officer
Serving the U.S. and Canada with 24 hour service through 250 offices in 48 states.
Visit us on the Web at www.custard.com
Covering 75 mile radius of Springfield/ Branson.

Montana

BILLINGS–Adjusters

CUSTARD INSURANCE ADJUSTERS, INC.

Automobile, Trucking Liability, Property, Casualty, Fire & Allied Lines, Workers' Compensation, Heavy Equipment, Product Liability, Bonds, and Appraisals.

1302 24th Street West, PMB 306
Billings, MT 59102
Phone: (406) 652-3255
Fax: (406) 652-2701
Custard Hotline Center (24 hours)
1-800-457-3390
Head Office: Atlanta, Georgia
Rick Linville, Chairman of the Board
Charlie Peek, Chief Executive Officer
Serving the U.S. and Canada with 24 hour service through 250 offices in 48 states.
Visit us on the Web at www.custard.com
Covering 75 mile radius of Billings.

BOZEMAN–Adjusters

CUSTARD INSURANCE ADJUSTERS, INC.

Automobile, Trucking Liability, Property, Casualty, Fire & Allied Lines, Workers' Compensation, Heavy Equipment, Product Liability, Bonds, and Appraisals.

90 West Madison Avenue
Suite 4
PMB 144
Belgrade, MT 59714
Phone: (406) 586-8427
Fax: (406) 586-9600
Custard Hotline Center (24 hours)
1-800-457-3390
Head Office: Atlanta, Georgia
Rick Linville, Chairman of the Board
Charlie Peek, Chief Executive Officer
Serving the U.S. and Canada with 24 hour service through 250 offices in 48 states.
Visit us on the Web at www.custard.com
Covering 75 mile radius of Bozeman.

HELENA–Adjusters

CUSTARD INSURANCE ADJUSTERS, INC.

Automobile, Trucking Liability, Property, Casualty, Fire & Allied Lines, Workers' Compensation, Heavy Equipment, Product Liability, Bonds, and Appraisals.

2047 N. Last Chance Gulch No. 336
Helena, MT 59601
Phone: (406) 442-6248
Fax: (406) 204-0214
Custard Hotline Center (24 hours)
1-800-457-3390
Head Office: Atlanta, Georgia
Rick Linville, Chairman of the Board
Charlie Peek, Chief Executive Officer
Serving the U.S. and Canada with 24 hour service through 250 offices in 49states.
Visit us on the Web at www.custard.com
Covering 75 mile radius of Helena.

MISSOULA–Adjusters

CUSTARD INSURANCE ADJUSTERS, INC.

Automobile, Trucking Liability, Property, Casualty, Fire & Allied Lines, Workers' Compensation, Heavy Equipment, Product Liability, Bonds, and Appraisals.

1008 Burlington Avenue, Suite A
Missoula, MT 59801
Phone: (406) 542-8727
Fax: (406) 542-8842
Custard Hotline Center (24 hours)
1-800-457-3390
Head Office: Atlanta, Georgia
Rick Linville, Chairman of the Board
Charlie Peek, Chief Executive Officer
Serving the U.S. and Canada with 24 hour service through 250 offices in 48 states.
Visit us on the Web at www.custard.com
Covering 75 mile radius of Missoula.

SIDNEY–Adjusters

CUSTARD INSURANCE ADJUSTERS, INC.

Automobile, Trucking Liability, Property, Casualty, Fire & Allied Lines, Workers' Compensation, Heavy Equipment, Product Liability, Bonds, and Appraisals.

609 10th Street S.E.
Sidney, MT 59270
Phone: (406) 482-9030
Fax: (406) 482-9031
Custard Hotline Center (24 hours)
1-800-457-3390
Head Office: Atlanta, Georgia
Rick Linville, Chairman of the Board
Charlie Peek, Chief Executive Officer
Serving the U.S. and Canada with 24 hour service through 250 offices in 48 states.
Visit us on the Web at www.custard.com
Covering 75 mile radius of Sidney.

Nebraska

GRAND ISLAND–Adjusters

CUSTARD INSURANCE ADJUSTERS, INC.

Automobile, Trucking Liability, Property, Casualty, Fire & Allied Lines, Workers' Compensation, Heavy Equipment, Product Liability, Bonds, and Appraisals.

P.O. Box 841
Grand Island, NE 68802
Phone: (308) 398-1864
Fax: (402) 858-6096
Custard Hotline Center (24 hours)
1-800-457-3390
Head Office: Atlanta, Georgia
Rick Linville, Chairman of the Board
Charlie Peek, Chief Executive Officer
Serving the U.S. and Canada with 24 hour service through 250 offices in 48 states.
Visit us on the Web at www.custard.com
Covering 75 mile radius of Grand Island.

OMAHA–Adjusters

CUSTARD INSURANCE ADJUSTERS, INC.

Automobile, Trucking Liability, Property, Casualty, Fire & Allied Lines, Workers' Compensation, Heavy Equipment, Product Liability, Bonds, and Appraisals.

1002 South 48th Street, Suite A
Omaha, NE 68137
Phone: (402) 891-0500
Fax: (402) 891-0514
Custard Hotline Center (24 hours)
1-800-457-3390
Head Office: Atlanta, Georgia
Rick Linville, Chairman of the Board
Charlie Peek, Chief Executive Officer
Serving the U.S. and Canada with 24 hour service through 250 offices in 48 states.
Visit us on the Web at www.custard.com
Covering 75 mile radius of Omaha.

Nevada

LAS VEGAS–Adjusters

CUSTARD INSURANCE ADJUSTERS, INC.

Automobile, Trucking Liability, Property, Casualty, Fire & Allied Lines, Workers' Compensation, Heavy Equipment, Product Liability, Bonds, and Appraisals.

1771 East Flamingo, Suite 117B
Las Vegas, NV 89119
Phone: (702) 434-2444
Fax: (702) 434-2002
Custard Hotline Center (24 hours)
1-800-457-3390
Head Office: Atlanta, Georgia
Rick Linville, Chairman of the Board
Charlie Peek, Chief Executive Officer
Serving the U.S. and Canada with 24 hour service through 250 offices in 48 states.
Visit us on the Web at www.custard.com
Covering 75 mile radius of Las Vegas.

RENO–Adjusters

CUSTARD INSURANCE ADJUSTERS, INC.

Automobile, Trucking Liability, Property, Casualty, Fire & Allied Lines, Workers' Compensation, Heavy Equipment, Product Liability, Bonds, and Appraisals.

P.O. Box 51776
Sparks, NV 89435
Phone: (775) 348-8117
Fax: (775) 828-9377
Custard Hotline Center (24 hours)
1-800-457-3390
Head Office: Atlanta, Georgia
Rick Linville, Chairman of the Board
Charlie Peek, Chief Executive Officer
Serving the U.S. and Canada with 24 hour service through 250 offices in 48 states.
Visit us on the Web at www.custard.com
Covering 75 mile radius of Reno.

New Hampshire

MANCHESTER–Adjusters

CUSTARD INSURANCE ADJUSTERS, INC.

Automobile, Trucking Liability, Property, Casualty, Fire & Allied Lines, Workers' Compensation, Heavy Equipment, Product Liability, Bonds, and Appraisals.

1600 Candia Road, Suite 10
Manchester, NH 03109
Phone: (603) 628-1970
Fax: (603) 647-9668
Custard Hotline Center (24 hours)
1-800-457-3390
Head Office: Atlanta, Georgia
Rick Linville, Chairman of the Board
Charlie Peek, Chief Executive Officer
Serving the U.S. and Canada with 24 hour service through 250 offices in 48 states.
Visit us on the Web at www.custard.com
Covering 75 mile radius of Manchester.

New Jersey

CHERRY HILL–Adjusters

CUSTARD INSURANCE ADJUSTERS, INC.

Automobile, Trucking Liability, Property, Casualty, Fire & Allied Lines, Workers' Compensation, Heavy Equipment, Product Liability, Bonds, and Appraisals.

168 Barclay Farms Shopping Center
1409 Marlton Pike East, Suite 310
Cherry Hill, NJ 08034
Phone: (856) 424-5471
Fax: (856) 424-5273
Custard Hotline Center (24 hours)
1-800-457-3390
Head Office: Atlanta, Georgia
Rick Linville, Chairman of the Board
Charlie Peek, Chief Executive Officer
Serving the U.S. and Canada with 24 hour service through 250 offices in 48 states.
Visit us on the Web at www.custard.com
Covering 75 mile radius of Cherry Hill.

CRANFORD–Adjusters

CUSTARD INSURANCE ADJUSTERS, INC.
Automobile, Trucking Liability, Property, Casualty, Fire & Allied Lines, Workers' Compensation, Heavy Equipment, Product Liability, Bonds, and Appraisals.
16 South Avenue West, Suite 183
Cranford, NJ 07016
Phone: (973) 439-9004
Fax: (973) 439-9064
Custard Hotline Center (24 hours)
1-800-457-3390
Head Office: Atlanta, Georgia
Rick Linville, Chairman of the Board
Charlie Peek, Chief Executive Officer
Serving the U.S. and Canada with 24 hour service through 250 offices in 48 states.
Visit us on the Web at www.custard.com
Covering 75 mile radius of Cranford.

NEWARK–Adjusters

CUSTARD INSURANCE ADJUSTERS, INC.
Automobile, Trucking Liability, Property, Casualty, Fire & Allied Lines, Workers' Compensation, Heavy Equipment, Product Liability, Bonds, and Appraisals.
P.O. Box 1973
Newark, NJ 07101-1155
Phone: (973) 733-2065
Fax: (973) 733-2799
Custard Hotline Center (24 hours)
1-800-457-3390
Head Office: Atlanta, Georgia
Rick Linville, Chairman of the Board
Charlie Peek, Chief Executive Officer
Serving the U.S. and Canada with 24 hour service through 250 offices in 48 states.
Visit us on the Web at www.custard.com
Covering 75 mile radius of Newark.

PARSIPPANY–Adjusters

CUSTARD INSURANCE ADJUSTERS, INC.
Automobile, Trucking Liability, Property, Casualty, Fire & Allied Lines, Workers' Compensation, Heavy Equipment, Product Liability, Bonds, and Appraisals.
141 New Road, 2nd Floor – F2
Parsippany, NJ 07054
Phone: (973) 439-9004
Fax: (973) 439-9064
Custard Hotline Center (24 hours)
1-800-457-3390
Head Office: Atlanta, Georgia
Rick Linville, Chairman of the Board
Charlie Peek, Chief Executive Officer
Serving the U.S. and Canada with 24 hour service through 250 offices in 48 states.
Visit us on the Web at www.custard.com
Covering 75 mile radius of Parsippany.

New Mexico

ALBUQUERQUE–Adjusters

CUSTARD INSURANCE ADJUSTERS, INC.
Automobile, Trucking Liability, Property, Casualty, Fire & Allied Lines, Workers' Compensation, Heavy Equipment, Product Liability, Bonds, and Appraisals.
3705 Ellison Boulevard, Suite B1-384
Albuquerque, NM 87114
Phone: (505) 323-2355
Fax: (505) 323-2455
Custard Hotline Center (24 hours)
1-800-457-3390
Head Office: Atlanta, Georgia
Rick Linville, Chairman of the Board
Charlie Peek, Chief Executive Officer
Serving the U.S. and Canada with 24 hour service through 250 offices in 48 states.
Visit us on the Web at www.custard.com
Covering 150 mile radius of Albuquerque.

LAS CRUCES–Adjusters

CUSTARD INSURANCE ADJUSTERS, INC.

Automobile, Trucking Liability, Property, Casualty, Fire & Allied Lines, Workers' Compensation, Heavy Equipment, Product Liability, Bonds, and Appraisals.

P.O. Box 8
Las Cruces, NM 88004
Phone: (575) 524-9200
Fax: (575) 524-9210
Custard Hotline Center (24 hours)
1-800-457-3390
Head Office: Atlanta, Georgia
Rick Linville, Chairman of the Board
Charlie Peek, Chief Executive Officer
Serving the U.S. and Canada with 24 hour service through 250 offices in 48 states.
Visit us on the Web at www.custard.com
Covering 75 mile radius of Las Cruces.

New York

ALBANY–Adjusters

CUSTARD INSURANCE ADJUSTERS, INC.

Automobile, Trucking Liability, Property, Casualty, Fire & Allied Lines, Workers' Compensation, Heavy Equipment, Product Liability, Bonds, and Appraisals.

911 Central Avenue, Box 252
Albany, NY 12206
Phone: (518) 454-0020
Fax: (518) 454-0022
Custard Hotline Center (24 hours)
1-800-457-3390
Head Office: Atlanta, Georgia
Rick Linville, Chairman of the Board
Charlie Peek, Chief Executive Officer
Serving the U.S. and Canada with 24 hour service through 250 offices in 48 states.
Visit us on the Web at www.custard.com
Covering 75 mile radius of Albany.

BINGHAMTON–Adjusters

CUSTARD INSURANCE ADJUSTERS, INC.

Automobile, Trucking Liability, Property, Casualty, Fire & Allied Lines, Workers' Compensation, Heavy Equipment, Product Liability, Bonds, and Appraisals.

1235 Upper Front Street, PMB 231
Binghamton, NY 13905
Phone: (607) 772-0035
Fax: (607) 772-1721
Custard Hotline Center (24 hours)
1-800-457-3390
Head Office: Atlanta, Georgia
Rick Linville, Chairman of the Board
Charlie Peek, Chief Executive Officer
Serving the U.S. and Canada with 24 hour service through 250 offices in 48 states.
Visit us on the Web at www.custard.com
Covering 75 mile radius of Binghamton.

BUFFALO–Adjusters

CUSTARD INSURANCE ADJUSTERS, INC.

Automobile, Trucking Liability, Property, Casualty, Fire & Allied Lines, Workers' Compensation, Heavy Equipment, Product Liability, Bonds, and Appraisals.

15 Webster Street
2nd Floor, Suite 8
N. Tonawanda, NY 14120
Phone: (716) 693-2914
Fax: (716) 693-1835
Custard Hotline Center (24 hours)
1-800-457-3390
Head Office: Atlanta, Georgia
Rick Linville, Chairman of the Board
Charlie Peek, Chief Executive Officer
Serving the U.S. and Canada with 24 hour service through 250 offices in 48 states.
Visit us on the Web at www.custard.com
Covering western New York including 75 mile radius of Buffalo.

BUFFALO–Continued

A.E. MAHONEY & COMPANY INC.

Casualty, Auto Phy. Damage & Liability, OLT, Products, Liquor Liab., Fire & Allied Lines (including large commercial), Inland Marine & Cargo, Marine Losses, Marine Surveys, Heavy Equipment, Farm Losses, Mobile Homes, Excess – Surplus Lines Sub Standard Risks.

17 Limestone Drive, Suite 4
Buffalo, NY 14221
Phone: (716) 633-3570 or
1-800-856-8716
Fax: (716) 633-3575
Nights: (716) 864-3745
Todd D. Mahoney, Manager
E-mail: todd@aemahoney.com or
claims@aemahoney.com
Website: www.aemahoney.com
24 Hour Service in Western New York '10 counties'
Member: National Association of Independent Insurance Adjusters, New York State Assn. of Independent Adjusters, Loss Executives Assn.

JERICHO–Adjusters

CUSTARD INSURANCE ADJUSTERS, INC.

Automobile, Trucking Liability, Property, Casualty, Fire & Allied Lines, Workers' Compensation, Heavy Equipment, Product Liability, Bonds, and Appraisals.

55 Jericho Turnpike, Suite 101
Jericho, NY 11753
Phone: (516) 333-2123
Fax: (516) 333-6004
Custard Hotline Center (24 hours)
1-800-457-3390
Head Office: Atlanta, Georgia
Rick Linville, Chairman of the Board
Charlie Peek, Chief Executive Officer
Serving the U.S. and Canada with 24 hour service through 250 offices in 48 states.
Visit us on the Web at www.custard.com
Covering 75 mile radius of New York City.

LONG ISLAND–Adjusters

CUSTARD INSURANCE ADJUSTERS, INC.

Automobile, Trucking Liability, Property, Casualty, Fire & Allied Lines, Workers' Compensation, Heavy Equipment, Product Liability, Bonds, and Appraisals.

654 N. Wellwood Avenue, Suite D
No. 260
Lindenhurst, NY 11757-1672
Phone: (631) 224-1400
Fax: (631) 224-5835
Custard Hotline Center (24 hours)
1-800-457-3390
Head Office: Atlanta, Georgia
Rick Linville, Chairman of the Board
Charlie Peek, Chief Executive Officer
Serving the U.S. and Canada with 24 hour service through 250 offices in 48 states.
Visit us on the Web at www.custard.com
Covering 75 mile radius of Long Island.

NANUET–Adjusters

A.E. MAHONEY & COMPANY INC.

Casualty, Auto Phy. Damage & Liability, OLT, Products, Liquor Liab., Fire & Allied Lines (including large commercial), Inland Marine & Cargo, Marine Losses, Marine Surveys, Heavy Equipment, Farm Losses, Mobile Homes, Excess – Surplus Lines Sub Standard Risks.

146 Avalon Drive
Nanuet, NY 10954
Phone: (518) 265-6762 or 1-800-856-8716
Fax: (716) 633-3575
Nights: (716) 864-3745
Todd D. Mahoney, Manager
E-mail: todd@aemahoney.com or
claims@aemahoney.com
Website: www.aemahoney.com
Hudson Valley including Rockland and Westchester Counties
Member: National Association of Independent Insurance Adjusters, New York State Assn. of Independent Adjusters, Loss Executives Assn.

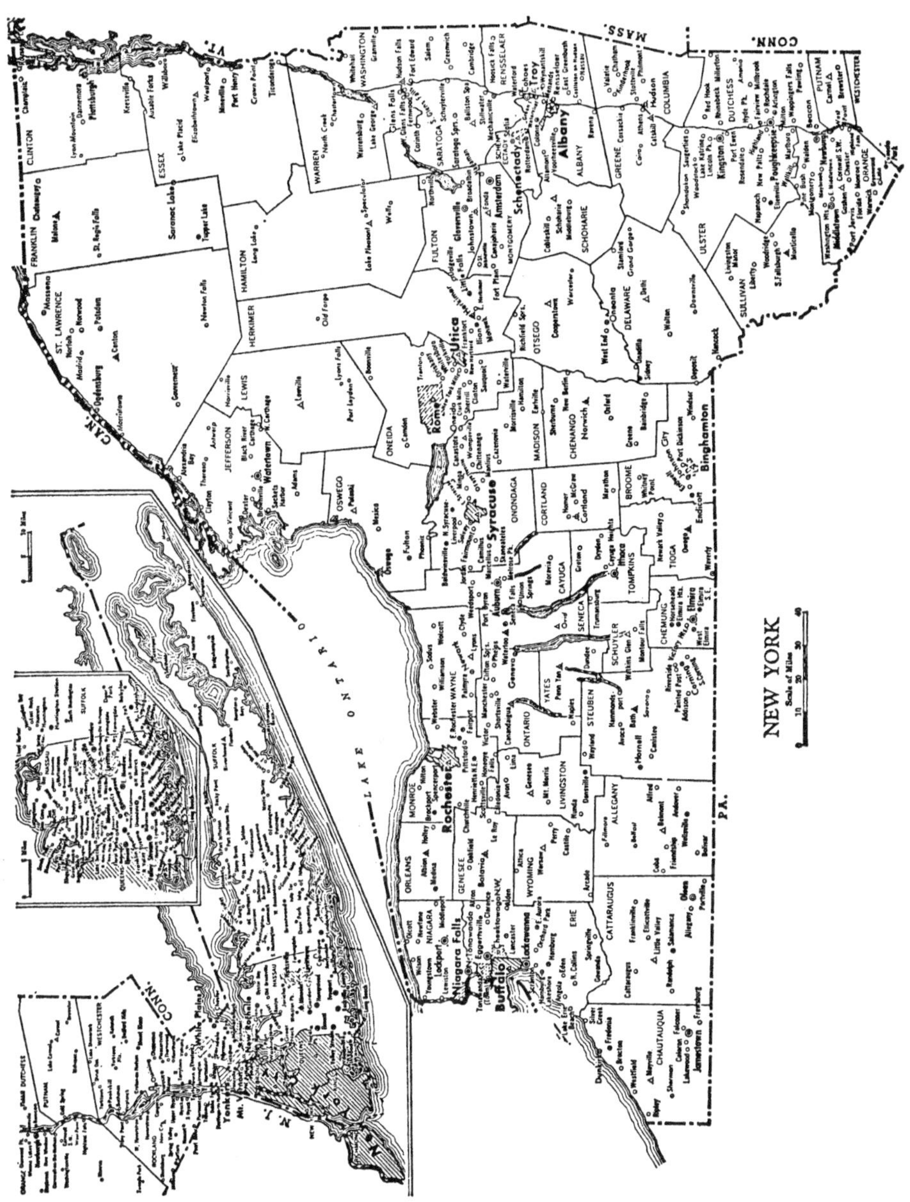
NEW YORK
Scale of Miles
LAKE ONTARIO
CAN.
VT.
MASS.
CONN.
PA.
N.J.

NEW PALTZ (Hudson Valley)–Adjusters

CUSTARD INSURANCE ADJUSTERS, INC.

Automobile, Trucking Liability, Property, Casualty, Fire & Allied Lines, Workers' Compensation, Heavy Equipment, Product Liability, Bonds, and Appraisals.
602 Route 299
Highland, NY 12528
Phone: (845) 834-2880
Fax: (845) 834-2884
Custard Hotline Center (24 hours)
1-800-457-3390
Head Office: Atlanta, Georgia
Rick Linville, Chairman of the Board
Charlie Peek, Chief Executive Officer
Serving the U.S. and Canada with 24 hour service through 250 offices in 48 states.
Visit us on the Web at www.custard.com
Covering 75 mile radius of New Paltz.

CUSTARD INSURANCE ADJUSTERS, INC. – TPA OFFICE

Automobile, Trucking Liability, Property, Casualty, Fire & Allied Lines, Workers' Compensation, Heavy Equipment, Product Liability, Bonds, and Appraisals.
602 Route 299
Highland, NY 12528
Phone: (845) 834-2880
Fax: (845) 834-2884
Custard Hotline Center (24 hours)
1-800-457-3390
Head Office: Atlanta, Georgia
Rick Linville, Chairman of the Board
Charlie Peek, Chief Executive Officer
Serving the U.S. and Canada with 24 hour service through 250 offices in 48 states.
Visit us on the Web at www.custard.com
Covering 75 mile radius of New York City.

ROCHESTER–Adjusters

A.E. MAHONEY & COMPANY INC.

Casualty, Auto Phy. Damage & Liability, OLT, Products, Liquor Liab., Fire & Allied Lines (including large commercial), Inland Marine & Cargo, Marine Losses, Marine Surveys, Heavy Equipment, Farm Losses, Mobile Homes, Excess – Surplus Lines Sub Standard Risks.
97 Canal Landing, Suite 8
Rochester, NY 14626
Phone: (585) 368-0035 or
1-800-856-8716
Fax: (585) 368-0036
Nights: (716) 864-3745
Todd D. Mahoney, Manager
E-mail: todd@aemahoney.com or
claims@aemahoney.com
Website: www.aemahoney.com
24 Hour Service in Western New York '10 counties'
Member: National Association of Independent Insurance Adjusters, New York State Assn. of Independent Adjusters, Loss Executives Assn.

SYRACUSE–Adjusters

CUSTARD INSURANCE ADJUSTERS, INC.

Automobile, Trucking Liability, Property, Casualty, Fire & Allied Lines, Workers' Compensation, Heavy Equipment, Product Liability, Bonds, and Appraisals.
4465 East Genesee Street
Suite 187
Dewitt, NY 13214
Phone: (315) 457-4380
Fax: (315) 457-4375
Custard Hotline Center (24 hours)
1-800-457-3390
Head Office: Atlanta, Georgia
Rick Linville, Chairman of the Board
Charlie Peek, Chief Executive Officer
Serving the U.S. and Canada with 24 hour service through 250 offices in 48 states.
Visit us on the Web at www.custard.com
Covering 75 mile radius of Syracuse.

North Carolina

ASHEVILLE–Adjusters

CUSTARD INSURANCE ADJUSTERS, INC.

Automobile, Trucking Liability, Property, Casualty, Fire & Allied Lines, Workers' Compensation, Heavy Equipment, Product Liability, Bonds, and Appraisals.

1854 Hendersonville Road
Suite A, PMB 247
Asheville, NC 28803
Phone: (828) 252-1036
Fax: (828) 252-1408
Custard Hotline Center (24 hours)
1-800-457-3390
Head Office: Atlanta, Georgia
Rick Linville, Chairman of the Board
Charlie Peek, Chief Executive Officer
Serving the U.S. and Canada with 24 hour service through 250 offices in 48 states.
Visit us on the Web at www.custard.com
Covering 75 mile radius of Asheville.

CHARLOTTE–Adjusters

CUSTARD INSURANCE ADJUSTERS, INC.

Automobile, Trucking Liability, Property, Casualty, Fire & Allied Lines, Workers' Compensation, Heavy Equipment, Product Liability, Bonds, and Appraisals.

P.O. Box 481288
Charlotte, NC 28269
Phone: (704) 565-5224
Fax: (704) 565-5240
Custard Hotline Center (24 hours)
1-800-457-3390
Head Office: Atlanta, Georgia
Rick Linville, Chairman of the Board
Charlie Peek, Chief Executive Officer
Serving the U.S. and Canada with 24 hour service through 250 offices in 48 states.
Visit us on the Web at www.custard.com
Covering 75 mile radius of Charlotte.

GREENSBORO–Adjusters

CUSTARD INSURANCE ADJUSTERS, INC.

Automobile, Trucking Liability, Property, Casualty, Fire & Allied Lines, Workers' Compensation, Heavy Equipment, Product Liability, Bonds, and Appraisals.

1903 – B Ashwood Court
Greensboro, NC 27455
Phone: (336) 288-0770
Fax: (336) 574-2860
Custard Hotline Center (24 hours)
1-800-457-3390
Head Office: Atlanta, Georgia
Rick Linville, Chairman of the Board
Charlie Peek, Chief Executive Officer
Serving the U.S. and Canada with 24 hour service through 250 offices in 48 states.
Visit us on the Web at www.custard.com
Covering 75 mile radius of Greensboro.

RALEIGH–Adjusters

CUSTARD INSURANCE ADJUSTERS, INC.

Automobile, Trucking Liability, Property, Casualty, Fire & Allied Lines, Workers' Compensation, Heavy Equipment, Product Liability, Bonds, and Appraisals.

3803 B Computer Drive, Suite 105
Raleigh, NC 27609
Phone: (919) 782-5781
Fax: (919) 782-4957
Custard Hotline Center (24 hours)
1-800-457-3390
Head Office: Atlanta, Georgia
Rick Linville, Chairman of the Board
Charlie Peek, Chief Executive Officer
Serving the U.S. and Canada with 24 hour service through 250 offices in 48 states.
Visit us on the Web at www.custard.com
Covering 75 mile radius of Raleigh.

RALEIGH–Continued

SPECIALTY GROUP, INC.

Auto Liability, Auto Physical Damage, Cargo, Casualty, Construction Defect Liability, Construction Defect Mediation, E&O, Fidelity Bonds, Inter-Company Arbitration, Liquor Liability, Long Haul Trucking, Longshore & Harborworkers, Malpractice, OLT, Products Liability, Workers' Compensation, Surveillance, Full Service SIU and Data Services.

3737 Glenwood Avenue
Suite 100
Raleigh, NC 27612
Phone: 1-888-888-9989
Fax: 1-866-537-3097
Toll-free: 1-888-888-9989
Nights: 1-888-888-9989
E-mail:
ncsales@specialtygroupinc.com
Website: www.specialtygroupinc.com
Jeffrey A. Kaiser, President

WILMINGTON–Adjusters

CUSTARD INSURANCE ADJUSTERS, INC.

Automobile, Trucking Liability, Property, Casualty, Fire & Allied Lines, Workers' Compensation, Heavy Equipment, Product Liability, Bonds, and Appraisals.

P.O. Box 15722
Wilmington, NC 28408
Phone: (910) 343-0750
Fax: (910) 338-3132
Custard Hotline Center (24 hours)
1-800-457-3390
Head Office: Atlanta, Georgia
Rick Linville, Chairman of the Board
Charlie Peek, Chief Executive Officer
Serving the U.S. and Canada with 24 hour service through 250 offices in 48 states.
Visit us on the Web at www.custard.com
Covering 75 mile radius of Wilmington.

North Dakota

BISMARCK/FARGO–Adjusters

CUSTARD INSURANCE ADJUSTERS, INC.

Automobile, Trucking Liability, Property, Casualty, Fire & Allied Lines, Workers' Compensation, Heavy Equipment, Product Liability, Bonds, and Appraisals.

P.O. Box 657
Bismarck, ND 58502
Phone: (701) 297-4009
Fax: (701) 205-3195
Custard Hotline Center (24 hours)
1-800-457-3390
Head Office: Atlanta, Georgia
Rick Linville, Chairman of the Board
Charlie Peek, Chief Executive Officer
Serving the U.S. and Canada with 24 hour service through 250 offices in 48 states.
Visit us on the Web at www.custard.com
Covering 75 mile radius of Fargo.

Ohio

AKRON–Adjusters

CUSTARD INSURANCE ADJUSTERS, INC.

Automobile, Trucking Liability, Property, Casualty, Fire & Allied Lines, Workers' Compensation, Heavy Equipment, Product Liability, Bonds, and Appraisals.

5339 Ridge Road, Suite 202
Cleveland, OH 44236
Phone: (330) 678-4999
Fax: (330) 678-4889
Custard Hotline Center (24 hours)
1-800-457-3390
Head Office: Atlanta, Georgia
Rick Linville, Chairman of the Board
Charlie Peek, Chief Executive Officer
Serving the U.S. and Canada with 24 hour service through 250 offices in 48 states.
Visit us on the Web at www.custard.com
Covering 75 mile radius of Akron.

CINCINNATI–Adjusters

CUSTARD INSURANCE ADJUSTERS, INC.

Automobile, Trucking Liability, Property, Casualty, Fire & Allied Lines, Workers' Compensation, Heavy Equipment, Product Liability, Bonds, and Appraisals.
110 Boggs Lane, Suite 320
Cincinnati, OH 45246
Phone: (513) 326-5900
Fax: (513) 326-5909
Custard Hotline Center (24 hours)
1-800-457-3390
Head Office: Atlanta, Georgia
Rick Linville, Chairman of the Board
Charlie Peek, Chief Executive Officer
Serving the U.S. and Canada with 24 hour service through 250 offices in 48 states.
Visit us on the Web at www.custard.com
Covering 75 mile radius of Cincinnati.

METRO ADJUSTING SERVICE/ AmeriClaim of KY

Automobile (all lines); Fire & Allied Lines; General Liability (bodily injury, physical damage, Workers' Compensation).
34 West 6th Street
Covington, KY 41011
Phone: (859) 491-6333
Toll-free: 1-800-685-4567
Fax: (859) 491-2520
Nights: (859) 491-6333
E-mail: info@metroadjusting.com
Website: www.metroadjusting.com
David P. Meisner, President
Serving Cincinnati, Dayton and Columbus, Ohio metropolitan areas; Northern & Central KY including Louisville and Lexington, KY; Southeastern Indiana.
Member: N.A.I.I.A., N.S.P.I.I., Dayton and Cincinnati, Ohio Claims Associations, Blue Grass Claims Assn., and Columbus, Ohio Claims Assn., Northern Kentucky Claims Assn., Kentucky Claims Assn.

CLEVELAND–Adjusters

CUSTARD INSURANCE ADJUSTERS, INC.

Automobile, Trucking Liability, Property, Casualty, Fire & Allied Lines, Workers' Compensation, Heavy Equipment, Product Liability, Bonds, and Appraisals.
5339 Ridge Road, Suite 202
Parma, OH 44129-1420
Phone: (440) 888-6007
Fax: (440) 888-6009
Custard Hotline Center (24 hours)
1-800-457-3390
Head Office: Atlanta, Georgia
Rick Linville, Chairman of the Board
Charlie Peek, Chief Executive Officer
Serving the U.S. and Canada with 24 hour service through 250 offices in 48 states.
Visit us on the Web at www.custard.com
Covering 75 mile radius of Cleveland.

COLUMBUS–Adjusters

CUSTARD INSURANCE ADJUSTERS, INC.

Automobile, Trucking Liability, Property, Casualty, Fire & Allied Lines, Workers' Compensation, Heavy Equipment, Product Liability, Bonds, and Appraisals.
6161 Busch Boulevard, Suite 312
Columbus, OH 43229
Phone: (614) 431-1328
Fax: (614) 431-0866
Custard Hotline Center (24 hours)
1-800-457-3390
Head Office: Atlanta, Georgia
Rick Linville, Chairman of the Board
Charlie Peek, Chief Executive Officer
Serving the U.S. and Canada with 24 hour service through 250 offices in 48 states.
Visit us on the Web at www.custard.com
Covering 75 mile radius of Columbus.

DAYTON–Adjusters

CUSTARD INSURANCE ADJUSTERS, INC.
Automobile, Trucking Liability, Property, Casualty, Fire & Allied Lines, Workers' Compensation, Heavy Equipment, Product Liability, Bonds, and Appraisals.
110 Boggs Lane
Cincinnati, OH 45246
Phone: (937) 291-3710
Fax: (937) 291-3717
Custard Hotline Center (24 hours)
1-800-457-3390
Head Office: Atlanta, Georgia
Rick Linville, Chairman of the Board
Charlie Peek, Chief Executive Officer
Serving the U.S. and Canada with 24 hour service through 250 offices in 48 states.
Visit us on the Web at www.custard.com
Covering 75 mile radius of Dayton.

METRO ADJUSTING SERVICE/ AmeriClaim of KY
See Cincinnati, Ohio, listing
Phone: (859) 491-6333

FINDLAY–Adjusters

CUSTARD INSURANCE ADJUSTERS, INC.
Automobile, Trucking Liability, Property, Casualty, Fire & Allied Lines, Workers' Compensation, Heavy Equipment, Product Liability, Bonds, and Appraisals.
P.O. Box 124
Ada, OH 45810
Phone: (419) 558-0162
Fax: (419) 634-0255
Custard Hotline Center (24 hours)
1-800-457-3390
Head Office: Atlanta, Georgia
Rick Linville, Chairman of the Board
Charlie Peek, Chief Executive Officer
Serving the U.S. and Canada with 24 hour service through 250 offices in 48 states.
Visit us on the Web at www.custard.com
Covering 75 mile radius of Findlay.

MANSFIELD–Adjusters

CUSTARD INSURANCE ADJUSTERS, INC.
Automobile, Trucking Liability, Property, Casualty, Fire & Allied Lines, Workers' Compensation, Heavy Equipment, Product Liability, Bonds, and Appraisals.
1130 East Main Street, Suite 190
Ashland, OH 44805
Phone: (419) 522-6992
Fax: (419) 522-6997
Custard Hotline Center (24 hours)
1-800-457-3390
Head Office: Atlanta, Georgia
Rick Linville, Chairman of the Board
Charlie Peek, Chief Executive Officer
Serving the U.S. and Canada with 24 hour service through 250 offices in 48 states.
Visit us on the Web at www.custard.com
Covering 75 mile radius of Mansfield.

MENTOR-PAINESVILLE–Adjusters

CUSTARD INSURANCE ADJUSTERS, INC.
Automobile, Trucking Liability, Property, Casualty, Fire & Allied Lines, Workers' Compensation, Heavy Equipment, Product Liability, Bonds, and Appraisals.
5339 Ridge Road, Suite 202
Parma, OH 44129
Phone: (440) 888-6007
Fax: (440) 888-6009
Custard Hotline Center (24 hours)
1-800-457-3390
Head Office: Atlanta, Georgia
Rick Linville, Chairman of the Board
Charlie Peek, Chief Executive Officer
Serving the U.S. and Canada with 24 hour service through 250 offices in 48 states.
Visit us on the Web at www.custard.com
Covering 75 mile radius of Mentor-Painesville.

TOLEDO–Adjusters

CUSTARD INSURANCE ADJUSTERS, INC.

Automobile, Trucking Liability, Property, Casualty, Fire & Allied Lines, Workers' Compensation, Heavy Equipment, Product Liability, Bonds, and Appraisals.
5339 Ridge Road, Suite 202
Parma, OH 44129
Phone: (419) 874-6612
Fax: (419) 874-6631
Custard Hotline Center (24 hours)
1-800-457-3390
Head Office: Atlanta, Georgia
Rick Linville, Chairman of the Board
Charlie Peek, Chief Executive Officer
Serving the U.S. and Canada with 24 hour service through 250 offices in 48 states.
Visit us on the Web at www.custard.com
Covering 75 mile radius of Toledo.

YOUNGSTOWN–Adjusters

CUSTARD INSURANCE ADJUSTERS, INC.

Automobile, Trucking Liability, Property, Casualty, Fire & Allied Lines, Workers' Compensation, Heavy Equipment, Product Liability, Bonds, and Appraisals.
143 Boardman Canfield Road
Suite 103
Boardman, OH 44512
Phone: (440) 888-6007
Fax: (440) 888-6009
Custard Hotline Center (24 hours)
1-800-457-3390
Head Office: Atlanta, Georgia
Rick Linville, Chairman of the Board
Charlie Peek, Chief Executive Officer
Serving the U.S. and Canada with 24 hour service through 250 offices in 48 states.
Visit us on the Web at www.custard.com
Covering 75 mile radius of Youngstown.

Oklahoma

OKLAHOMA CITY–Adjusters

CUSTARD INSURANCE ADJUSTERS, INC.

Automobile, Trucking Liability, Property, Casualty, Fire & Allied Lines, Workers' Compensation, Heavy Equipment, Product Liability, Bonds, and Appraisals.
2310 S.W. 89th Street, Suite E
Oklahoma City, OK 73159
Phone: (405) 692-5349
Fax: (405) 842-7192
Custard Hotline Center (24 hours)
1-800-457-3390
Head Office: Atlanta, Georgia
Rick Linville, Chairman of the Board
Charlie Peek, Chief Executive Officer
Serving the U.S. and Canada with 24 hour service through 250 offices in 48 states.
Visit us on the Web at www.custard.com
Covering 75 mile radius of Oklahoma City.

TULSA–Adjusters

CUSTARD INSURANCE ADJUSTERS, INC.

Automobile, Trucking Liability, Property, Casualty, Fire & Allied Lines, Workers' Compensation, Heavy Equipment, Product Liability, Bonds, and Appraisals.
6202 S. Lewis, Suite D1
Tulsa, OK 74136
Phone: (918) 712-8822
Fax: (918) 712-9552
Custard Hotline Center (24 hours)
1-800-457-3390
Head Office: Atlanta, Georgia
Rick Linville, Chairman of the Board
Charlie Peek, Chief Executive Officer
Serving the U.S. and Canada with 24 hour service through 250 offices in 48 states.
Visit us on the Web at www.custard.com
Covering 75 mile radius of Tulsa.

Oregon

PORTLAND–Adjusters

CUSTARD INSURANCE ADJUSTERS, INC.

Automobile, Trucking Liability, Property, Casualty, Fire & Allied Lines, Workers' Compensation, Heavy Equipment, Product Liability, Bonds, and Appraisals.

107 E. Historic Columbia River Highway
Suite 106
Troutdale, OR 97060
Phone: (503) 667-1600
Fax: (503) 667-1616
Custard Hotline Center (24 hours)
1-800-457-3390
Head Office: Atlanta, Georgia
Rick Linville, Chairman of the Board
Charlie Peek, Chief Executive Officer
Serving the U.S. and Canada with 24 hour service through 250 offices in 48 states.
Visit us on the Web at www.custard.com
Covering 75 mile radius of Portland.

ROSEBURG–Adjusters

CUSTARD INSURANCE ADJUSTERS, INC.

Automobile, Trucking Liability, Property, Casualty, Fire & Allied Lines, Workers' Compensation, Heavy Equipment, Product Liability, Bonds, and Appraisals.

P.O. Box 1204
Roseburg, OR 97470
Phone: (541) 673-9858
Fax: (541) 636-0208
Custard Hotline Center (24 hours)
1-800-457-3390
Head Office: Atlanta, Georgia
Rick Linville, Chairman of the Board
Charlie Peek, Chief Executive Officer
Serving the U.S. and Canada with 24 hour service through 250 offices in 48 states.
Visit us on the Web at www.custard.com
Covering 75 mile radius of Roseburg.

Pennsylvania

ALLENTOWN–Adjusters

CUSTARD INSURANCE ADJUSTERS, INC.

Automobile, Trucking Liability, Property, Casualty, Fire & Allied Lines, Workers' Compensation, Heavy Equipment, Product Liability, Bonds, and Appraisals.

Devonshire Plaza
PMB 304, 3440 Lehigh Street
Allentown, PA 18103
Phone: (610) 437-3691
Fax: (610) 437-3692
Custard Hotline Center (24 hours)
1-800-457-3390
Head Office: Atlanta, Georgia
Rick Linville, Chairman of the Board
Charlie Peek, Chief Executive Officer
Serving the U.S. and Canada with 24 hour service through 250 offices in 48 states.
Visit us on the Web at www.custard.com
Covering 75 mile radius of Allentown.

CHAMBERSBURG–Adjusters

CUSTARD INSURANCE ADJUSTERS, INC.

Automobile, Trucking Liability, Property, Casualty, Fire & Allied Lines, Workers' Compensation, Heavy Equipment, Product Liability, Bonds, and Appraisals.

975 Wayne Avenue Plaza, Suite 244
Chambersburg, PA 17201
Phone: (717) 267-2347
Fax: (717) 267-2387
Custard Hotline Center (24 hours)
1-800-457-3390
Head Office: Atlanta, Georgia
Rick Linville, Chairman of the Board
Charlie Peek, Chief Executive Officer
Serving the U.S. and Canada with 24 hour service through 250 offices in 48 states.
Visit us on the Web at www.custard.com
Covering 75 mile radius of Chambersburg.

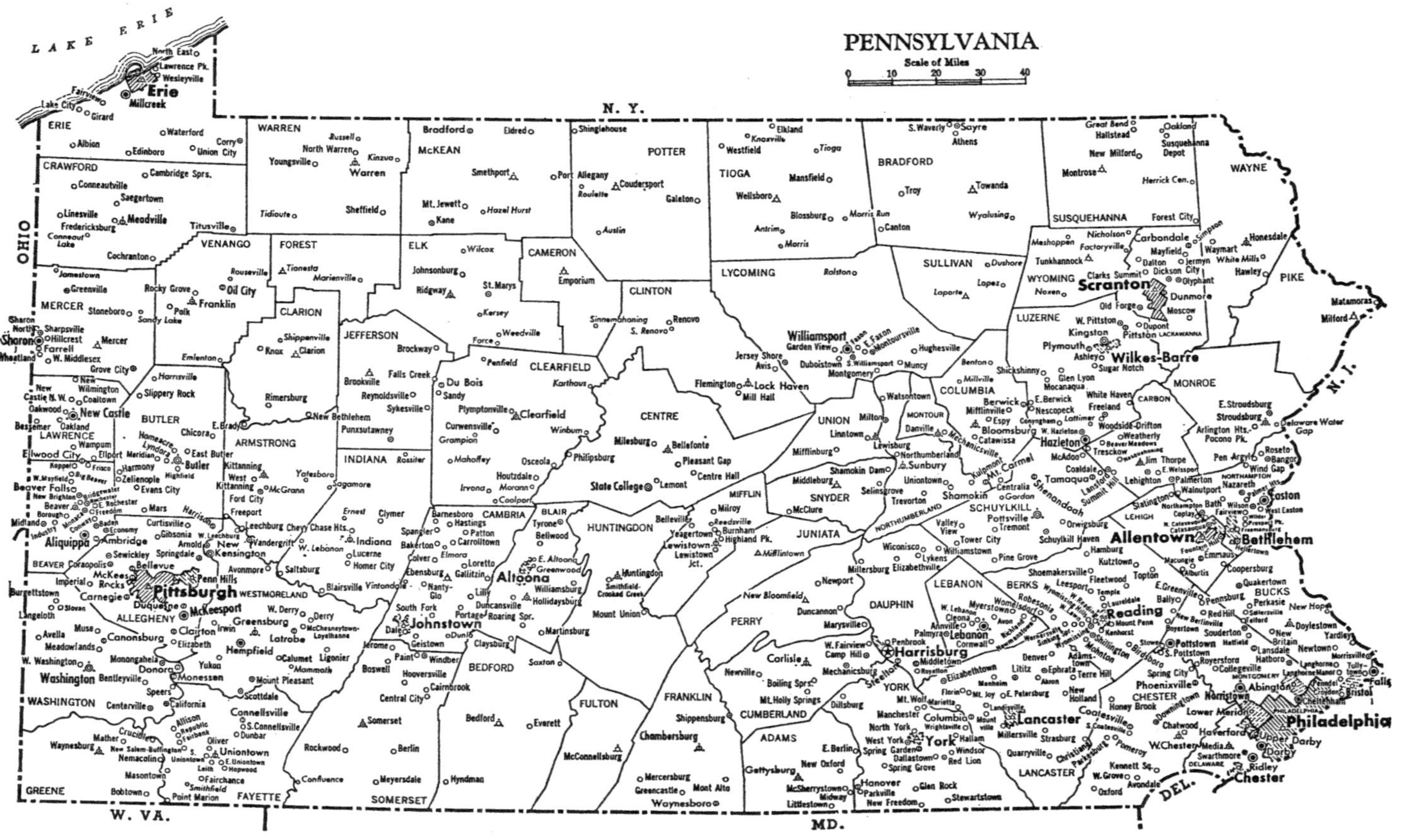
PENNSYLVANIA
Scale of Miles
0 10 20 30 40
N. Y.
LAKE ERIE
OHIO
W. VA.
MD.
DEL.
N. J.
ERIE
CRAWFORD
MERCER
LAWRENCE
BEAVER
WASHINGTON
GREENE
WARREN
VENANGO
BUTLER
ALLEGHENY
FAYETTE
FOREST
CLARION
ARMSTRONG
WESTMORELAND
SOMERSET
McKEAN
ELK
JEFFERSON
INDIANA
CAMBRIA
BEDFORD
POTTER
CAMERON
CLEARFIELD
BLAIR
HUNTINGDON
FULTON
TIOGA
CLINTON
CENTRE
MIFFLIN
JUNIATA
FRANKLIN
LYCOMING
UNION
SNYDER
PERRY
CUMBERLAND
ADAMS
BRADFORD
SULLIVAN
COLUMBIA
MONTOUR
NORTHUMBERLAND
DAUPHIN
YORK
SUSQUEHANNA
WYOMING
LUZERNE
SCHUYLKILL
LEBANON
LANCASTER
WAYNE
PIKE
MONROE
CARBON
LEHIGH
BERKS
CHESTER
NORTHAMPTON
BUCKS
MONTGOMERY
DELAWARE
Erie
Pittsburgh
Altoona
Johnstown
Williamsport
Harrisburg
Scranton
Wilkes-Barre
Hazleton
Allentown
Bethlehem
Reading
Lancaster
York
Philadelphia
Chester

HARRISBURG–Adjusters

CUSTARD INSURANCE ADJUSTERS, INC.

Automobile, Trucking Liability, Property, Casualty, Fire & Allied Lines, Workers' Compensation, Heavy Equipment, Product Liability, Bonds, and Appraisals.

5072 Ritter Road
Suite 100
Mechanicsburg, PA 17055
Phone: (717) 730-7477
Fax: (717) 730-7478
Custard Hotline Center (24 hours)
1-800-457-3390
Head Office: Atlanta, Georgia
Rick Linville, Chairman of the Board
Charlie Peek, Chief Executive Officer
Serving the U.S. and Canada with 24 hour service through 250 offices in 48 states.
Visit us on the Web at www.custard.com
Covering 75 mile radius of Harrisburg.

PHILADELPHIA–Adjusters

CUSTARD INSURANCE ADJUSTERS, INC.

Automobile, Trucking Liability, Property, Casualty, Fire & Allied Lines, Workers' Compensation, Heavy Equipment, Product Liability, Bonds, and Appraisals.

408 East Fourth Street, Suite 104
Bridgeport, PA 19405
Phone: (610) 313-5525
Fax: (610) 313-5526
Custard Hotline Center (24 hours)
1-800-457-3390
Head Office: Atlanta, Georgia
Rick Linville, Chairman of the Board
Charlie Peek, Chief Executive Officer
Serving the U.S. and Canada with 24 hour service through 250 offices in 48 states.
Visit us on the Web at www.custard.com
Covering 75 mile radius of Philadelphia/ Bridgeport.

PITTSBURGH–Adjusters

CUSTARD INSURANCE ADJUSTERS, INC.

Automobile, Trucking Liability, Property, Casualty, Fire & Allied Lines, Workers' Compensation, Heavy Equipment, Product Liability, Bonds, and Appraisals.

204 Kenmar Drive, Suite 2
Monroeville, PA 15146
Phone: (412) 856-1139
Fax: (412) 856-1829
Custard Hotline Center (24 hours)
1-800-457-3390
Head Office: Atlanta, Georgia
Rick Linville, Chairman of the Board
Charlie Peek, Chief Executive Officer
Serving the U.S. and Canada with 24 hour service through 250 offices in 48 states.
Visit us on the Web at www.custard.com
Covering 75 mile radius of Pittsburgh.

PITTSTON–Adjusters

CUSTARD INSURANCE ADJUSTERS, INC.

Automobile, Trucking Liability, Property, Casualty, Fire & Allied Lines, Workers' Compensation, Heavy Equipment, Product Liability, Bonds, and Appraisals.

Global Auto Building
1007 Oak Street
Pittston, PA 18640
Phone: (570) 654-4500
Fax: (570) 383-9331
Custard Hotline Center (24 hours)
1-800-457-3390
Head Office: Atlanta, Georgia
Rick Linville, Chairman of the Board
Charlie Peek, Chief Executive Officer
Serving the U.S. and Canada with 24 hour service through 250 offices in 48 states.
Visit us on the Web at www.custard.com
Covering 75 mile radius of Dickson City.

SCRANTON–Adjusters

CUSTARD INSURANCE ADJUSTERS, INC.

Automobile, Trucking Liability, Property, Casualty, Fire & Allied Lines, Workers' Compensation, Heavy Equipment, Product Liability, Bonds, and Appraisals.

512 Northampton Street, Suite 145
Edwardsville, PA 18704
Phone: (570) 969-2692
Fax: (570) 969-2693
Custard Hotline Center (24 hours)
1-800-457-3390
Head Office: Atlanta, Georgia
Rick Linville, Chairman of the Board
Charlie Peek, Chief Executive Officer
Serving the U.S. and Canada with 24 hour service through 250 offices in 48 states.
Visit us on the Web at www.custard.com
Covering 75 mile radius of Pittsburgh.

Rhode Island

PROVIDENCE–Adjusters

CUSTARD INSURANCE ADJUSTERS, INC.

Automobile, Trucking Liability, Property, Casualty, Fire & Allied Lines, Workers' Compensation, Heavy Equipment, Product Liability, Bonds, and Appraisals.

P.O. Box 3211
Pawtucket, RI 02861
Phone: (401) 415-9589
Fax: (401) 272-2353
Custard Hotline Center (24 hours)
1-800-457-3390
Head Office: Atlanta, Georgia
Rick Linville, Chairman of the Board
Charlie Peek, Chief Executive Officer
Serving the U.S. and Canada with 24 hour service through 250 offices in 48 states.
Visit us on the Web at www.custard.com
Covering 75 mile radius of Providence.

South Carolina

CHARLESTON–Adjusters

CUSTARD INSURANCE ADJUSTERS, INC.

Automobile, Trucking Liability, Property, Casualty, Fire & Allied Lines, Workers' Compensation, Heavy Equipment, Product Liability, Bonds, and Appraisals.

P.O. Box 22466
Charleston, SC 29413
Phone: (843) 216-2063
Fax: (843) 856-2105
Custard Hotline Center (24 hours)
1-800-457-3390
Head Office: Atlanta, Georgia
Rick Linville, Chairman of the Board
Charlie Peek, Chief Executive Officer
Serving the U.S. and Canada with 24 hour service through 250 offices in 48 states.
Visit us on the Web at www.custard.com
Covering 75 mile radius of Charleston.

COLUMBIA–Adjusters

CUSTARD INSURANCE ADJUSTERS, INC.

Automobile, Trucking Liability, Property, Casualty, Fire & Allied Lines, Workers' Compensation, Heavy Equipment, Product Liability, Bonds, and Appraisals.

P.O. Box 372
Columbia, SC 29202
Phone: (803) 739-1815
Fax: (803) 739-1816
Custard Hotline Center (24 hours)
1-800-457-3390
Head Office: Atlanta, Georgia
Rick Linville, Chairman of the Board
Charlie Peek, Chief Executive Officer
Serving the U.S. and Canada with 24 hour service through 250 offices in 48 states.
Visit us on the Web at www.custard.com
Covering 75 mile radius of Columbia.

COLUMBIA–Adjusters

SPECIALTY GROUP, INC.

Auto Liability, Auto Physical Damage, Cargo, Casualty, Construction Defect Liability, Construction Defect Mediation, E&O, Fidelity Bonds, Inter-Company Arbitration, Liquor Liability, Long Haul Trucking, Longshore & Harborworkers, Malpractice, OLT, Products Liability, Workers' Compensation, Surveillance, Full Service SIU and Data Services.

1201 Main Street
Suite 1980
Columbia, SC 29201
Phone: 1-888-888-9989
Fax: 1-866-537-3097
Toll-free: 1-888-888-9989
Nights: 1-888-888-9989
E-mail:
scsales@specialtygroupinc.com
Website: www.specialtygroupinc.com
Jeffrey A. Kaiser, President
Member: South Carolina Association of Licensed Investigators (SCALI).

GREENVILLE–Adjusters

CUSTARD INSURANCE ADJUSTERS, INC.

Automobile, Trucking Liability, Property, Casualty, Fire & Allied Lines, Workers' Compensation, Heavy Equipment, Product Liability, Bonds, and Appraisals.

150 Executive Center Drive
Suite 217, P.O. Box 54
Greenville, SC 29615
Phone: (864) 329-9972
Fax: (864) 329-9973
Custard Hotline Center (24 hours)
1-800-457-3390
Head Office: Atlanta, Georgia
Rick Linville, Chairman of the Board
Charlie Peek, Chief Executive Officer
Serving the U.S. and Canada with 24 hour service through 250 offices in 48 states.
Visit us on the Web at www.custard.com
Covering 75 mile radius of Greenville.

FLORENCE–Adjusters

CUSTARD INSURANCE ADJUSTERS, INC.

Automobile, Trucking Liability, Property, Casualty, Fire & Allied Lines, Workers' Compensation, Heavy Equipment, Product Liability, Bonds, and Appraisals.

P.O. Box 372
Columbia, SC 29202
Phone: (843) 662-8118
Fax: (843) 662-8119
Custard Hotline Center (24 hours)
1-800-457-3390
Head Office: Atlanta, Georgia
Rick Linville, Chairman of the Board
Charlie Peek, Chief Executive Officer
Serving the U.S. and Canada with 24 hour service through 250 offices in 48 states.
Visit us on the Web at www.custard.com
Covering 75 mile radius of Florence.

MYRTLE BEACH–Adjusters

CUSTARD INSURANCE ADJUSTERS, INC.

Automobile, Trucking Liability, Property, Casualty, Fire & Allied Lines, Workers' Compensation, Heavy Equipment, Product Liability, Bonds, and Appraisals.

P.O. Box 975
Myrtle Beach, SC 29578
Phone: (843) 626-7570
Fax: (843) 626-7571
Custard Hotline Center (24 hours)
1-800-457-3390
Head Office: Atlanta, Georgia
Rick Linville, Chairman of the Board
Charlie Peek, Chief Executive Officer
Serving the U.S. and Canada with 24 hour service through 250 offices in 48 states.
Visit us on the Web at www.custard.com
Covering 75 mile radius of Myrtle Beach.

South Dakota

RAPID CITY–Adjusters

CUSTARD INSURANCE ADJUSTERS, INC.
Automobile, Trucking Liability, Property, Casualty, Fire & Allied Lines, Workers' Compensation, Heavy Equipment, Product Liability, Bonds, and Appraisals.
P.O. Box 1351
Rapid City, SD 57709
Phone: (605) 787-1008
Fax: (605) 385-0367
Custard Hotline Center (24 hours)
1-800-457-3390
Head Office: Atlanta, Georgia
Rick Linville, Chairman of the Board
Charlie Peek, Chief Executive Officer
Serving the U.S. and Canada with 24 hour service through 250 offices in 48 states.
Visit us on the Web at www.custard.com
Covering 75 mile radius of Rapid City.

SIOUX FALLS–Adjusters

CUSTARD INSURANCE ADJUSTERS, INC.
Automobile, Trucking Liability, Property, Casualty, Fire & Allied Lines, Workers' Compensation, Heavy Equipment, Product Liability, Bonds, and Appraisals.
P.O. Box 89206
Sioux Falls, SD 57109
Phone: (605) 338-2478
Fax: (605) 385-0358
Custard Hotline Center (24 hours)
1-800-457-3390
Head Office: Atlanta, Georgia
Rick Linville, Chairman of the Board
Charlie Peek, Chief Executive Officer
Serving the U.S. and Canada with 24 hour service through 250 offices in 48 states.
Visit us on the Web at www.custard.com
Covering 75 mile radius of Sioux Falls.

Tennessee

CHATTANOOGA–Adjusters

APPALACHIAN CLAIMS SERVICE
Multi Line
Central Correspondence Office
1110 West Clinch Avenue
P.O. Drawer 3490 (37927)
Knoxville, TN 37916
Phone: (865) 523-0461
Toll-free: 1-800-777-2779
Fax: (865) 525-2635
E-mail: acsclaims@claims1.com
Appalachian Claims Service is committed to quality claims handling in all areas of Tennessee and Southwest Virginia.
Member: Chattanooga Claims Association, Tennessee Claims Association, Atlanta Claims Association, National Association of Independent Insurance Adjusters.

CUSTARD INSURANCE ADJUSTERS, INC.
Automobile, Trucking Liability, Property, Casualty, Fire & Allied Lines, Workers' Compensation, Heavy Equipment, Product Liability, Bonds, and Appraisals.
5959 Shallowford Road, Suite 209 – 5
Chattanooga, TN 37421
Phone: (423) 899-1552
Fax: (423) 899-3797
Custard Hotline Center (24 hours)
1-800-457-3390
Head Office: Atlanta, Georgia
Rick Linville, Chairman of the Board
Charlie Peek, Chief Executive Officer
Serving the U.S. and Canada with 24 hour service through 250 offices in 48 states.
Visit us on the Web at www.custard.com
Covering 75 mile radius of Chattanooga.

CLEVELAND–Adjusters

APPALACHIAN CLAIMS SERVICE

Multi Line
Central Correspondence Office
1110 West Clinch Avenue
P.O. Drawer 3490 (37927)
Knoxville, TN 37916
Phone: (865) 523-0461
Toll-free: 1-800-777-2779
Fax: (865) 525-2635
E-mail: acsclaims@claims1.com
Appalachian Claims Service is committed to quality claims handling in all areas of Tennessee and Southwest Virginia.

Member: Tennessee Claims Association, Chattanooga Claims Association, Atlanta Claims Association, National Association of Independent Insurance Adjusters.

CROSSVILLE–Adjusters

APPALACHIAN CLAIMS SERVICE

Multi Line
Central Correspondence Office
1110 West Clinch Avenue
P.O. Drawer 3490 (37927)
Knoxville, TN 37916
Phone: (865) 523-0461
Toll-free: 1-800-777-2779
Fax: (865) 525-2635
E-mail: acsclaims@claims1.com
Appalachian Claims Service is committed to quality claims handling in all areas of Tennessee and Southwest Virginia.
Member: Tennessee Claims Association, National Association of Independent Insurance Adjusters.

GRAY–Adjusters

APPALACHIAN CLAIMS SERVICE

Multi Line
Central Correspondence Office
1110 West Clinch Avenue
P.O. Drawer 3490 (37927)
Knoxville, TN 37916
Phone: (865) 523-0461
Toll-free: 1-800-777-2779
Fax: (865) 525-2635
E-mail: acsclaims@claims1.com
Appalachian Claims Service is committed to quality claims handling in all areas of Tennessee and Southwest Virginia.
Member: Tri-Cities Claims Association, Tennessee Claims Association, National Association of Independent Insurance Adjusters.

JACKSON–Adjusters

APPALACHIAN CLAIMS SERVICE

Multi Line
Central Correspondence Office
1110 West Clinch Avenue
P.O. Drawer 3490 (37927)
Knoxville, TN 37916
Phone: (865) 523-0461
Toll-free: 1-800-777-2779
Fax: (865) 525-2635
E-mail: acsclaims@claims1.com
Appalachian Claims Service is committed to quality claims handling in all areas of Tennessee and Southwest Virginia.
Member: Tennessee Claims Association, National Association of Independent Insurance Adjusters.

KNOXVILLE–Adjusters

APPALACHIAN CLAIMS SERVICE

Multi Line
Home Office
1110 West Clinch Avenue
P.O. Drawer 3490 (37927)
Knoxville, TN 37916
Phone: (865) 523-0461
Toll-free: 1-800-777-2779
Fax: (865) 525-2635
E-mail: acsclaims@claims1.com
Appalachian Claims Service is committed to quality claims handling in all areas of Tennessee and Southwest Virginia.
Member: Knoxville Claims Association, Atlanta Claims Association, National Association of Independent Insurance Adjusters, Canadian Independent Adjusters Association.

CUSTARD INSURANCE ADJUSTERS, INC.

Automobile, Trucking Liability, Property, Casualty, Fire & Allied Lines, Workers' Compensation, Heavy Equipment, Product Liability, Bonds, and Appraisals.
186 Airport Plaza
Suite B
Alcoa, TN 37701
Phone: (865) 233-7003
Fax: (865) 577-0684
Custard Hotline Center (24 hours)
1-800-457-3390
Head Office: Atlanta, Georgia
Rick Linville, Chairman of the Board
Charlie Peek, Chief Executive Officer
Serving the U.S. and Canada with 24 hour service through 250 offices in 48 states.
Visit us on the Web at www.custard.com
Covering 75 mile radius of Knoxville.

MEMPHIS–Adjusters

CUSTARD INSURANCE ADJUSTERS, INC.

Automobile, Trucking Liability, Property, Casualty, Fire & Allied Lines, Workers' Compensation, Heavy Equipment, Product Liability, Bonds, and Appraisals.
2893 South Mendenhall, Suite 2
Memphis, TN 38115
Phone: (901) 366-5998
Fax: (901) 794-2345
Custard Hotline Center (24 hours)
1-800-457-3390
Head Office: Atlanta, Georgia
Rick Linville, Chairman of the Board
Charlie Peek, Chief Executive Officer
Serving the U.S. and Canada with 24 hour service through 250 offices in 48 states.
Visit us on the Web at www.custard.com
Covering 75 mile radius of Memphis.

MORRISTOWN–Adjusters

APPALACHIAN CLAIMS SERVICE

Multi Line
Central Correspondence Office
1110 West Clinch Avenue
P.O. Drawer 3490 (37927)
Knoxville, TN 37916
Phone: (865) 523-0461
Toll-free: 1-800-777-2779
Fax: (865) 525-2635
E-mail: acsclaims@claims1.com
Appalachian Claims Service is committed to quality claims handling in all areas of Tennessee and Southwest Virginia.
Member: Knoxville Claims Association, Tennessee Claims Association, National Association of Independent Insurance Adjusters.

NASHVILLE–Adjusters

APPALACHIAN CLAIMS SERVICE

Multi Line

Central Correspondence Office
1110 West Clinch Avenue
P.O. Drawer 3490 (37927)
Knoxville, TN 37916
Phone: (865) 523-0461
Toll-free: 1-800-777-2779
Fax: (865) 525-2635
E-mail: acsclaims@claims1.com

Appalachian Claims Service is committed to quality claims handling in all areas of Tennessee and Southwest Virginia.

Member: Tennessee Claims Association, National Association of Independent Insurance Adjusters.

CUSTARD INSURANCE ADJUSTERS, INC.

Automobile, Trucking Liability, Property, Casualty, Fire & Allied Lines, Workers' Compensation, Heavy Equipment, Product Liability, Bonds, and Appraisals.

1121 Airport Center Drive, Suite 102
Nashville, TN 37214
Phone: (615) 882-9005
Fax: (615) 882-9060
Custard Hotline Center (24 hours)
1-800-457-3390
Head Office: Atlanta, Georgia
Rick Linville, Chairman of the Board
Charlie Peek, Chief Executive Officer

Serving the U.S. and Canada with 24 hour service through 250 offices in 48 states.
Visit us on the Web at www.custard.com
Covering 75 mile radius of Nashville.

TRI-CITIES AREA–Adjusters

CUSTARD INSURANCE ADJUSTERS, INC.

Automobile, Trucking Liability, Property, Casualty, Fire & Allied Lines, Workers' Compensation, Heavy Equipment, Product Liability, Bonds, and Appraisals.

1735 W. State of Franklin Road
Suite 5, No. 251
Johnson City, TN 37604
Phone: (423) 979-0307
Fax: (423) 979-0308
Custard Hotline Center (24 hours)
1-800-457-3390
Head Office: Atlanta, Georgia
Rick Linville, Chairman of the Board
Charlie Peek, Chief Executive Officer

Serving the U.S. and Canada with 24 hour service through 250 offices in 48 states.
Visit us on the Web at www.custard.com
Covering 75 mile radius of Kingsport, Bristol, Johnson City.

Texas

ABILENE–Adjusters

CUSTARD INSURANCE ADJUSTERS, INC.

Automobile, Trucking Liability, Property, Casualty, Fire & Allied Lines, Workers' Compensation, Heavy Equipment, Product Liability, Bonds, and Appraisals.

3301 North 3rd Street
Suite 115
Abilene, TX 79603
Phone: (325) 672-6296
Fax: (325) 672-5289
Custard Hotline Center (24 hours)
1-800-457-3390
Head Office: Atlanta, Georgia
Rick Linville, Chairman of the Board
Charlie Peek, Chief Executive Officer

Serving the U.S. and Canada with 24 hour service through 250 offices in 48 states.
Visit us on the Web at www.custard.com
Covering 75 mile radius of Abilene.

AMARILLO–Adjusters

CUSTARD INSURANCE ADJUSTERS, INC.

Automobile, Trucking Liability, Property, Casualty, Fire & Allied Lines, Workers' Compensation, Heavy Equipment, Product Liability, Bonds, and Appraisals.

1616 S. Kentucky Street
Suite D-120
Amarillo, TX 79102
Phone: (806) 354-8368
Fax: (806) 354-2756
Custard Hotline Center (24 hours)
1-800-457-3390
Head Office: Atlanta, Georgia
Rick Linville, Chairman of the Board
Charlie Peek, Chief Executive Officer
Serving the U.S. and Canada with 24 hour service through 250 offices in 48 states.
Visit us on the Web at www.custard.com
Covering 75 mile radius of Amarillo.

AUSTIN–Adjusters

CUSTARD INSURANCE ADJUSTERS, INC.

Automobile, Trucking Liability, Property, Casualty, Fire & Allied Lines, Workers' Compensation, Heavy Equipment, Product Liability, Bonds, and Appraisals.

2101 S. IH 35, Suite 221
Austin, TX 78741
Phone: (512) 458-2180
Fax: (512) 458-2254
Custard Hotline Center (24 hours)
1-800-457-3390
Head Office: Atlanta, Georgia
Rick Linville, Chairman of the Board
Charlie Peek, Chief Executive Officer
Serving the U.S. and Canada with 24 hour service through 250 offices in 48 states.
Visit us on the Web at www.custard.com
Covering 75 mile radius of Austin.

BEAUMONT–Adjusters

CUSTARD INSURANCE ADJUSTERS, INC.

Automobile, Trucking Liability, Property, Casualty, Fire & Allied Lines, Workers' Compensation, Heavy Equipment, Product Liability, Bonds, and Appraisals.

P.O. Box 367
Orange, TX 77631
Phone: (409) 886-5170
Fax: (409) 886-5179
Custard Hotline Center (24 hours)
1-800-457-3390
Head Office: Atlanta, Georgia
Rick Linville, Chairman of the Board
Charlie Peek, Chief Executive Officer
Serving the U.S. and Canada with 24 hour service through 250 offices in 48 states.
Visit us on the Web at www.custard.com
Covering 75 mile radius of Beaumont.

CORPUS CHRISTI–Adjusters

CUSTARD INSURANCE ADJUSTERS, INC.

Automobile, Trucking Liability, Property, Casualty, Fire & Allied Lines, Workers' Compensation, Heavy Equipment, Product Liability, Bonds, and Appraisals.

5151 Flynn Parkway, Suite 412–S
Corpus Christi, TX 78411
Phone: (361) 853-0449
Fax: (361) 853-0259
Custard Hotline Center (24 hours)
1-800-457-3390
Head Office: Atlanta, Georgia
Rick Linville, Chairman of the Board
Charlie Peek, Chief Executive Officer
Serving the U.S. and Canada with 24 hour service through 250 offices in 48 states.
Visit us on the Web at www.custard.com
Covering 75 mile radius of Corpus Christi.

DALLAS–Adjusters

CUSTARD INSURANCE ADJUSTERS, INC.

Automobile, Trucking Liability, Property, Casualty, Fire & Allied Lines, Workers' Compensation, Heavy Equipment, Product Liability, Bonds, and Appraisals.

P.O. Box 36283
Dallas, TX 75235
Phone: (214) 630-6171
Fax: (214) 631-4525
Custard Hotline Center (24 hours)
1-800-457-3390
Head Office: Atlanta, Georgia
Rick Linville, Chairman of the Board
Charlie Peek, Chief Executive Officer
Serving the U.S. and Canada with 24 hour service through 250 offices in 48 states.
Visit us on the Web at www.custard.com
Covering 75 mile radius of Dallas.

EL PASO–Adjusters

CUSTARD INSURANCE ADJUSTERS, INC.

Automobile, Trucking Liability, Property, Casualty, Fire & Allied Lines, Workers' Compensation, Heavy Equipment, Product Liability, Bonds, and Appraisals.

444 Executive Center Boulevard
Suite 126
El Paso, TX 79902
Phone: (915) 351-9431
Fax: (915) 351-9432
Custard Hotline Center (24 hours)
1-800-457-3390
Head Office: Atlanta, Georgia
Rick Linville, Chairman of the Board
Charlie Peek, Chief Executive Officer
Serving the U.S. and Canada with 24 hour service through 250 offices in 48 states.
Visit us on the Web at www.custard.com
Covering 75 mile radius of El Paso.

FORT WORTH–Adjusters

CUSTARD INSURANCE ADJUSTERS, INC.

Automobile, Trucking Liability, Property, Casualty, Fire & Allied Lines, Workers' Compensation, Heavy Equipment, Product Liability, Bonds, and Appraisals.

P.O. Box 36283
Dallas, TX 75235
Phone: (817) 268-5444
Fax: (817) 268-4929
Custard Hotline Center (24 hours)
1-800-457-3390
Head Office: Atlanta, Georgia
Rick Linville, Chairman of the Board
Charlie Peek, Chief Executive Officer
Serving the U.S. and Canada with 24 hour service through 250 offices in 48 states.
Visit us on the Web at www.custard.com
Covering 75 mile radius of Fort Worth.

HOUSTON–Adjusters

CUSTARD INSURANCE ADJUSTERS, INC.

Automobile, Trucking Liability, Property, Casualty, Fire & Allied Lines, Workers' Compensation, Heavy Equipment, Product Liability, Bonds, and Appraisals.

10333 Northwest Freeway, Suite 201
Houston, TX 77092
Phone: (713) 686-8885
Fax: (713) 686-9379
Custard Hotline Center (24 hours)
1-800-457-3390
Head Office: Atlanta, Georgia
Rick Linville, Chairman of the Board
Charlie Peek, Chief Executive Officer
Serving the U.S. and Canada with 24 hour service through 250 offices in 48 states.
Visit us on the Web at www.custard.com
Covering 75 mile radius of Houston/ Galveston.

HOUSTON–Continued

SPECIALTY GROUP, INC.

Auto Liability, Auto Physical Damage, Cargo, Casualty, Construction Defect Liability, Construction Defect Mediation, E&O, Fidelity Bonds, Inter-Company Arbitration, Liquor Liability, Long Haul Trucking, Longshore & Harborworkers, Malpractice, OLT, Products Liability, Workers' Compensation, Surveillance, Full Service SIU and Data Services.

4606 FM 1960 Road West
Suite 400
Houston, TX 77069
Phone: 1-888-888-9989
Fax: 1-866-537-3097
Toll-free: 1-888-888-9989
Nights: 1-888-888-9989
E-mail:
txsales@specialtygroupinc.com
Website: www.specialtygroupinc.com
Jeffrey A. Kaiser, President

LAKE CHARLES–Adjusters

CUSTARD INSURANCE ADJUSTERS, INC.

Automobile, Trucking Liability, Property, Casualty, Fire & Allied Lines, Workers' Compensation, Heavy Equipment, Product Liability, Bonds, and Appraisals.

P.O. Box 367
Orange, TX 77631
Phone: (337) 433-6577
Fax: (337) 433-6578
Custard Hotline Center (24 hours)
1-800-457-3390
Head Office: Atlanta, Georgia
Rick Linville, Chairman of the Board
Charlie Peek, Chief Executive Officer
Serving the U.S. and Canada with 24 hour service through 250 offices in 48 states.
Visit us on the Web at www.custard.com
Covering 75 mile radius of Lake Charles.

LAREDO–Adjusters

CUSTARD INSURANCE ADJUSTERS, INC.

Automobile, Trucking Liability, Property, Casualty, Fire & Allied Lines, Workers' Compensation, Heavy Equipment, Product Liability, Bonds, and Appraisals.

2801 East Montgomery
Suite 203
Laredo, TX 78043
Phone: (956) 753-6444
Fax: (956) 753-7848
Custard Hotline Center (24 hours)
1-800-457-3390
Head Office: Atlanta, Georgia
Rick Linville, Chairman of the Board
Charlie Peek, Chief Executive Officer
Serving the U.S. and Canada with 24 hour service through 250 offices in 48 states.
Visit us on the Web at www.custard.com
Covering 75 mile radius of Laredo.

LUBBOCK–Adjusters

CUSTARD INSURANCE ADJUSTERS, INC.

Automobile, Trucking Liability, Property, Casualty, Fire & Allied Lines, Workers' Compensation, Heavy Equipment, Product Liability, Bonds, and Appraisals.

7921 Indiana Drive, Suite E
Lubbock, TX 79423
Phone: (806) 788-1791
Fax: (806) 744-9091
Custard Hotline Center (24 hours)
1-800-457-3390
Head Office: Atlanta, Georgia
Rick Linville, Chairman of the Board
Charlie Peek, Chief Executive Officer
Serving the U.S. and Canada with 24 hour service through 250 offices in 48 states.
Visit us on the Web at www.custard.com
Covering 75 mile radius of Lubbock.

MARSHALL–Adjusters

CUSTARD INSURANCE ADJUSTERS, INC.

Automobile, Trucking Liability, Property, Casualty, Fire & Allied Lines, Workers' Compensation, Heavy Equipment, Product Liability, Bonds, and Appraisals.

P.O. Box 98
Marshall, TX 75671
Phone: (903) 934-8327
Fax: (903) 934-8319
Custard Hotline Center (24 hours)
1-800-457-3390
Head Office: Atlanta, Georgia
Rick Linville, Chairman of the Board
Charlie Peek, Chief Executive Officer
Serving the U.S. and Canada with 24 hour service through 250 offices in 48 states.
Visit us on the Web at www.custard.com
Covering 75 mile radius of Marshall.

McALLEN–Adjusters

CUSTARD INSURANCE ADJUSTERS, INC.

Automobile, Trucking Liability, Property, Casualty, Fire & Allied Lines, Workers' Compensation, Heavy Equipment, Product Liability, Bonds, and Appraisals.

3600 North 23rd Street, Suite 207
McAllen, TX 78501
Phone: (956) 972-1448
Fax: (956) 972-1449
Custard Hotline Center (24 hours)
1-800-457-3390
Head Office: Atlanta, Georgia
Rick Linville, Chairman of the Board
Charlie Peek, Chief Executive Officer
Serving the U.S. and Canada with 24 hour service through 250 offices in 48 states.
Visit us on the Web at www.custard.com
Covering 75 mile radius of McAllen.

MIDLAND–Adjusters

CUSTARD INSURANCE ADJUSTERS, INC.

Automobile, Trucking Liability, Property, Casualty, Fire & Allied Lines, Workers' Compensation, Heavy Equipment, Product Liability, Bonds, and Appraisals.

PMB 175
3323 N. Midland Drive, No. 113
Midland, TX 79707
Phone: (432) 561-8786
Fax: (432) 561-5372
Custard Hotline Center (24 hours)
1-800-457-3390
Head Office: Atlanta, Georgia
Rick Linville, Chairman of the Board
Charlie Peek, Chief Executive Officer
Serving the U.S. and Canada with 24 hour service through 250 offices in 48 states.
Visit us on the Web at www.custard.com
Covering 75 mile radius of Midland.

SAN ANTONIO–Adjusters

CUSTARD INSURANCE ADJUSTERS, INC.

Automobile, Trucking Liability, Property, Casualty, Fire & Allied Lines, Workers' Compensation, Heavy Equipment, Product Liability, Bonds, and Appraisals.

2929 Mossrock Drive, Suite 207
San Antonio, TX 78230
Phone: (210) 366-9990
Fax: (210) 366-9991
Custard Hotline Center (24 hours)
1-800-457-3390
Head Office: Atlanta, Georgia
Rick Linville, Chairman of the Board
Charlie Peek, Chief Executive Officer
Serving the U.S. and Canada with 24 hour service through 250 offices in 48 states.
Visit us on the Web at www.custard.com
Covering 75 mile radius of San Antonio.

TEXARKANA–Adjusters

CUSTARD INSURANCE ADJUSTERS, INC.

Automobile, Trucking Liability, Property, Casualty, Fire & Allied Lines, Workers' Compensation, Heavy Equipment, Product Liability, Bonds, and Appraisals.
P.O. Box 124
Hooks, TX 75561
Phone: (903) 667-5819
Fax: (903) 667-2974
Custard Hotline Center (24 hours)
1-800-457-3390
Head Office: Atlanta, Georgia
Rick Linville, Chairman of the Board
Charlie Peek, Chief Executive Officer
Serving the U.S. and Canada with 24 hour service through 250 offices in 48 states.
Visit us on the Web at www.custard.com
Covering 75 mile radius of Texarkana.

TYLER–Adjusters

CUSTARD INSURANCE ADJUSTERS, INC.

Automobile, Trucking Liability, Property, Casualty, Fire & Allied Lines, Workers' Compensation, Heavy Equipment, Product Liability, Bonds, and Appraisals.
P.O. Box 280
Frankston, TX 75763
Phone: (903) 769-1013
Fax: (903) 769-1015
Custard Hotline Center (24 hours)
1-800-457-3390
Head Office: Atlanta, Georgia
Rick Linville, Chairman of the Board
Charlie Peek, Chief Executive Officer
Serving the U.S. and Canada with 24 hour service through 250 offices in 48 states.
Visit us on the Web at www.custard.com
Covering 75 mile radius of Tyler.

Utah

SALT LAKE CITY–Adjusters

CUSTARD INSURANCE ADJUSTERS, INC.

Automobile, Trucking Liability, Property, Casualty, Fire & Allied Lines, Workers' Compensation, Heavy Equipment, Product Liability, Bonds, and Appraisals.
8282 South State Street, Suite 21
Midvale, UT 84047
Phone: (801) 566-5315
Fax: (801) 566-5365
Custard Hotline Center (24 hours)
1-800-457-3390
Head Office: Atlanta, Georgia
Rick Linville, Chairman of the Board
Charlie Peek, Chief Executive Officer
Serving the U.S. and Canada with 24 hour service through 250 offices in 48 states.
Visit us on the Web at www.custard.com
Covering 75 mile radius of Salt Lake City.

Vermont

RUTLAND–Adjusters

CUSTARD INSURANCE ADJUSTERS, INC.

Auto Liability, General Liability, Trucking, Workers' Compensation, Public Entities, Product Liability, Commercial Property, and Non-trucking.
P.O. Box 6453
Rutland, VT 05702
Phone: (802) 773-1051
Fax: (802) 773-1038
Custard Hotline Center (24 hours)
1-800-457-3390
Head Office: Atlanta, Georgia
Rick Linville, Chairman of the Board
Charlie Peek, Chief Executive Officer
Serving the U.S. and Canada with 24 hour service through 250 offices in 48 states.
Visit us on the Web at www.custard.com
Covering 75 mile radius of Rutland.

Virginia

CHANTILLY–Adjusters

CUSTARD INSURANCE ADJUSTERS, INC.
Auto Liability, General Liability, Trucking, Workers' Compensation, Public Entities, Product Liability, Commercial Property, and Non-trucking.
14150 Willard Road, Suite 205
Chantilly, VA 20151
Phone: (703) 263-9334
Fax: (703) 263-9335
Custard Hotline Center (24 hours)
1-800-457-3390
Head Office: Atlanta, Georgia
Rick Linville, Chairman of the Board
Charlie Peek, Chief Executive Officer
Serving the U.S. and Canada with 24 hour service through 250 offices in 48 states.
Visit us on the Web at www.custard.com
Covering 75 mile radius of Fairfax/Springfield.

FREDERICKSBURG AREA–Adjusters

CUSTARD INSURANCE ADJUSTERS, INC.
Automobile, Trucking Liability, Property, Casualty, Fire & Allied Lines, Workers' Compensation, Heavy Equipment, Product Liability, Bonds, and Appraisals.
2215 Pland Road, Suite 293
Fredericksburg, VA 22401
Phone: (540) 371-8804
Fax: (540) 371-8843
Custard Hotline Center (24 hours)
1-800-457-3390
Head Office: Atlanta, Georgia
Rick Linville, Chairman of the Board
Charlie Peek, Chief Executive Officer
Serving the U.S. and Canada with 24 hour service through 250 offices in 48 states.
Visit us on the Web at www.custard.com
Covering 75 mile radius of Fredericksburg.

HARRISONBURG–Adjusters

CUSTARD INSURANCE ADJUSTERS, INC.
Automobile, Trucking Liability, Property, Casualty, Fire & Allied Lines, Workers' Compensation, Heavy Equipment, Product Liability, Bonds, and Appraisals.
1866 C. East Market Street
PMB 307
Harrisonburg, VA 22801
Phone: (540) 564-6117
Fax: (540) 564-6122
Custard Hotline Center (24 hours)
1-800-457-3390
Head Office: Atlanta, Georgia
Rick Linville, Chairman of the Board
Charlie Peek, Chief Executive Officer
Serving the U.S. and Canada with 24 hour service through 250 offices in 48 states.
Visit us on the Web at www.custard.com
Covering 75 mile radius of Harrisonburg.

RICHMOND–Adjusters

CUSTARD INSURANCE ADJUSTERS, INC.
Automobile, Trucking Liability, Property, Casualty, Fire & Allied Lines, Workers' Compensation, Heavy Equipment, Product Liability, Bonds, and Appraisals.
1911 Huguenot Road
Suite 300
Richmond, VA 23235
Phone: (804) 594-0812
Fax: (804) 594-0814
Custard Hotline Center (24 hours)
1-800-457-3390
Head Office: Atlanta, Georgia
Rick Linville, Chairman of the Board
Charlie Peek, Chief Executive Officer
Serving the U.S. and Canada with 24 hour service through 250 offices in 48 states.
Visit us on the Web at www.custard.com
Covering 75 mile radius of Richmond.

ROANOKE–Adjusters

CUSTARD INSURANCE ADJUSTERS, INC.

Automobile, Trucking Liability, Property, Casualty, Fire & Allied Lines, Workers' Compensation, Heavy Equipment, Product Liability, Bonds, and Appraisals.
3735 Franklin Road S.W.
Box 225
Roanoke, VA 24014
Phone: (540) 342-2496
Fax: (540) 342-2497
Custard Hotline Center (24 hours)
1-800-457-3390
Head Office: Atlanta, Georgia
Rick Linville, Chairman of the Board
Charlie Peek, Chief Executive Officer
Serving the U.S. and Canada with 24 hour service through 250 offices in 48 states.
Visit us on the Web at www.custard.com
Covering 75 mile radius of Roanoke.

VIRGINIA BEACH–Adjusters

CUSTARD INSURANCE ADJUSTERS, INC.

Automobile, Trucking Liability, Property, Casualty, Fire & Allied Lines, Workers' Compensation, Heavy Equipment, Product Liability, Bonds, and Appraisals.
P.O. Box 56072
Virginia Beach, VA 23456
Phone: (757) 340-3674
Fax: (757) 340-3675
Custard Hotline Center (24 hours)
1-800-457-3390
Head Office: Atlanta, Georgia
Rick Linville, Chairman of the Board
Charlie Peek, Chief Executive Officer
Serving the U.S. and Canada with 24 hour service through 250 offices in 48 states.
Visit us on the Web at www.custard.com
Covering 75 mile radius of Virginia Beach.

WINCHESTER–Adjusters

CUSTARD INSURANCE ADJUSTERS, INC.

Automobile, Trucking Liability, Property, Casualty, Fire & Allied Lines, Workers' Compensation, Heavy Equipment, Product Liability, Bonds, and Appraisals.
4 Weems Lane, Suite 188
Winchester, VA 22601
Phone: (540) 665-9470
Fax: (540) 665-9471
Custard Hotline Center (24 hours)
1-800-457-3390
Head Office: Atlanta, Georgia
Rick Linville, Chairman of the Board
Charlie Peek, Chief Executive Officer
Serving the U.S. and Canada with 24 hour service through 250 offices in 48 states.
Visit us on the Web at www.custard.com
Covering 75 mile radius of Winchester.

WYTHEVILLE–Adjusters

APPALACHIAN CLAIMS SERVICE

Multi Line
Central Correspondence Office
1110 West Clinch Avenue
P.O. Drawer 3490 (37927)
Knoxville, TN 37916
Phone: (865) 523-0461
Toll-free: 1-800-777-2779
Fax: (865) 525-2635
E-mail: acsclaims@claims1.com
Appalachian Claims Service is committed to quality claims handling in all areas of Tennessee and Southwest Virginia.
Member: Tennessee Claims Association, National Association of Independent Insurance Adjusters.

Washington

MOUNT VERNON–Adjusters

CUSTARD INSURANCE ADJUSTERS, INC.

Automobile, Trucking Liability, Property, Casualty, Fire & Allied Lines, Workers' Compensation, Heavy Equipment, Product Liability, Bonds, and Appraisals.

1500 East College Way
Suite A, PMB 420
Mount Vernon, WA 98273
Phone: (360) 428-8658
Fax: (360) 336-5396
Custard Hotline Center (24 hours)
1-800-457-3390
Head Office: Atlanta, Georgia
Rick Linville, Chairman of the Board
Charlie Peek, Chief Executive Officer
Serving the U.S. and Canada with 24 hour service through 250 offices in 48 states.
Visit us on the Web at www.custard.com
Covering 75 mile radius of Mount Vernon.

OLYMPIA–Adjusters

CUSTARD INSURANCE ADJUSTERS, INC.

Automobile, Trucking Liability, Property, Casualty, Fire & Allied Lines, Workers' Compensation, Heavy Equipment, Product Liability, Bonds, and Appraisals.

1001 Cooper Point Road SW
Suite 140, PMB 393
Olympia, WA 98502-1107
Phone: (360) 754-2397
Fax: (360) 754-2670
Custard Hotline Center (24 hours)
1-800-457-3390
Head Office: Atlanta, Georgia
Rick Linville, Chairman of the Board
Charlie Peek, Chief Executive Officer
Serving the U.S. and Canada with 24 hour service through 250 offices in 48 states.
Visit us on the Web at www.custard.com
Covering 75 mile radius of Olympia.

SEATTLE–Adjusters

CUSTARD INSURANCE ADJUSTERS, INC.

Automobile, Trucking Liability, Property, Casualty, Fire & Allied Lines, Workers' Compensation, Heavy Equipment, Product Liability, Bonds, and Appraisals.

PMB 4465
10002 Aurora Avenue North, Suite 36
Seattle, WA 98133-9334
Phone: (206) 527-4285
Fax: (206) 522-2816
Custard Hotline Center (24 hours)
1-800-457-3390
Head Office: Atlanta, Georgia
Rick Linville, Chairman of the Board
Charlie Peek, Chief Executive Officer
Serving the U.S. and Canada with 24 hour service through 250 offices in 48 states.
Visit us on the Web at www.custard.com
Covering 75 mile radius of Seattle.

SPOKANE–Adjusters

CUSTARD INSURANCE ADJUSTERS, INC.

Automobile, Trucking Liability, Property, Casualty, Fire & Allied Lines, Workers' Compensation, Heavy Equipment, Product Liability, Bonds, and Appraisals.

1314 S. Grand Boulevard
Suite 2, PMB 338
Spokane, WA 99202
Phone: (509) 838-9684
Fax: (509) 838-9784
Custard Hotline Center (24 hours)
1-800-457-3390
Head Office: Atlanta, Georgia
Rick Linville, Chairman of the Board
Charlie Peek, Chief Executive Officer
Serving the U.S. and Canada with 24 hour service through 250 offices in 48 states.
Visit us on the Web at www.custard.com
Covering 75 mile radius of Spokane.

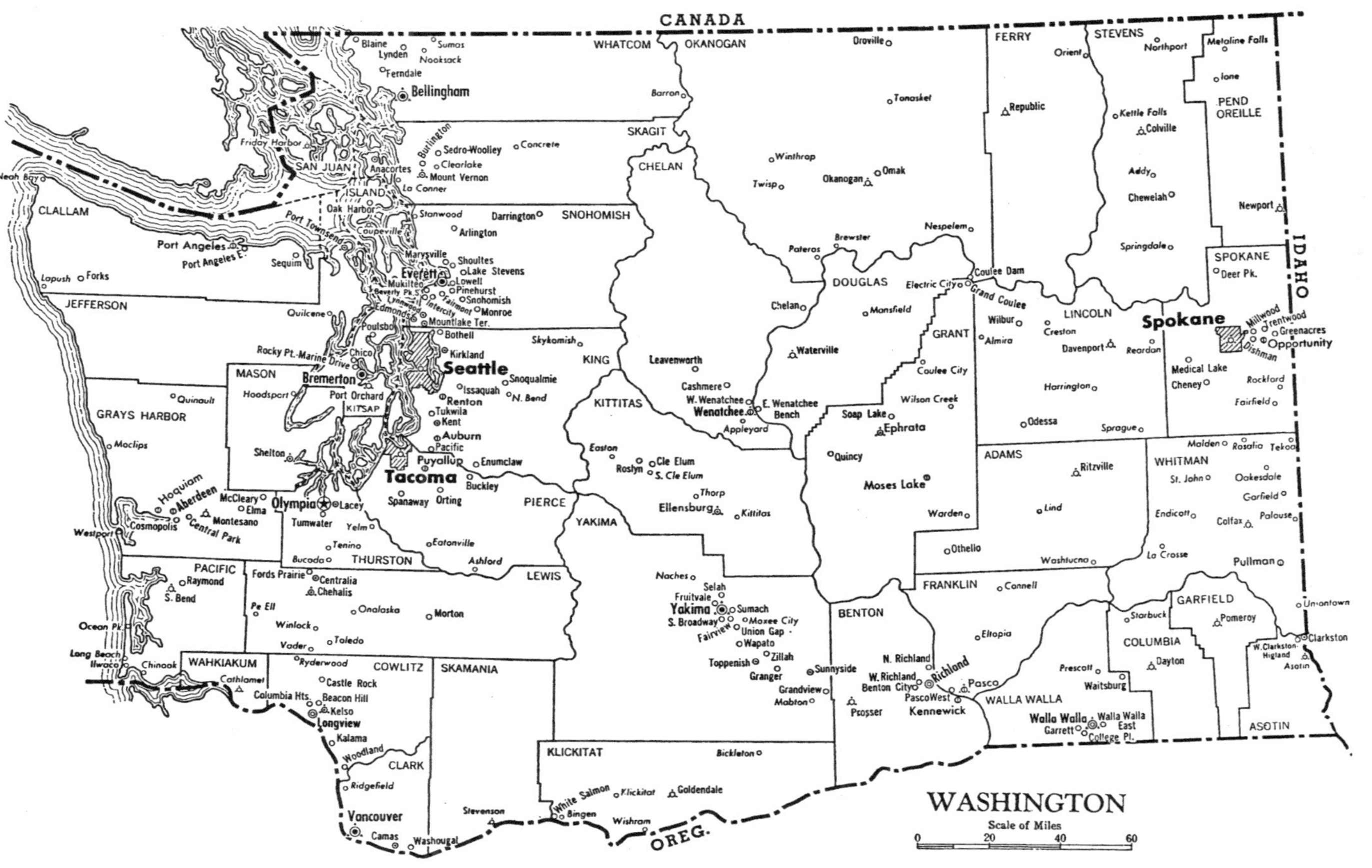
CANADA
IDAHO
OREG.
WASHINGTON
Scale of Miles
0
20
40
60
WHATCOM
OKANOGAN
FERRY
STEVENS
PEND OREILLE
SPOKANE
SKAGIT
SAN JUAN
ISLAND
CHELAN
SNOHOMISH
CLALLAM
JEFFERSON
DOUGLAS
LINCOLN
KING
GRANT
MASON
KITSAP
GRAYS HARBOR
KITTITAS
ADAMS
WHITMAN
PIERCE
YAKIMA
THURSTON
PACIFIC
LEWIS
FRANKLIN
GARFIELD
BENTON
COLUMBIA
WAHKIAKUM
COWLITZ
SKAMANIA
WALLA WALLA
ASOTIN
KLICKITAT
CLARK
Blaine
Lynden
Sumas
Nooksack
Ferndale
Bellingham
Oroville
Tonasket
Republic
Orient
Northport
Metaline Falls
Ione
Kettle Falls
Colville
Addy
Chewelah
Springdale
Newport
Barron
Friday Harbor
Anacortes
Burlington
Sedro-Woolley
Concrete
Clearlake
Mount Vernon
La Conner
Neah Bay
Oak Harbor
Coupeville
Port Townsend
Stanwood
Darrington
Arlington
Winthrop
Twisp
Okanogan
Omak
Nespelem
Brewster
Pateros
Port Angeles
Port Angeles E.
Sequim
Lapush
Forks
Marysville
Shoultes
Lake Stevens
Everett
Lowell
Mukilteo
Pinehurst
Snohomish
Monroe
Intercity
Edmonds
Mountlake Ter.
Bothell
Deer Pk.
Electric City
Coulee Dam
Grand Coulee
Chelan
Mansfield
Wilbur
Almira
Creston
Davenport
Reardan
Spokane
Millwood
Trentwood
Greenacres
Opportunity
Dishman
Quilcene
Poulsbo
Skykomish
Leavenworth
Waterville
Coulee City
Medical Lake
Cheney
Rockford
Fairfield
Rocky Pt.-Marine Drive
Chico
Kirkland
Seattle
Bremerton
Hoodsport
Port Orchard
Snoqualmie
Issaquah
N. Bend
Renton
Tukwila
Kent
Auburn
Pacific
Quinault
Cashmere
W. Wenatchee
E. Wenatchee Bench
Wenatchee
Appleyard
Wilson Creek
Harrington
Soap Lake
Ephrata
Odessa
Sprague
Moclips
Shelton
Puyallup
Enumclaw
Tacoma
Buckley
Easton
Roslyn
Cle Elum
S. Cle Elum
Quincy
Moses Lake
Ritzville
Malden
Rosalia
Tekoa
St. John
Oakesdale
Garfield
Hoquiam
Aberdeen
McCleary
Elma
Montesano
Central Park
Cosmopolis
Westport
Olympia
Lacey
Tumwater
Yelm
Tenino
Bucoda
Spanaway
Orting
Eatonville
Ashford
Thorp
Ellensburg
Kittitas
Warden
Lind
Endicott
Colfax
Palouse
Othello
Washtucna
La Crosse
Pullman
Raymond
S. Bend
Fords Prairie
Centralia
Chehalis
Pe Ell
Onalaska
Morton
Winlock
Toledo
Vader
Naches
Selah
Fruitvale
Yakima
Sumach
S. Broadway
Fairview
Moxee City
Union Gap
Wapato
Zillah
Toppenish
Granger
Sunnyside
Grandview
Mabton
Connell
Eltopia
Starbuck
Pomeroy
Uniontown
Clarkston
W. Clarkston-Highland
Asotin
Dayton
Ocean Pk.
Long Beach
Ilwaco
Chinook
Cathlamet
Ryderwood
Castle Rock
Columbia Hts.
Beacon Hill
Kelso
Longview
Kalama
Woodland
Ridgefield
Vancouver
Camas
Washougal
Stevenson
White Salmon
Bingen
Klickitat
Goldendale
Wishram
Bickleton
N. Richland
W. Richland
Benton City
Richland
Pasco
PascoWest
Kennewick
Prosser
Prescott
Waitsburg
Walla Walla
Walla Walla East
Garrett
College Pl.

TACOMA–Adjusters

CUSTARD INSURANCE ADJUSTERS, INC.
Automobile, Trucking Liability, Property, Casualty, Fire & Allied Lines, Workers' Compensation, Heavy Equipment, Product Liability, Bonds, and Appraisals.
2602 South 38th Street
PMB 48
Tacoma, WA 98409
Phone: (253) 475-4174
Fax: (253) 475-4815
Custard Hotline Center (24 hours)
1-800-457-3390
Head Office: Atlanta, Georgia
Rick Linville, Chairman of the Board
Charlie Peek, Chief Executive Officer
Serving the U.S. and Canada with 24 hour service through 250 offices in 48 states.
Visit us on the Web at www.custard.com
Covering 75 mile radius of Tacoma.

VANCOUVER–Adjusters

CUSTARD INSURANCE ADJUSTERS, INC.
Automobile, Trucking Liability, Property, Casualty, Fire & Allied Lines, Workers' Compensation, Heavy Equipment, Product Liability, Bonds, and Appraisals.
13023 N.E. Hwy. 99
Suite 7, PMB 348
Vancouver, WA 98686
Phone: (360) 334-6023
Fax: (360) 859-4559
Custard Hotline Center (24 hours)
1-800-457-3390
Head Office: Atlanta, Georgia
Rick Linville, Chairman of the Board
Charlie Peek, Chief Executive Officer
Serving the U.S. and Canada with 24 hour service through 250 offices in 48 states.
Visit us on the Web at www.custard.com
Covering 75 mile radius of Vancouver.

West Virginia

CHARLESTON–Adjusters

CUSTARD INSURANCE ADJUSTERS, INC.
Automobile, Trucking Liability, Property, Casualty, Fire & Allied Lines, Workers' Compensation, Heavy Equipment, Product Liability, Bonds, and Appraisals.
101 Carriage Way
Route 34, Suite 303
Hurricane, WV 25526
Phone: (304) 760-1044
Fax: (304) 760-1046
Custard Hotline Center (24 hours)
1-800-457-3390
Head Office: Atlanta, Georgia
Rick Linville, Chairman of the Board
Charlie Peek, Chief Executive Officer
Serving the U.S. and Canada with 24 hour service through 250 offices in 48 states.
Visit us on the Web at www.custard.com
Covering 75 mile radius of Charleston.

MARTINSBURG–Adjusters

CUSTARD INSURANCE ADJUSTERS, INC.
Automobile, Trucking Liability, Property, Casualty, Fire & Allied Lines, Workers' Compensation, Heavy Equipment, Product Liability, Bonds, and Appraisals.
484 Williamsport Pike, Suite 114
Martinsburg, WV 25402
Phone: (304) 267-1260
Fax: (304) 267-1261
Custard Hotline Center (24 hours)
1-800-457-3390
Head Office: Atlanta, Georgia
Rick Linville, Chairman of the Board
Charlie Peek, Chief Executive Officer
Serving the U.S. and Canada with 24 hour service through 250 offices in 48 states.
Visit us on the Web at www.custard.com
Covering 75 mile radius of Martinsburg.

MORGANTOWN–Adjusters

CUSTARD INSURANCE ADJUSTERS, INC.

Automobile, Trucking Liability, Property, Casualty, Fire & Allied Lines, Workers' Compensation, Heavy Equipment, Product Liability, Bonds, and Appraisals.

364 Patterson Drive, Suite 281
Morgantown, WV 26505
Phone: (304) 284-0752
Fax: (304) 284-0753
Custard Hotline Center (24 hours)
1-800-457-3390
Head Office: Atlanta, Georgia
Rick Linville, Chairman of the Board
Charlie Peek, Chief Executive Officer
Serving the U.S. and Canada with 24 hour service through 250 offices in 48 states.
Visit us on the Web at www.custard.com
Covering 75 mile radius of Morgantown.

WHEELING–Adjusters

CUSTARD INSURANCE ADJUSTERS, INC.

Automobile, Trucking Liability, Property, Casualty, Fire & Allied Lines, Workers' Compensation, Heavy Equipment, Product Liability, Bonds, and Appraisals.

47 Washington Avenue, Suite 117
Wheeling, WV 26003
Phone: (304) 233-0791
Fax: (304) 233-0792
Custard Hotline Center (24 hours)
1-800-457-3390
Head Office: Atlanta, Georgia
Rick Linville, Chairman of the Board
Charlie Peek, Chief Executive Officer
Serving the U.S. and Canada with 24 hour service through 250 offices in 48 states.
Visit us on the Web at www.custard.com
Covering 75 mile radius of Wheeling.

Wisconsin

APPLETON–Adjusters

CUSTARD INSURANCE ADJUSTERS, INC.

Automobile, Trucking Liability, Property, Casualty, Fire & Allied Lines, Workers' Compensation, Heavy Equipment, Product Liability, Bonds, and Appraisals.

P.O. Box 1111
Appleton, WI 54812
Phone: (920) 954-6860
Fax: (920) 954-6861
Custard Hotline Center (24 hours)
1-800-457-3390
Head Office: Atlanta, Georgia
Rick Linville, Chairman of the Board
Charlie Peek, Chief Executive Officer
Serving the U.S. and Canada with 24 hour service through 250 offices in 48 states.
Visit us on the Web at www.custard.com
Covering 75 mile radius of Appleton.

DULUTH–Adjusters

CUSTARD INSURANCE ADJUSTERS, INC.

Automobile, Trucking Liability, Property, Casualty, Fire & Allied Lines, Workers' Compensation, Heavy Equipment, Product Liability, Bonds, and Appraisals.

P.O. Box 828
Iron River, WI 54847
Phone: (218) 216-9200
Fax: (218) 249-0785
Custard Hotline Center (24 hours)
1-800-457-3390
Head Office: Atlanta, Georgia
Rick Linville, Chairman of the Board
Charlie Peek, Chief Executive Officer
Serving the U.S. and Canada with 24 hour service through 250 offices in 48 states.
Visit us on the Web at www.custard.com
Covering 75 mile radius of Duluth.

EAU CLAIRE–Adjusters

CUSTARD INSURANCE ADJUSTERS, INC.

Automobile, Trucking Liability, Property, Casualty, Fire & Allied Lines, Workers' Compensation, Heavy Equipment, Product Liability, Bonds, and Appraisals.

P.O. Box 448
Eau Claire, WI 54702
Phone: (715) 836-7099
Fax: (715) 318-0770
Custard Hotline Center (24 hours)
1-800-457-3390
Head Office: Atlanta, Georgia
Rick Linville, Chairman of the Board
Charlie Peek, Chief Executive Officer
Serving the U.S. and Canada with 24 hour service through 250 offices in 48 states.
Visit us on the Web at www.custard.com
Covering 75 mile radius of Eau Claire.

LA CROSSE–Adjusters

CUSTARD INSURANCE ADJUSTERS, INC.

Automobile, Trucking Liability, Property, Casualty, Fire & Allied Lines, Workers' Compensation, Heavy Equipment, Product Liability, Bonds, and Appraisals.

P.O. Box 507
Holmen, WI 54636
Phone: (608) 249-5199
Fax: (608) 249-1399
Custard Hotline Center (24 hours)
1-800-457-3390
Head Office: Atlanta, Georgia
Rick Linville, Chairman of the Board
Charlie Peek, Chief Executive Officer
Serving the U.S. and Canada with 24 hour service through 250 offices in 48 states.
Visit us on the Web at www.custard.com
Covering 75 mile radius of La Crosse.

GREEN BAY–Adjusters

CUSTARD INSURANCE ADJUSTERS, INC.

Automobile, Trucking Liability, Property, Casualty, Fire & Allied Lines, Workers' Compensation, Heavy Equipment, Product Liability, Bonds, and Appraisals.

P.O. Box 1111
Appleton, WI 54912
Phone: (920) 498-2825
Fax: (920) 498-0815
Custard Hotline Center (24 hours)
1-800-457-3390
Head Office: Atlanta, Georgia
Rick Linville, Chairman of the Board
Charlie Peek, Chief Executive Officer
Serving the U.S. and Canada with 24 hour service through 250 offices in 48 states.
Visit us on the Web at www.custard.com
Covering 75 mile radius of Green Bay.

MADISON–Adjusters

CUSTARD INSURANCE ADJUSTERS, INC.

Automobile, Trucking Liability, Property, Casualty, Fire & Allied Lines, Workers' Compensation, Heavy Equipment, Product Liability, Bonds, and Appraisals.

2317 International Lane, Suite 102
Madison, WI 53704
Phone: (608) 249-5199
Fax: (608) 249-1399
Custard Hotline Center (24 hours)
1-800-457-3390
Head Office: Atlanta, Georgia
Rick Linville, Chairman of the Board
Charlie Peek, Chief Executive Officer
Serving the U.S. and Canada with 24 hour service through 250 offices in 48 states.
Visit us on the Web at www.custard.com
Covering 75 mile radius of Madison.

MILWAUKEE–Adjusters

CUSTARD INSURANCE ADJUSTERS, INC.

Automobile, Trucking Liability, Property, Casualty, Fire & Allied Lines, Workers' Compensation, Heavy Equipment, Product Liability, Bonds, and Appraisals.
275 Regency Court, Suite 102
Brookfield, WI 53045
Phone: (262) 439-9576
Fax: (262) 780-3919
Custard Hotline Center (24 hours)
1-800-457-3390
Head Office: Atlanta, Georgia
Rick Linville, Chairman of the Board
Charlie Peek, Chief Executive Officer
Serving the U.S. and Canada with 24 hour service through 250 offices in 48 states.
Visit us on the Web at www.custard.com
Covering 75 mile radius of Milwaukee.

NORTH CENTRAL WISCONSIN/ WAUSAU–Adjusters

CUSTARD INSURANCE ADJUSTERS, INC.

Automobile, Trucking Liability, Property, Casualty, Fire & Allied Lines, Workers' Compensation, Heavy Equipment, Product Liability, Bonds, and Appraisals.
P.O. Box 935
Merrill, WI 54452
Phone: (715) 536-8326
Fax: (715) 539-8427
Custard Hotline Center (24 hours)
1-800-457-3390
Head Office: Atlanta, Georgia
Rick Linville, Chairman of the Board
Charlie Peek, Chief Executive Officer
Serving the U.S. and Canada with 24 hour service through 250 offices in 48 states.
Visit us on the Web at www.custard.com
Covering 75 mile radius of Wausau.

Wyoming

CHEYENNE–Adjusters

CUSTARD INSURANCE ADJUSTERS, INC.

Automobile, Trucking Liability, Property, Casualty, Fire & Allied Lines, Workers' Compensation, Heavy Equipment, Product Liability, Bonds, and Appraisals.
1740H Dell Range Boulevard
Suite 123
Cheyenne, WY 82009
Phone: (307) 638-8294
Fax: (307) 638-8298
Custard Hotline Center (24 hours)
1-800-457-3390
Head Office: Atlanta, Georgia
Rick Linville, Chairman of the Board
Charlie Peek, Chief Executive Officer
Serving the U.S. and Canada with 24 hour service through 250 offices in 48 states.
Visit us on the Web at www.custard.com
Covering 75 mile radius of Cheyenne.

Insurance Associations and Governing Bodies

INSURANCE ASSOCIATIONS

ADVOCIS
390 Queens Quay West
Suite 209
Toronto, ON M5V 3A2
Phone: (416) 444-5251
Toll-free: 1-800-563-5822
Fax: (416) 444-8031
info@advocis.ca
www.advocis.ca
President and Chief Executive Officer: Greg Pollock

CANADA SAFETY COUNCIL
1020 Thomas Spratt Place
Ottawa, ON K1G 5L5
Phone: (613) 739-1535
Fax: (613) 739-1566
csc@safety-council.org
www.canadasafetycouncil.org
President: Jack Smith

CANADIAN ASSOCIATION OF DIRECT RELATIONSHIP INSURERS
250 Consumer Road
Suite 301
Toronto, ON M2J 4V6
Phone: (416) 773-0101
Fax: (416) 495-8723
cadri@cadri.com
www.cadri.com
Chief Executive Officer and Chairperson: Alain Thibault

THE CANADIAN ASSOCIATION OF FINANCIAL INSTITUTIONS IN INSURANCE
21 St. Clair Avenue East, Suite 802
Toronto, ON M4T 1L9
Phone: (416) 494-9224
Fax: (416) 967-6320
info@cafii.com
www.cafii.com
Executive Directors: Brendan Wycks and Keith Martin

CANADIAN ASSOCIATION OF INSURANCE WOMEN
c/o Donna Payne, Secretary
RBC Insurance Agency Ltd.
c/o 21 Fairweather Avenue
Mount Pearl, NL A1N 2S5
Phone: (709) 693-1362
domma.payne@rbc..com
www.caiw-acfa.com
President: Deborah MacDougall

CANADIAN COUNCIL OF INSURANCE REGULATORS
5160 Yonge Street
Box 85
Toronto, ON M2N 6L9
Phone: (416) 590-7290
Fax: (416) 226-7878
ccir-ccrra@fsco.gov.on.ca
www.ccir-ccrra.org
Policy Manager: Martin Boyle

... continued on next page

INSURANCE ASSOCIATIONS (continued)

CANADIAN FIRE SAFETY ASSOCIATION
2800 – 14th Avenue
Suite 210
Markham, ON L3R 0E4
Phone: (416) 492-9417
Fax: (416) 491-1670
cfsa@associationconcepts.ca
www.canadianfiresafety.com
President: David Morris
Administrator: Carolyne Vigon

CHARTERED INSURANCE PROFESSIONALS' SOCIETY
18 King Street East
6th Floor
Toronto, ON M5C 1C4
Phone: (416) 362-8586
Toll-free: 1-866-362-8585
Fax: (416) 362-8081
cips@insuranceinstitute.ca
www.insuranceinstitute.ca
Director: Margaret Parent, BA

INSURANCE BROKERS ASSOCIATION OF CANADA
18 King Street East
Suite 1210
Toronto, ON M5C 1C4
Phone: (416) 367-1831
Fax: (416) 367-3687
ibac@ibac.ca
www.ibac.ca
President: Scott Treasure
Chief Executive Officer: Peter Braid

INSURANCE BUREAU OF CANADA
777 Bay Street, Suite 2400, Box 121
Toronto, ON M5G 2C8
Phone: (416) 362-2031
Fax: (416) 361-5952
www.ibc.ca
President and Chief Executive Officer:
Don Forgeron

THE INSURANCE INSTITUTE OF CANADA
18 King Street East, 6th Floor
Toronto, ON M5C 1C4
Phone: (416) 362-8586
Fax: (416) 362-1126
Toll-free: 1-866-362-8585
IICmail@insuranceinstitute.ca
www.insuranceinstitute.ca
President and Chief Executive Officer:
Peter Hohman, MBA, FCIP, ICD.D

NATIONAL ASSOCIATION OF INDEPENDENT INSURANCE ADJUSTERS
1880 Radcliff Court
Tracy, CA 95376
Phone: 1-877-344-0624
Fax: (269) 978-9078
admin@naiia.com
www.naiia.com
Executive Director: Brenda Reisinger

TORONTO INSURANCE WOMEN'S ASSOCIATION
31 Adelaide Street East
P.O. Box 861
Toronto, ON M5C 2K1
president@tiwa.org
www.tiwa.org
President: Vinita Jajware, B.Comm,
CMS, CRM

CANADIAN INDEPENDENT ADJUSTERS' ASSOCIATION

Incorporated under Part 2 of the Canadian Companies Act

2017–2018

NATIONAL EXECUTIVE

President	MONICA KUZYK, FCIP, CRM
1st Vice-President	TROY QUIGLEY, BBA, CIP
2nd Vice-President	SARAH HIRST, CIP, CRM, FCIP
Secretary	CHRISTOPHER BARTLETT, BA, CIP
Treasurer	JEFF EDGE, CIP, CFEI
Past President	HEATHER MATTHEWS, CIP, CRM, CIOP
Executive Director	PATRICIA M. BATTLE
Director	PAUL FÉRON, FCIP, CRM
Director	SEAN FORGIE, BA, CIP, CFEI
Director	JAMES B. ESO, CIP, CIOP
Director	E. GRANT KING, BA, B.ED, CIP
Director	ALBERT POON, CIP
Director	TROY QUIGLEY, BBA, CIP
Director	MARIE C. GALLAGHER, FCIP, CRM
Director	GARY ELLIS, BBA, FCIP, RF, FCLA, FCIAA, FIFAA
Director	BALU NAIDU, B.COMM., FCIP, CRM
Newfoundland/Labrador Region President	GEJAPATHY GOPAL, CRM
Nova Scotia Region President	M. KENNETH MACLEOD, CIP
N.B. and PEI Region President	GREG POTTEN, BPE, CIP, CFEI, CRM, CLA
Quebec Region President	MICHEL LACELLE, PAA/CIP
Ontario Region President	NIKI MCCONNELL, BA (Hons.), CIP, CRM
Manitoba Region President	CRAIG SHANKS, BA, CIP
Saskatchewan Region President	LEE DIXON, B.COMM., CIP
Western Region President	JODY SCHMIDT, B.COMM., CIP
Pacific Region President	PAT LODEWIJKX, FCIP, CRM

NATIONAL STANDING COMMITTEES

ADVISORY	TROY QUIGLEY, BBA, CIP
	SARAH HIRST, CIP, CRM, FCIP
	HEATHER MATTHEWS, CIP, CRM, CIOP
	PAUL FÉRON, FCIP, CRM
	SEAN FORGIE, BA, CIP, CFEI
	JAMES B. ESO, CIP, CIOP
	E. GRANT KING, BA, B.ED, CIP
	ALBERT POON, CIP
	MARIE C. GALLAGHER, FCIP, CRM
	BALU NAIDU, B.COMM., FCIP, CRM

... continued on next page

CANADIAN INDEPENDENT ADJUSTERS' ASSOCIATION
(Continued)

CAREER RECRUITMENT PLANNING	RICHARD SWIERCZYNSKI, BA, CIP
COMMUNICATIONS	RICHARD SWIERCZYNSKI, BA, CIP
	JOHN D. SEYLER, CIP
CONSTITUTION & RULES	PAUL FÉRON, FCIP, CRM
CONVENTION	TROY QUIGLEY, BBA, CIP
DESIGNATION/EDUCATION	GARY ELLIS, BBA, FCIP, RF, FCLA, FCIAA, FIFAA
	ROBERT V. PEARSON, CLA, FCIAA
	LORNE MONTGOMERY, CIP, FCIAA, FCLA
EDITORIAL	MARY CHARMAN, CIP
	JOHN M. SHAROUN, FCIP, FCIAA, CRM
EMERGENCY MEASURES	RICHARD VAN HORNE
FINANCE	JEFF EDGE, CIP, CFEI
	MONICA KUZYK, FCIP, CRM
	HEATHER MATTHEWS, CIP, CRM, CIOP
IBC: LIAISON, LEGISLATIVE & FORMS	LEE POWELL
LICENSING	J. MILES O. BARBER, B.COMM. (Hons.), FCIP, CRM, RF
MEMBERSHIP & QUALIFICATIONS	MARIE C. GALLAGHER, FCIP, CRM
NOMINATING	HEATHER MATTHEWS, CIP, CRM, CIOP
	MONICA KUZYK, FCIP, CRM
	PAUL FÉRON, FCIP, CRM
	TROY QUIGLEY, BBA, CIP
	BALU NAIDU, B.COMM., FCIP, CRM
PRIVACY	JAMES B. ESO, CIP, CIOP
	KEITH P. EDWARDS, FCILA, CLA, FUEDI-ELAE
PROFESSIONAL PRACTICES	HEATHER MATTHEWS, CIP, CRM, CIOP

Correspondence may be addressed to the Executive Director:
Patricia M. Battle
Centennial Centre,
5401 Eglinton Avenue West,
Suite 100
Etobicoke, ON M9C 5K6
Phone: (416) 621-6222
Toll-free: 1-877-255-5589
www.ciaa-adjusters.ca
E-mail: info@ciaa-adjusters.ca

FIRE MARSHALS AND FIRE COMMISSIONERS IN CANADA

Alberta
Kevan D. Jess
Executive Director and Fire Commissioner
Municipal Affairs
Rpp, 19D, Commerce Place
10155 – 102 Street
Edmonton, AB T5J 4L4
Phone: (780) 427-4860
Fax: (780) 422-0214

British Columbia
Gordon Anderson
Fire Commissioner
Emergency Management B.C.
P.O. Box 9201
Stn. Prov. Govt.
Victoria, BC V8W 9J1
Phone: (250) 952-4913
Fax: (250) 952-4888

Manitoba
David Schafer
Fire Commissioner
Manitoba Labour & Immigration
508 – 401 York Avenue
Winnipeg, MB R3C 0P8
Phone: (204) 945-3322
Fax: (204) 948-2089

New Brunswick
Douglas Browne
Fire Marshal
Public Safety
Province of New Brunswick
Victoria Health Centre
P.O. Box 6000
Fredericton, NB E3B 5H1
Phone: (506) 453-2004
Fax: (506) 457-4899

Newfoundland and Labrador
Derek Simmons
Fire Commissioner and Director of Fire Services
Department of Municipal and Provincial Affairs
25 Hallett Crescent
P.O. Box 8700
St. John's, NL A1B 4J6
Phone: (709) 729-1608
Fax: (709) 729-2524

Northwest Territories
Chucker Dewar
Fire Marshal
Municipal and Community Affairs
Government of the NWT
N.W. Tower, 600
5201 50th Avenue, P.O. Box 1320
Yellowknife, NT X1A 3S9
Phone: (867) 767-9161, ext. 21026
Fax: (867) 873-0260

Nova Scotia
Fred Jeffers
Fire Marshal
Office of Municipal Affairs
Building & Fire Safety
P.O. Box 231
Halifax Central, NS B3J 2M4
Phone: (902) 424-5721
Fax: (902) 424-3239

Nunavut
Ed Zebedee, Director of Nunavut Emergency Management
Department of Community and Government Services
Nunavut Protection Services
P.O. Box 1000, Station 700
Iqaluit, NU X0A 0H0
Phone: (867) 975-5477
Fax: (867) 979-4221

... continued on next page

FIRE MARSHALS AND FIRE COMMISSIONERS IN CANADA
(Continued)

Ontario
Ross Nichols
Fire Marshal and Chief of Emergency Management
Community Safety and Correctional Services
25 Morton Shulman Avenue
Toronto, ON M3M 0B1
Phone: (647) 329-1200
Fax: (647) 329-1143

Prince Edward Island
David Rossiter
Fire Marshal
Office of Public Safety
P.O. Box 2000
J. Elmer Blanchard Building
Charlottetown, PE C1A 7N8
Phone: (902) 368-4869
Fax: (902) 368-5526

Quebec
Mme. Liette Larrivée
Sous-ministre associé à la sécurité civile et la sécurité incendie
Ministère de la sécurité publique
2525, boulevard Laurier, 5e étage
Tour des Laurentides
Sainte-Foy, QC G1V 2L2
Phone: (418) 646-6777
Fax: (418) 643-0275

Saskatchewan
Duane McKay
Commissioner and Executive Director
Energy Management and Fire Safety
Government Relations
500 – 1855 Victoria Street
Regina, SK S4P 3T2
Phone: (306) 787-4516
Fax: (306) 787-7107

Yukon
James Patterson
Director and Fire Marshal
Community Services
Protective Services
91788 Alaska Highway
Whitehorse, YT Y1A 5X7
Phone: (867)
Fax: (403) 667-3165

Fire Commissioner of Canada
Marcia J. Edgar
Manager, OHS Compliance and Operations Unit
HRSDC Operations
165 Hôtel-de-Ville Street
Gatineau, QC K1A 0J2
Phone: (819) 654-4431
Fax: (819) 956-7521

National Defence Fire Marshal
Patrice Bouffard
Canadian Forces Fire Marshal
Department of National Defence
101 Colonel By Drive
Ottawa, ON K1A 0K2
Phone: (613) 995-1959
Fax: (613) 996-1753

SUPERINTENDENTS OF INSURANCE
FOR THE PROVINCES AND TERRITORIES OF CANADA

Alberta
Nilam Jetha
Superintendent of Financial Institutions Insurance, and Pensions
4th Floor, Terrace Building
9515 – 107 Street
Edmonton, AB T5K 2C3
TEL: (403) 427-8322
FAX: (403) 420-0752
E-mail: nilam.jetha@gov.ab.ca
Website: www.finance.gov.ab.ca

British Columbia
Tara Richards
Interim Chief Executive Officer & Superintendent
Financial Institutions Commission
Suite 1200, 13450 – 102nd Avenue
Surrey, BC V3T 5X3
TEL: (604) 660-3631
FAX: (604) 660-3365
E-mail: ficom@ficom.bc.ca
Website: www.ficom.bc.ca

Manitoba
Scott Moore
Superintendent of Financial Institutions
Financial Institutions Regulation Branch
400 St. Mary Avenue, Suite 207
Winnipeg, MB R3C 4K5
TEL: (204) 945-2542
FAX: (204) 948-2268
E-mail: insurance@gov.mb.ca
Website: www.mbfinancialinstitutions.ca

New Brunswick
Angela Mazerolle
Superintendent of Insurance
Financial and Consumer Services Commission
225 King Street, Andal Building
Fredericton, NB E3B 1E1
TEL: (506) 453-8959
FAX: (506) 457-7266
E-mail: angela.mazerolle@fcnb.ca
Website: www.gnb.ca

Newfoundland and Labrador
Julian McCarthy
ADM/Superintendent of Insurance
Service NL
Consumer and Commercial Affairs Branch
P.O. Box 8700
St. John's, NL A1B 4J6
TEL: (709) 729-2570
FAX: (709) 729-4151
E-mail: jmccarthy@mail.gov.nl.ca
Website: www.gov.nl.ca

Northwest Territories
Louise Lavoie
Assistant Comptroller and Superintendent of Insurance
Office of the Comptroller General
Department of Finance
Govt. of the Northwest Territories
P.O. Box 1320
Yellowknife, NT X1A 2L9
TEL: (867) 767-9171, ext. 15080
FAX: (867) 920-4347
E-mail: louise_lavoie@gov.nt.ca
Website: www.gov.nt.ca

Nova Scotia
William Ngu
Superintendent of Financial Institutions Insurance
Finance and Treasury Board
P.O. Box 187, 1723 Hollis Street
Halifax, NS B3J 2N3
TEL: (902) 424-2787
FAX: (902) 424-1298
E-mail: William.Ngu@novascotia.ca
Website: www.gov.ns.ca/finance

... continued on next page

SUPERINTENDENTS OF INSURANCE
FOR THE PROVINCES AND TERRITORIES OF CANADA
(Continued)

Nunavut
Jeff Chown
Deputy Minister
Policy Planning, Dept. of Finance
Government of Nunavut
P.O. Box 1000, Station 330
Iqaluit, NU X0A 0H0
TEL: (867) 975-5801
FAX: (867) 975-5805
E-mail: JChown@gov.nu.ca
Website: www.gov.nu.ca/finance

Ontario
Brian Mills
Chief Executive Officer &
Superintendent of Financial
Services Commission
5160 Yonge Street, 17th Floor
Box 85
North York, ON M2N 6L9
TEL: (416) 590-7000
FAX: (416) 590-7070
E-mail: ceo@fsco.gov.on.ca
Website: www.fsco.gov.on.ca

Prince Edward Island
Robert A. Bradley
Superintendent of Insurance
Consumer, Labour and Financial
Services
Justice and Public Safety
Shaw Building, 4th Floor
P.O. Box 2000
Charlottetown, PE C1A 7N8
TEL: (902) 368-6478
FAX: (902) 368-5283
E-mail: rabradley@gov.pe.ca
Website: www.gov.pe.ca

Quebec
Louis Morisset
President and Chief Executive Officer
Autorité des marchés financiers
Place de la Cité, tour Cominar
2640, boulevard Laurier, bureau 400
Quebec, QC G1V 5C1

Quebec (continued)
TEL: (418) 525-0337
FAX: (418) 525-9512
Website: www.lautorite.qc.ca

Saskatchewan
Ian McIntosh
Director, Insurance and Real Estate
Division
Financial and Consumer Affairs
Authority
Government of Saskatchewan
601 – 1919 Saskatchewan Drive
Regina, SK S4P 4H2
TEL: (306) 787-5645
FAX: (306) 787-5899
E-mail: Ian.McIntosh@gov.sk.ca
Website: www.fcaa.gov.sk.ca

Yukon
Katherine White
Deputy Minister and Secretary to
Management Board
Department of Finance
Government of the Yukon
P.O. Box 2703
Whitehorse, YT Y1A 2C6
TEL: (867) 667-3571
FAX: (867) 393-6218
E-mail: Katherine.White@gov.yk.ca
Website: www.gov.yk.ca

Federal Government
Jeremy Rudin
Superintendent
Office of the Superintendent
of Financial Institutions
Kent Square
255 Albert Street
Ottawa, ON K1A 0H2
TEL: (613) 990-3667
TOLL-FREE: 1-800-385-8647
FAX: (613) 993-6782
E-mail: jeremy.rudin@osfi-bsif.gc.ca
Website: www.osfi-bsif.gc.ca

ONTARIO INSURANCE ADJUSTERS ASSOCIATION

29 De Jong Drive, Mississauga, ON L5M 1B9

Business Manager: Jackie Johnston (905) 542-0576
Toll Free: 1-888-259-1555
Fax: (905) 542-1301
E-mail: jackie@oiaa.com

EXECUTIVE COUNCIL 2017–2018

President: Jennifer Graham, CIP
1st Vice-Pres.: Michael McLeod, CIP
2nd Vice-Pres.: Leanne Hardman, B.Sc. (Hons.), CIP
Treasurer: Simone Cybulski
Secretary: Rue Sherrard
Past President: Ian Gallagher, CIP

COUNCIL MEMBERS

Georgian Bay: Greg Doerr, CIP
Hamilton: Tom Pooler
Kawartha/Durham: Ray Proctor, BA, CIP
Kitchener/Waterloo: Stephen Tucker, MA, FCIP, CRM
London: Kyle Case, FCIP, CRM
Niagara: Craig Ozog, CIP
Northen: Mike Bottan, CIP, CFEI
Ottawa: Cindy Bridge, CIP, CRM
Thousand Islands: Terry Doherty, CFEI
Thunder Bay: Geoff Sullivan, CIP, CFEI, CFE, CCFI-C
Toronto:
Carrie Evans, CIP, CRM
Shawna Gillen, CIP
Matthew Rienzo
Windsor: Michael Hoffman, BA, CIP, CRM

Insurance Companies

AIG Insurance Company of Canada
120 Bremmer Boulevard, Suite 2200
Toronto, ON M5J 0A8

Affiliated FM Insurance Co.
165 Commerce Valley Drive West
Suite 500
Thornhill, ON L3T 7V8

Alberta Motor Association Insurance Company
10310 G.A. MacDonald (39A)
Edmonton, AB T6J 6R7

Allianz Global Risks US Insurance Company
130 Adelaide Street West, Suite 1600
Toronto, ON M5H 3P5

Allied World Specialty Insurance Company
200 King Street West, Suite 1600
Toronto, ON M5H 3T4

Allstate Insurance Company of Canada
27 Allstate Parkway, Suite 100
Markham, ON L3R 5P8

American Agricultural Insurance Company
1145 Nicholson Road, Unit 2
Newmarket, ON L3Y 9C3

American Bankers Insurance Company of Florida
5000 Yonge Street, Suite 2000
Toronto, ON M2N 7E9

The American Road Insurance Company
1145 Nicholson Road, Unit 2
Newmarket, ON L3Y 9C3

Antigonish Farmers' Mutual Fire Insurance Company
188 Main Street, P.O. Box 1535
Antigonish, NS B2G 2B9

Arch Insurance Canada Ltd.
77 King Street West, Suite 3600
P.O. Box 308
Toronto, ON M5K 1K2

Arch Reinsurance Company
100 Wellington Street West, Suite 1210
Toronto, ON M5K 1J3

Ascentus Insurance Ltd.
18 York Street, Suite 800
Toronto, ON M5J 2T8

Aspen Insurance UK Limited
2100 Scotia Plaza, 40 King Street West
Toronto, ON M5H 3C2

Associated Electric and Gas Insurance Services Limited
2100 Scotia Plaza, 40 King Street West
Toronto, ON M5H 3C2

Aviva General Insurance Company
10 Aviva Way, Suite 100
Markham, ON L6G 0G1

Aviva Insurance Company of Canada
10 Aviva Way, Suite 100
Markham, ON L6G 0G1

AXA Art Insurance Corporation
44 Victoria Street, Suite 1103
Toronto, ON M5C 1Y2

AXA Insurance Company
44 Victoria Street, Suite 1103
Toronto, ON M5C 1Y2

AXIS Reinsurance Company (Canada)
70 York Street, Suite 1010
Toronto, ON M5J 1S9

Berkley Insurance Company
145 King Street West, Suite 1000
Toronto, ON M5H 1J8

Boiler Inspection and Insurance Company of Canada
390 Bay Street, Suite 2000
Toronto, ON M5H 2Y2

CAA Insurance Company (Ontario)
60 Commerce Valley Drive East
Thornhill, ON L3T 7P9

Canadian Direct Insurance Incorporated
700 University Avenue, Suite 1500A
Toronto, ON M5G 0A1

Canadian Northern Shield Insurance Co.
18 York Street, Suite 800
Toronto, ON M5J 2T8

La Capitale assurances générales inc.
625 rue Jacques-Parizeau
Québec, QC G1R 2G5

Catalina General Insurance Ltd.
200 University Avenue, 14th Floor
Toronto, ON M5H 3C6

Certas Direct Insurance Company
1 Complexe Desjardins
South Tower, 17th Floor
Montreal, QC H5B 1B1

Certas Home and Auto Insurance Co.
333 First Commerce Drive
Aurora, ON L4G 8A4

Cherokee Insurance Company
4285 Industrial Drive, Room 208
Windsor, ON N9C 3R9

Chubb Insurance Company of Canada
199 Bay Street, Suite 2500
P.O. Box 139, Commerce Court P.S.
Toronto, ON M5L 1E2

Clare Mutual Insurance Company
3300 Highway 1, Belliveau Cove
Digby County, NS B0W 1J0

Continental Casualty Company
66 Wellingston Street West, Suite 3700
Toronto, ON M5K 1J5

Co-operators General Insurance Company
Priory Square, 130 Macdonnell Street
Guelph, ON N1H 6P8

CorePointe Insurance Company
1145 Nicholson Road, Unit 2
Newmarket, ON L3Y 9C3

Coseco Insurance Company
Priory Square, 130 Macdonnell Street
Guelph, ON N1H 6P8

CUMIS General Insurance Company
151 North Service Road, P.O. Box 5065
Burlington, ON L7R 4C2

Dominion of Canada General Insurance Company
165 University Avenue
Toronto, ON M5H 3B9

Ecclesiastical Insurance Office P.L.C.
20 Eglinton Avenue West, Suite 2200
Box 2004
Toronto, ON M4R 1K8

Echelon Insurance
2680 Matheson Boulevard East, Suite 300
Mississauga, ON L4W 0A5

Economical Mutual Insurance Company
111 Westmount Rd. South, P.O. Box 2000
Waterloo, ON N2J 4S4

Electric Insurance Company
2100 Scotia Plaza, 40 King Street West
Toronto, ON M5H 3C2

Elite Insurance Company
10 Aviva Way
Markham, ON L6G 0G1

Employers Insurance Company of Wausau
c/o Garth Pepper
181 Bay Street, Brookfield Place
Suite 1000
Toronto, ON M5J 2T3

Esurance Insurance Company of Canada
27 Allstate Parkway
Suite 100
Markham, ON L3R 5P8

Everest Insurance Company of Canada
130 King Street West
Toronto, ON M5X 1C7

Everest Reinsurance Company
130 King Street West
Suite 2520
Box 431
Toronto, ON M5X 1E3

Factory Mutual Insurance Company
165 Commerce Valley Drive West
Suite 500
Thornhill, ON L3T 7V8

FCT Insurance Company Ltd.
2235 Sheridan Garden Drive
Oakville, ON L6J 7Y5

Federal Insurance Company
199 Bay Street, Suite 2500
Toronto, ON M5L 1E2

Federated Insurance Company of Canada
255 Commerce Drive
P.O. Box 5800, Stn. Main
Winnipeg, MB R3C 3C9

First North American Insurance Company
250 Bloor Street East, 6th Floor
Toronto, ON M4W 1E5

Foresters Indemnity Company
789 Don Mills Road
Don Mills, ON M3C 1T9

Fundy Mutual Insurance Company
1022 Main Street
Sussex, NB E2E 2M3

General Reinsurance Corporation
1 First Canadian Place, Suite 5705
P.O. Box 471
Toronto, ON M5X 1E4

Gore Mutual Insurance Company
252 Dundas Street North, P.O. Box 70
Cambridge, ON N1R 5T3

Great American Insurance Co./Great American Insurance Company of N.Y.
2100 Scotia Plaza, 40 King Street West
Toronto, ON M5H 3C2

Guarantee Company of North America
4950 Yonge Street, Suite 1400
Toronto, ON M2N 6K1

Hannover Rück SE
220 Bay Street, Suite 400
Toronto, ON M5J 2W4

Hartford Fire Insurance Company
1145 Nicholson Road, Unit 2
Newmarket, ON L3Y 9C3

Heartland Farm Mutual
100 Erb Street East
Waterloo, ON N2J 1L9

HDI Global SE
181 University Avenue
Suite 1900
Toronto, ON M5H 3M7

Insurance Corporation of British Columbia
151 West Esplanade Avenue
North Vancouver, BC V7M 3H9

Intact Insurance Company
700 University Avenue
Suite 1500-A
Toronto, ON M5G 0A1

International Insurance Company of Hannover SE
220 Bay Street, Suite 400
Toronto, ON M5J 2W4

Ironshore Insurance Ltd.
333 Bay Street
Toronto, ON M5H 4A6

Jevco Insurance Company
700 University Avenue
Suite 1500-A (legal)
Toronto, ON M5G 0A1

Jewellers Mutual Insurance Company
2100 Scotia Plaza, 40 King Street West
Toronto, ON M5H 3C2

The Kings Mutual Insurance Company
220 Commercial Street
P.O. Box 10
Berwick, NS B0P 1E0

Legacy General Insurance Company
5000 Yonge Street
Toronto, ON M2N 7J8

Liberty Mutual Insurance Company
181 Bay Street, Brookfield Place
Suite 1000
Toronto, ON M5J 2T3

Lloyd's Underwriters
1155 Metcalfe Street
Suite 2220
Montreal, QC H3B 2V6

The Manitoba Public Insurance Corporation
234 Donald Street
Room B100,
Box 6300
Winnipeg, MB R3C 4A4

Mapfre Re Compania de Reaseguros, S.A.
2100 Scotia Plaza, 40 King Street West
Toronto, ON M5H 3C2

The Missisquoi Insurance Company
111 Westmount Road South
P.O. Box 2000
Waterloo, ON N2J 4S4

Mitsui Sumitomo Insurance Company Limited
199 Bay Street, Suite 2500
Toronto, ON M5L 1E2

Motors Insurance Corporation
8500 Leslie Street, Suite 101
P.O. Box 6000
Thornhill, ON L3T 7M8

Munich Reinsurance America, Inc.
390 Bay Street
22nd Floor
Toronto, ON M5H 2Y2

Munich Reinsurance Company of Canada
390 Bay Street
22nd Floor
Toronto, ON M5H 2Y2

The Mutual Fire Insurance Company of British Columbia
9366 – 200A Street, Suite 201
Langley, BC V1M 4B3

National Liability & Fire Insurance Company
200 Bay Street, 15th Floor
Toronto, ON M5H 2J2

Nationwide Mutual Insurance Company
c/o John Milnes and Associates
1300 Bay Street, 4th Floor
Toronto, ON M5R 3K8

The Nordic Insurance Company of Canada
700 University Avenue, Suite 1500-A
Toronto, ON M5G 0A1

Northbridge General Insurance Corporation
105 Adelaide Street West
Toronto, ON M5H 1P9

Northbridge Personal Insurance Corporation
105 Adelaide Street West
Toronto, ON M5H 1P9

Novex Insurance Company
700 University Avenue, Suite 1500-A
Toronto, ON M5G 0A1

Odyssey Reinsurance Company
55 University Avenue, Suite 1600
Toronto, ON M5J 2H7

Old Republic Insurance Company of Canada
100 King Street West
Box 557, Station LCD1
Hamilton, ON L8N 3K9

Omega General Insurance Company
34 King Street East, Suite 1200
Toronto, ON M5C 2X8

Ontario Mutual Insurance Association
350 Pinebush Road
Cambridge, ON N1T 1Z6

Ontario School Board's Insurance Exchange
91 Westmount Road
Guelph, ON N1H 5J2

Pafco Insurance Company
27 Allstate Parkway
Suite 100
Markham, ON L3R 5P8

Partner Reinsurance Company of the United States
123 Front Street West
Suite 909
Toronto, ON M5J 2M2

Prince Edward Island Mutual Insurance Company
116 Walker Avenue
Summerside, PE C1N 6V9

Pembridge Insurance Company
27 Allstate Parkway
Suite 100
Markham, ON L3R 5P8

Personal Insurance Company
1 Complexe Desjardins
South Tower, 17th Floor
Montreal, QC H5B 1B1

Perth Insurance Company
111 Westmount Road South
P.O. Box 2000
Waterloo, ON N2J 4S4

Petline Insurance Company
111 Westmount Road South
P.O. Box 2000
Waterloo, ON N2J 4S4

Pilot Insurance Company
100 Aviva Way
Suite 100
Markham, ON L6G 0G1

Portage La Prairie Mutual Insurance of Canada
749 Saskatchewan Avenue East
P.O. Box 340, Stn. Main
Portage La Prairie, MB R1N 3B8

Primmum Insurance Company/
Primmum compagnie d'assurance
50 Crémazie Place
12th Floor
Montreal, QC H2P 1B6

Protective Insurance Company
34 King Street East
Suite 1200
Toronto, ON M5C 2X8

Quebec Assurance Company
18 York Street, Suite 800
Toronto, ON M5J 2T8

RBC Insurance Company of Canada
200 Bay Street
South Tower, 9th Floor
Toronto, ON M5J 2J5

Royal & Sun Alliance Insurance
Company of Canada
18 York Street, Suite 800
Toronto, ON M5J 2T8

S&Y Insurance Company
10 Aviva Way, Suite 100
Markham, ON L0G 0G1

Safety National Casualty Corporation
2100 Scotia Plaza, 40 King Street West
Toronto, ON M5H 3C2

St. Paul Fire and Marine Insurance
Company
165 University Avenue
Toronto, ON M5H 3B9

Saskatchewan Auto Fund
2260 – 11th Avenue
Regina, SK S4P 0J9

Saskatchewan Mutual Insurance Company
279 Third Avenue North
Saskatoon, SK S7K 2H8

SCOR Canada Reinsurance Company
Commerce Court West
199 Bay Street, Suite 2800
P.O. Box 329
Toronto, ON M5J 1G1

SCOR UK Company Limited
Commerce Court West
199 Bay Street, Suite 2800
P.O. Box 329
Toronto, ON M5J 1G1

Scotia General Insurance Company
100 Yonge Street, 4th Floor
Toronto, ON M5H 1H1

Scottish & York Insurance Co. Limited
10 Aviva Way, Suite 100
Markham, ON L0G 0G1

Security National Insurance Company
50 Crémazie Place, 12th Floor
Montreal, QC H2P 1B6

Sentry Insurance, A Mutual Company
2100, Scotia Tower, 40 King Street West
Toronto, ON M5H 3C2

SGI Canada
2260 – 11th Avenue
Regina, SK S4P 0J9

Sirius American Insurance Company
80 Bloor Street West, Suite 1202
Toronto, ON M5S 2V1

Sompo Japan Insurance Inc.
199 Bay Street, Suite 2500
Box 139
Toronto, ON M5L 1E2

Sonnet Insurance Company
111 Westmount Road South
P.O. Box 2000
Waterloo, ON N2J 4S4

Sovereign General Insurance Co.
6700 Macleod Trail S.E.
Suite 140
Calgary, AB T2H 0L3

SSQ, Société d'assurances générales inc.
2515 boulevard Laurier
C.P. 1053, Succ. Sainte-Foy
Québec, QC G1V 0A5

Starr Insurance & Reinsurance Limited
200 King Street West, Suite 1200
P.O. Box 16
Toronto, ON M5H 3T4

Suecia Reinsurance Company
427 Donlands Avenue
Toronto, ON M4J 3S2

Sunderland Marine Insurance Company Limited
890 West Pender Street
Suite 701
Vancouver, BC V6C 1J9

Swiss Reinsurance Company
150 King Street West
Suite 1000
P.O. Box 50
Toronto, ON M5H 1J9

TD Direct Insurance Inc.
50 Crémazie Place, 12th Floor
Montreal, QC H2P 1B6

TD General Insurance Company
50 Crémazie Place, 12th Floor
Montreal, QC H2P 1B6

TD Home and Auto Insurance Company
50 Crémazie Place, 12th Floor
Montreal, QC H2P 1B6

Technology Insurance Company Inc.
1145 Nicholson Street, Unit 2
Newmarket, ON L3Y 9C3

Temple Insurance Company
390 Bay Street, 22nd Floor
Toronto, ON M5H 2Y2

T.H.E. Insurance Company
200 University Avenue, 14th Floor
Toronto, ON M5H 3C6

TOA Reinsurance Company of America
55 University Avenue, Suite 1700
P.O. Box 53
Toronto, ON M5J 2H7

Tokio Marine & Nichido Fire Insurance Company Limited
105 Adelaide Street West, 3rd Floor
Toronto, ON M5H 1P9

Traders General Insurance Company
10 Aviva Way, Suite 100
Markham, ON L0G 0G1

Trafalgar Insurance Company of Canada
700 University Avenue
Suite 1500-A Legal
Toronto, ON M5G 0A1

Transatlantic Reinsurance Company
95 Wellington Street West, Suite 1110
Toronto, ON M5J 2N7

Travelers Insurance Company of Canada
165 University Avenue
Toronto, ON M5H 3B9

Trisura Guarantee Insurance Company
333 Bay Street, Suite 1610
Toronto, ON M5H 2R2

Triton Insurance Company
380 Wellington Street, Suite 1420
London, ON N6A 5B5

Unifund Assurance Company
10 Factory Lane
St. John's, NL A1C 6H5

Virginia Surety Company, Inc.
34 King Street East, Suite 1200
Toronto, ON M5C 2X8

Waterloo Insurance Company
111 Westmount Road South
P.O. Box 2000
Waterloo, ON N2J 4S4

Wawanesa Mutual Insurance Company
191 Broadway, Suite 900
Winnipeg, MB R3C 3P1

Western Assurance Company
18 York Street, Suite 800
Toronto, ON M5J 2T8

Western Surety Company
1881 Scarth Street, Suite 2100
Regina, SK S4P 4K9

Westport Insurance Corporation
150 King Street West, Suite 1000
Toronto, ON M5H 1J9

Wynward Insurance Group
1240 One Lombard Place
Winnipeg, MB R3B 0V9

XL Reinsurance America Inc.
100 Yonge Street, Suite 1200
Toronto, ON M5C 2W1

XL Specialty Insurance Company
100 Yonge Street, Suite 1200
Toronto, ON M5C 2W1

Zenith Insurance Company
105 Adelaide Street West
Toronto, ON M5H 1P9

Zurich Insurance Company Ltd.
100 King Street West, Suite 5500
Toronto, ON M5X 1C9

General Index

www.ingramcontent.com/pod-product-compliance
Lightning Source LLC
LaVergne TN
LVHW020440080826
844660LV00033B/1343
9781487523008